The Central Office Supervisor of Curriculum and Instruction: Setting the Stage for Success

The Central Office Supervisor of Curriculum and Instruction

SETTING THE STAGE FOR SUCCESS

Edward Pajak
THE UNIVERSITY OF GEORGIA

SOCIAL SCIENCE & HISTORY DIVISION
EDUCATION & PHILOSOPHY SECTION

Allyn and Bacon, Inc.
BOSTON   LONDON   SYDNEY   TORONTO

Copyright © 1989 by Allyn and Bacon, Inc.
A Division of Simon & Schuster
160 Gould Street
Needham Heights, Massachusetts 02194

All rights reserved. No part of the material protected by this copyright notice may be reproduced or utilized in any form or by any means, electronic or mechanical, including photocopying, recording, or by any information storage and retrieval system, without written permission from the copyright owner.

Library of Congress Cataloging-in-Publication Data

Pajak, Edward, 1947–
 The central office supervisor of curriculum and instruction: setting the stage for success / Edward Pajak.
   p.   cm.
 Bibliography: p.
 Includes index.
 ISBN 0-205-11710-4
 1. School supervision—United States. 2. Teacher-principal relationships.   I. Title.
 LB2806.4.P35 1989
 371.2′013–dc19   88-14575
                                                                 CIP

Printed in the United States of America
10 9 8 7 6 5 4 3 2 1   92 91 90 89 88

TO ALEXANDRA

Contents

Preface	xi
1 MAKING SENSE OF DIVERSITY	**1**
A Puzzling Role	2
A Generic Job Description	4
Some Recent Research	7
Making Sense for Oneself	9
The Supervisor as Medium	14
References	16
2 PROBLEMS, FRUSTRATIONS, SATISFACTIONS, AND SOLUTIONS	**19**
The Problem of Social and Psychological Distance	20
Frustrations	23
Satisfaction	28
Reducing Role Conflict	32
Importance of Norms and Goals	35
References	36
3 ORGANIZATIONAL CULTURE AND SOCIAL STRUCTURE	**38**
Organizational Culture	40
The Four Components of Social Action	42
The Social Components, Collective Behavior, and Schools	44
Social Structure and Central Office Supervision	48
References	50
4 PROMOTING AND MAINTAINING NORMS OF ORGANIZATIONAL EFFECTIVENESS	**52**
Modeling Professional Norms	55
Cooperation, Fairness, and Reciprocity	56

	Managing Conflict	57
	Exchanging Credit	62
	References	69
5	**MOBILIZING EFFORT AND COORDINATING ROLES**	**70**
	Coordination and Communication	72
	Standardization	73
	Planning and Goal Setting	77
	Organizing Networks	81
	Bounded Rationality	85
	References	87
6	**CLARIFYING TASKS AND OUTCOMES**	**88**
	Securing Resources for Instructional Improvement	88
	Locating Materials and Information	92
	Improving Skills Through Training	94
	Validating Worth	96
	Building Confidence	100
	Developing a System of Support	102
	References	103
7	**INVOLVING TEACHERS IN CHANGE**	**105**
	Top–Down or Bottom–Up?	106
	Changing Instructional Practice	108
	A Contrary Example	110
	Normative Change and Professional Growth	112
	Structuring Involvement	116
	Change and Credibility	118
	Balancing Conformity with Innovation	121
	References	124
8	**WORKING WITH PRINCIPALS**	**125**
	Similarities and Differences	126
	Understanding and Credibility	128
	Earning Credibility	130
	Predictability and Reciprocity	131
	The Central Office and the Local School	133
	Power and Teamwork	136
	References	143
9	**TRANSACTIONAL AND TRANSFORMING LEADERSHIP**	**144**
	Reciprocal Influence of Supervisors	145
	Delegation	149

Developing Others 151
The Inadequacy of Popular Models of Leadership 153
Transactional Leadership 156
Toward a Reciprocal Model of Central Office
  Supervision 159
References 160

10 WORKING WITH THE SUPERINTENDENT 162
Integration and Adaptation 163
The Effective Working Relationship 164
Support 169
Principals 171
School Board 174
Perceptions of the Superintendency 175
Commitment to the Superintendent 176
References 178

11 THE DILEMMA OF INVISIBILITY 179
Ambiguity and Remoteness 181
Intangibility of Instructional and Supervisory Tasks 184
Functional Outcomes of Invisibility 189
Becoming More Visible 191
References 195

12 THE BACKSTAGE WORLD OF CLASSROOM SUPERVISION 196
Upgrading Instructional Materials and Techniques 197
Communicating Informally 199
Organizing Groups 199
Initiating and Facilitating Innovation 200
Training Staff 202
Rehearsing Presentations to the School Board 203
The Role of Teacher 204
The Supervisor as Theatrical Director 205
On Classroom Observation 209
References 211

13 THE BACKSTAGE WORLD OF CENTRAL OFFICE SUPERVISION 213
The Backstage Perspective 214
Working Backstage with Principals 216
Working Backstage with the Superintendent 218
Working Backstage with the School Board 221

x CONTENTS

    What Is Reality? 222
    Actors and Audiences 225
    References 227

14 MAKING SENSE OF IT ALL **229**
    References 235

INDEX **237**

Preface

Anthropologists, it has been said, document the demise of the societies they study, for they themselves are harbingers of the technological and bureaucratic processes that eventually undermine and transform even the most complex and stable cultures. In preparing to write this book, I have relied heavily upon interviews with central office instructional supervisors, somewhat as an anthropologist might use informants when studying an alien culture. It is my hope that the description presented here will help to preserve the position of central office instructional supervisor by drawing attention to its uniqueness and what would be lost to school districts and students if it did not exist.

This book is unique in several respects. As far as I can determine, it is the only book ever written specifically about the position of central office supervisor of curriculum and instruction. In fact, many practitioners with whom I have spoken have remarked, "Finally, someone is paying attention to us!"

This book also represents a departure from the bureaucratic descriptions of how schools function and the technical prescriptions, so prevalent in the education literature, for how schools can be improved. This departure is carefully considered and arises from a conviction that the reality of being a district level instructional supervisor can only be understood within a social context. In order to comprehend the contributions that district level supervisors make to the school systems they serve, it is necessary to understand the nature of the relationships they have with other people. Bureaucracy and technology simply do not provide sufficient and appropriate vantage points from which to view and understand the complexity of the central office supervisor's position.

Finally, this is one of only a few books in the field of educational supervision that is based upon original data. However, because it is written primarily for people who currently hold or aspire to the position of district level supervisor of curriculum and instruction, the format is not typical of a research report. It is necessary, therefore, to outline the rationale and criteria for selection of the participants and the methodology employed in collecting and analyzing the data.

The central office supervisor of curriculum and instruction is defined here as the individual who is responsible for maintaining and improving the overall instructional program of the school district in which he or she is employed. The participants in the study upon which this book is based were selected, therefore, on the basis of their job function rather than their job title.

Although the participants all shared similar work responsibilities, their official titles differed considerably. Included among the participants, for example, were assistant and associate superintendents for instruction and curriculum, curriculum directors, curriculum coordinators, and directors of education or instructional services. Differences in titles seem to depend more on the size of the district than on the specific responsibilities associated with the job.

Perceptions of practicing instructional supervisors, university professors who spend much time working in the public schools, and members of the general public were taken into consideration when making judgments concerning whom to include as participants in this study. Ten practicing central office supervisors of instruction—five men and five women, five from New York and five from Georgia—were selected on the basis of their reputations as successful practitioners. Geographical convenience was a consideration, but a determined effort was made to achieve a representative sample in terms of urban, suburban, and rural schools, as well as large and small districts.

One district supervisor who was selected had recently received an award as the outstanding supervisor of the year in her state. Another participant was chosen from a district featured, for its exemplary staff development program, on a videotape produced by the Association for Supervision and Curriculum Development. In several instances, supervisors were chosen from districts in which one or more schools were recipients of national "school of excellence" awards.

Interestingly, in two cases participants volunteered that they did not feel entirely successful about their work as supervisors and explained why this was so. In one instance the cause of frustration was the task of staff development. In the other the supervisor felt inadequate in working with principals. This mix of participant success was by no means a disadvantage. On the contrary, it provided a useful validity check. It also suggested that success and effectiveness have more facets than we often acknowledge.

Data collection proceeded in two stages. An unstructured interview was first conducted with each of the participants. Among the general questions I asked were: "What do I need to know to understand what your job is really like?" "What does being a supervisor of instruction mean to you personally?" "How do you know when you have been successful?"

As the participants responded, I asked them to clarify and give specific examples. Most interviews took approximately ninety minutes. All dialogue was tape recorded, and the recordings were transcribed and typed.

The data were analyzed using the constant-comparative method of coding phrases, sentences, or entire paragraphs according to their content. Each new unit of data was compared against units classified earlier. Categories of content thus emerged directly from the responses of the participants to the open-ended questions. Constructs were proposed and hypotheses formulated concerning possible relationships.

The major strength of the unstructured interview for collecting data is its focus on participants' language, which permits the researcher to develop an understanding of the unique meanings common to the group of "insiders." Other approaches that have been applied in the past, such as observations and surveys, would not have directly addressed the purpose of this study: to develop a detailed understanding of how district level instructional supervisors experience the work they do.

The second stage of data collection was more focused and systematic: A structured but open-ended survey was developed and mailed to each participant in order to verify the constructs derived from the interview data. A second interview was then held with each supervisor, with the open-ended survey serving as a focus for discussion. The purposes of this technique were to strengthen the existing categories with additional data and to allow the possibility of discovering new categories and relationships. Copies of the survey were also mailed to ten other instructional supervisors in five states. Again, data were analyzed according to the method described above.

Further corroboration of the tentative hypotheses and constructs was achieved through numerous phone calls and letters to the participants. Some of the participants also read and commented on drafts of early chapters. Finally, data from a separate study of three school districts in Georgia that had shown consistent improvement in student achievement over several years confirmed the findings derived from the original data.

The outcome of these procedures, which spanned three years, was a theoretical configuration of major and minor categories, concepts, and linkages that is grounded in data and that describes the position of the central office instructional supervisor as it is experienced and described by practitioners. The perspective that finally emerged, which is presented in the pages that follow, represents my attempt to understand and explain what central office supervisors have told me about what they do. These findings are not presented as an accurate picture of how *all* district level supervisors of instruction experience their work, but they do constitute a basic model for understanding the role as it is experienced and perceived by many practitioners.

I would like to thank, first of all, the many central office supervisors of curriculum and instruction who took time out of their busy schedules to answer patiently my innumerable questions. My colleague and friend Carl Glickman deserves special thanks for encouraging me to write a book on this topic. All of my colleagues in the Department of Curriculum and Supervision at the University of Georgia have been supportive throughout this effort, especially Ray Bruce and Gerald Firth. With Carl, they offered insightful comments and suggestions on several chapters. Joseph Blase and Helen Hazi helped me to clarify methodological and conceptual issues in the early stages of the project, suggested relevant references, and critiqued drafts of some chapters.

A number of secretaries and many students who passed through the Department of Curriculum and Supervision at Georgia in recent years have contributed to this book by transcribing taped interviews, tracking down references, and proofreading. To avoid the risk of omitting anyone, my thanks go to them collectively for their help. Special thanks are extended to the students enrolled in my summer 1987 Supervision Theory class for their careful reading of the first draft of the completed manuscript and their critical observations and suggestions.

My greatest debt is to my family, who patiently tolerated considerable inconvenience as I struggled with this tome. Without their understanding, support, and encouragement, this book would not have been written.

The Central Office Supervisor of Curriculum and Instruction: Setting the Stage for Success

1
Making Sense of Diversity

Posted above the sign-out sheet for central office personnel in a school district I visited is a series of drawings of children's faces. Just below these drawings is written the admonition: "Remember, this is why we are here." In order to understand effective central office supervision, one must appreciate the importance of the essential truth contained in that short message. It represents nothing less than a pivotal value around which all else revolves. It is the single constant in the ever changing world of public education. By remembering that students are "why we are here" and by frequently reminding others of this basic truth, effective central office supervisors of curriculum and instruction ensure that everything done in the name of schooling has both meaning and focus for everyone involved.

It is commonly observed that district level supervisors serve as an important link between teachers and new materials, ideas, and policies developed outside the classroom (Fullan, 1982; Cox, 1983). This is certainly true. But effective central office supervisors do more than passively relay resources and information from state education departments to teachers or facilitate the utilization of knowledge that originates at colleges and universities. Effective supervision seems to be closer to a process of interpretation in that supervisors actively engage in constructing meaning out of the diverse elements with which they work. In other words, materials, resources, ideas, policies, and events, that originate "out there," beyond the classroom, are interpreted, or given meaning, specifically in terms of their implications for the living, breathing students who inhabit the local schools.

This construction of meaning out of the various and often disjointed events and processes of schooling, however, is not done in isolation. It is a highly collaborative activity that requires the supervisor to work in close association with teachers, principals, and the superintendent and to encourage their active involvement. By emphasizing the common value of benefiting students through instruction in the work they do with others, effective central office supervisors provide and reinforce both a purpose and a focus to the efforts of people within the system, thereby ensuring that the district is more than simply an aggregation of one-room schoolhouses or a loose confederation of autonomous buildings. By working to provide students with the best instructional experiences possible, effective supervisors simultaneously ensure that the district bureaucracy remains responsive to the professional needs of teachers and principals and does not become overly rigid or intrusive.

Simply stated, the creation of meaning around the central value of providing high-quality instruction for students is what effective district level supervision is all about. How this creation of meaning occurs and how its enactment is facilitated by central office supervisors is the subject of this book generally and this chapter specifically.

A Puzzling Role

In the public school, the central office supervisor of curriculum or instruction is the individual responsible for maintaining and improving the overall quality of the local district's instructional program. Despite this obvious relevance and potential importance to the most fundamental process of schooling, the central office instructional supervisor's position may be, in fact, the least well understood and the most frequently overlooked of the professional roles that exist in schools (Wimpelberg, 1987).

It has long been recognized that the role of central office supervisor is poorly defined in both practice and theory (Harris, 1967). Various titles—such as assistant superintendent for instruction, supervisor of instruction, curriculum coordinator, and director of instruction—are used in different school systems to describe essentially the same position (Speiker, 1976). Job descriptions tend to be all-encompassing, so that specific task responsibilities can vary considerably among supervisors even when job titles are similar. A curriculum coordinator, for example, commented as follows about her role:

> This position is different in each district. We have a group [of supervisors] that meets regularly, and I know that each person has different responsibilities, does different things, works in different ways, and has different power or no power. It really is not as closely defined as other roles. Personnel people, they take

care of personnel, superintendents take care of the school district, principals do more or less what the superintendent wants. This position is not the same anywhere.

The lack of a satisfactory conceptual model of the role seems to have limited writing and research in the area. A commonly heard criticism of textbooks in the field of instructional supervision, for example, is that many simply list the things that supervisors do, should do, and are expected to do, without adequately explaining the dynamics of supervision. Several authors acknowledge that "confusion" and "uncertainty" remain concerning key issues affecting the role (Sergiovanni and Starrat, 1979) and that the role of the supervisor in education has not yet been clearly defined (Wiles and Bondi, 1980).

While the more familiar and clearly delineated positions of teacher, principal, and superintendent have received considerable attention from educational researchers and theorists, the position of central office supervisor has been generally neglected (Bridges, 1982; Fullan, 1982). Part of the reason for this neglect seems to be the difficulty of describing the work of district level supervisors in precise and measurable terms.

In 1982, the Association for Supervision and Curriculum Development established a Task Force on Research on Central Office Supervision to examine the possibility of documenting the effectiveness of supervisory personnel. In a final report the Task Force concluded that it may be impossible to develop a general measure of central office supervisor productivity and effectiveness. The variety of duties and expectations that comprise the supervisory role, according to the report, suggests that "questions of effectiveness must be answered in the specific situation and not through any sort of broad measuring instrument." The Task Force further observed that central office supervisors typically rely upon "personal measures" of effectiveness such as a "sense" of rapport with teachers and a "sense" of being welcome in a school, rather than any objectively definable standard of performance (Blumberg, 1984).

Despite the potential benefit to instructional quality implicit in the district level supervisory role, the obscurity of explicit outcomes makes the position difficult to justify. Tacit understandings and articles of faith appear inadequate to policymakers, such as school board members, legislators, and state education department officials, who tend to favor quantifiable measures of accountability. The absence of a clear conception of the role makes the position of central office supervisor vulnerable when resources are scarce, but it is tenuous even in prosperous times.

In California, for example, during the period from 1930 to 1970, when district level staffs grew larger with increased specialization according to function, the number of general instruction and curriculum-related positions increased (Rowan, 1982). However, the number of such positions lagged behind other staff positions responsible for managing more-tangible categories or for providing auxiliary services to children. Business and personnel positions showed the greatest overall gains during this period, with central office positions related to guidance and psychological services close behind. Most striking, however, is the finding that of seventeen district level staff position titles, those dealing with curriculum and instruction were the two least stable in terms of surviving from one five-year period to the next. The three most stable central office staff positions, in contrast, were those relating to the management of business affairs, cafeteria services, and health (Rowan, 1982).

According to another recent report, over the last ten years nationally, "the number of district-wide instructional supervisors has slowly but steadily declined" (Costa and Guditus, 1984). This situation is particularly ironic given recent calls for instructional improvement by various commissions, task forces, and governmental agencies. Although cutbacks in supervisory personnel may be partly attributable to declines in student enrollment, an undeniable factor is that the public, and even some educators, really do not understand the purposes and functions of central office supervision. Until a clearer understanding of the role and its functions is developed, the position of central office supervisor of curriculum and instruction is likely to continue to be considered expendable (Burch and Danley, 1980).

A Generic Job Description

The responsibilities of central office supervisors, curriculum coordinators, and directors of instruction may be described without exaggeration as being extremely diverse and global. These diverse responsibilities, combined with local variations in specific duties and work schedules that are often fragmented, defy simple interpretation and understanding. As one supervisor suggested, it is difficult for "people to understand what the role of curriculum director is, because it's a very fuzzy job description."

While no two job descriptions are exactly the same, those associated with supervisory positions typically include instruction-related tasks, such as coordinating the educational program, ensuring continuity in the kindergarten-through-twelfth-grade curriculum, supervising curriculum planning and development, coordinating program evaluation at the district level, coordinating staff supervision and evaluation, identifying staff development and in-service needs of teachers, planning for staff meetings and workshops for the improvement of instruction, and selecting and recommending textbooks and other teaching materials.

Another set of duties frequently mentioned in job descriptions is not strictly instructional. Many job descriptions, for example, include such items as gathering information and preparing reports required by governmental agencies, assisting in the development and administration of the district's budget, implementing the school and community relations program, and overseeing the production of district publications. Attending to instructional improvement and the curricular needs of the school district could easily take up all of a supervisor's time, but instructional issues constantly compete with these other duties. Especially in small districts, it seems, paperwork required by state and federal agencies can occupy an inordinate amount of the supervisor's time and attention. For example, one supervisor lamented:

> It's not just instruction but personnel, too. I have to do the record keeping, personnel applications, and processing of credentials— and the sorts of things that go along with personnel selection. And it takes time, time away from the curriculum end of the instructional program.

Complicating the situation further is a final catch-all statement appearing on virtually every central office instructional supervisor's job description that assigns the responsibility to "assist the superintendent in all other functions as required." While this phrase considerably broadens the scope of the supervisor's influence, it also presents an additional and potentially serious constraint upon the supervisor's autonomy in choosing where to allocate his or her time. An assistant superintendent explained:

> I get involved in a lot of special projects. When there's something new and big coming up, I generally tend to get stuck with it, if it can be related to instruction at all. And what I've decided over the period of time that I've been in this position is that anything the superintendent wants can be related to instruction. So you catch a lot of things. . . . Last summer we had a big push on job

descriptions and evaluation instruments. Well, obviously that relates to instruction, but it's also personnel. Anyway, I chaired the task force that handled that.

To an objective observer, the tasks that central office supervisors perform appear to be not only diverse but fragmented. A fairly typical day (which included a two-hour interview with the author) was described by a curriculum coordinator in this way:

> This morning, when I started out the day, it was with kindergarten screening; I set up the teams that would be working with the kindergarten screening. And then it was off to an in-service workshop for our librarians and reading teachers who are working with academically talented [students]; and then this afternoon it will be going over some materials for curriculum council next year.

Tasks performed by supervisors on a daily basis are usually comprised of scheduled events, such as attending meetings or completing paperwork, as well as unscheduled activities, such as responding to parental concerns or to requests for assistance from principals and teachers. This combination of planned and unplanned activities often requires supervisors to put in long hours and to be "constantly moving." The busyness of the supervisor's work schedule is evident in the quotation below:

> I put in more time on this job than I did as a principal because I'm normally here from eight o'clock in the morning to five-thirty at night, plus whatever night meetings I've got. And these can be considerable, because when we're running in-service during the school year we have four o'clock to seven o'clock meetings. . . . I've had three days off this summer, that's all I've had, because there's been one crisis or deadline after another. Chapter 1 has got to be in, Chapter 2 has to be in, the curriculum council has to be ready for the fall, and we've got all the reports to write for the summer programs.

Because of the diversity of and "fuzziness" concerning the responsibilities of central office supervisors, it is essential for people who occupy this supervisory role to have a clear personal sense of what they are about and what they are trying to accomplish. Otherwise their duties may be determined almost exclusively by other people and external agencies. Remembering that *students* are "why we are here" seems to help central office supervisors successfully maintain this needed focus.

Some Recent Research

Two fairly recent studies have sought to document in detail the work actually performed by district level supervisors of instruction and curriculum. Both studies relied upon the method of structured observation for gathering data to identify the tasks in which supervisors engage. In one study, Sullivan (1980, 1982) observed six instructional supervisors in a large metropolitan school district. In a similar study, involving central office curriculum directors in three school districts, Donmoyer and Neff (1983) supplemented descriptive behavioral categories with "high-inference" data in the form of field notes in order to gain insight into how behaviors might be related and contribute to supervisory effectiveness.

The studies by Sullivan and by Donmoyer and Neff complement each other well in several respects. Supervisors' work schedules in both instances were found to be typically comprised of a variety of brief and fragmented activities. Yet both Sullivan (1980) and Donmoyer and Neff (1983) also suggested that supervisors have more control over the pace of their work and personally initiate more of the tasks in which they engage than has been reported in similar studies of line administrative positions (e.g., Pitner, 1978; Martin and Willower, 1981). Rather than a pawn frantically responding to external forces, the central office instructional supervisor is depicted as being more proactive and as having considerable opportunity for individual interpretation and self-determination of behavior.

Both studies also found that the greatest proportion of time spent by central office supervisors is in verbal contacts that are usually self-initiated and involve people inside the school organization. This finding led the researchers in each case to highlight in their reports the "monitoring" function of management—that is, actively seeking and receiving a wide variety of information about the organization. Sullivan reported that supervisors also spend much time "disseminating information" and "allocating resources" to others within the school, leading her to conclude:

> The supervisor's primary position is that of information broker, or hub of communication, and the major task accomplished through the exchange and filtering of information is that of maintaining day-to-day operation of the school system as an organization. (1980, p. 37)

Sullivan speculates on the basis of her findings that the number and variety of individuals and organizational units with which supervisors interact represent an informal communication network constructed by the supervisor that facilitates the flow of information within the school district. The centrality of supervisors within this network, according to Sullivan (1980), enables them to control such processes as decision making by selectively regulating the flow and content of information as they transmit it to others.

Unlike Sullivan's analysis of purely observational data, which was essentially content neutral, Donmoyer and Neff's (1983) high-inference field notes documented that supervisors devote a large amount of their time to curriculum and instruction-related issues. Furthermore, many observed tasks that appeared superficially to be purely managerial were explained by the participants as relating directly to "the content and process of teaching" (p. 25). Donmoyer and Neff report that although considerable amounts of time and energy were often consumed by the resolution of immediate and concrete problems, supervisors actually view themselves as dealing primarily with abstract, long-range issues.

Donmoyer and Neff are fascinated by the degree of autonomy and flexibility supervisors appear to enjoy. Rather than portraying supervisors as victims of uncertainty and ambiguity, they view supervisors as actually benefiting from the lack of clearly prescribed duties, a situation that enables them to "choose to behave in a quite unmanagerial way and still meet the requirements of their role" (1983, p. 44). These authors suggest that more research is needed into how supervisors negotiate between "an action oriented environment of generally concrete problems and a substantive field often characterized by abstraction" (p. 24) and conclude that

> [T]he curriculum leader's role should be a focal point both for those interested in questions of knowledge utilization and for those who wish to conduct research which will examine more thoroughly linkages between the organizational aspects and the curricular and pedagogical functions of schools. (1983, p. 48)

Because the tasks in which supervisors engage and for which they are responsible may be characterized as fragmented, diverse, ambiguous, and even contradictory when described simply in terms of enacted behaviors, it sometimes can be difficult for supervisors to explain in a few words exactly what it is they do. Supervisors are quick to point out, however, that there is in fact an order and direction to their actions. While the rapidly shifting focus of a supervisor's attention may appear to an outsider to be scattered, and their energies may seem to be dispersed among seemingly overwhelming and sometimes conflicting tasks and responsibilities, the most important thing to consider may be how supervisors themselves go about making sense of what they do.

In other words, in order to comprehend what it is that supervisors do, it is necessary to broaden the focus of inquiry beyond simply identifying and describing behaviors and counting the frequency of their occurrence. The subjective experience of being a central office supervisor must also be included in any adequate conceptualization of the role. Only by considering objective and subjective realities simultaneously can the role of central office supervisor be fully appreciated and an understanding of what constitutes effectiveness in that role be achieved.

Making Sense for Oneself

Humans make sense of information through their unique capacity for symbolic abstraction, which is perhaps most commonly exhibited in the representation of reality through numbers and words. In organizations an attempt to represent reality numerically, for example, is evident in the practice of record keeping. Reality may be summed up, according to this view, by recording such things as student achievement test scores or the frequency of occurrence of behaviors exhibited by teachers in the classroom.

The major advantage of a numerical interpretation of reality is the degree to which it simplifies that which it describes. A complex situation seems less threatening and more manageable when numbers are attached to it because quantified measures give us a tangible sense of where we stand and how we are doing. The degree to which numbers simplify reality, however, is at the same time a major disadvantage. By eliminating complexity, a sense of context is also sacrificed and one's understanding of the totality is seriously limited.

The abstraction of information through language, on the other hand, can go beyond explicating reality by merely simplifying it. Language qualitatively transforms information by constructing images and myths. The creation of such visual and narrative symbols not only serves to summarize reality, it also enriches reality and may be considered the foundation of an organization's culture (Peters and Waterman, 1982).

Developments in linguistics (Campbell, 1982) and literary theory (Barthes, 1986) emphasize the centrality of meaning to the expression and interpretation of verbal communication and literary works. Recently Bruner (1986) proposed the "narrative mode" as a way of ordering experience and constructing reality that is distinct from the "paradigmatic mode" of science, which seeks causal explanation. Although central office supervisors of curriculum and instruction often end up devoting much of their time to such tasks as record keeping, they tend to view the aspects of their jobs that involve verbal communication as much more important because they directly relate to and influence what occurs at the classroom and school levels. It is worth taking a moment to explore how these processes of image making and storytelling seem to work.

If a single prevailing value or sentiment exists around which supervisors make sense of what they do, it might be expressed in these words of a central office leader in describing what he said was the essential guiding principle of his district: "A sincere concern for the well-being of children and a commitment to quality instruction for their benefit." Having a positive influence on larger numbers of students is often identified by supervisors, in fact, as the reason for their initially leaving the classroom and seeking a district level position. Many supervisors of instruction and curriculum, whether or not they have children of their own, often say that they judge the quality of an instructional program by asking themselves if they would be happy as parents to see their children enrolled in the program. Successful central office supervisors try to give expression to this fundamental ethic of service to children by representing, exemplifying, and embodying it in everything they do.

Related to the core value of strong personal concern for students and commitment to quality instruction is what might be described as a broad "system-wide" perspective concerning people that closely guides the actions of successful supervisors. When thinking about changes or improvements that may benefit students, for example, supervisors of instruction are likely to consider everyone who may be interested, influenced, or involved in some way, including students, teachers, administrators, the school board, and community members.

Supervisors are often extremely sensitive to anything that may enhance or undermine a sense of teamwork and cooperation among the various constituencies that comprise a school. A reason for this sensitivity is that the construction of images and narratives that give meaning to what goes on in schools is of necessity a collaborative activity that relies upon a continuous, open dialogue. Meaning is constructed around and focused upon the core value of providing quality instruction to students through the ongoing conversations among people within the school organization. Encouraging and facilitating such conversations is an essential element of effective central office supervision.

Another aspect of this system-wide perspective is a consideration of the full scope of processes operating within the district. Other student-oriented roles, such as those of teacher or principal, tend to generate a territorial point of view that is limited to the confines of the individual classroom or school. The district level supervisor, in contrast, enjoys a broad overview of the entire instructional program, which can include all subjects and all grade levels. Instructional supervisors report developing a strong appreciation for the value and legitimacy of other functional components of the district, including transportation, buildings and grounds, personnel, and the business office, all of which influence and are influenced by the instructional program.

Related to this system-wide perspective concerning people and processes is a long-term perspective of time. Supervisors consider not only where the system is at any time relative to its goals and objectives, but also how far it already has come. They look backward as well as forward when assessing their districts' achievements and measure personal satisfaction and success in terms of the cumulative long-range outcomes of what appears to be a series of minor accomplishments when viewed in the short term as isolated events. Supervisors thus construct a narrative of events to provide continuity and to make sense of what has happened in the past, what is happening now, and where the district is heading. A curriculum director explained:

> One of the things that I've learned is that you have to look back, and you have to be able to point to things that you feel were accomplished because you had a hand in them over the long period. You can't always look back and say, "OK, what kind of an impact did I make today?" But if you look back over a period of time, you can see. You try to look forward at where you're trying to go, but you also have to stop, I think, for your own sanity and be able to look backward and say, "This is where we were, and this is where we are, you know, and I did something here that made that change, or I did something here that let somebody else make a change."

Supervisors sometimes describe this inclusive view of people, processes, and events as "understanding the big—or the whole or the total—picture." This holistic perspective suggests an image that may be a key to understanding the psychological process by which supervisors make sense of the diversity of their role. When asked specifically why a seemingly minor responsibility was worth doing, for example, a district coordinator in New York State replied:

> It's one of the building blocks of taking things as you see them, doing them, and moving along to the next. It's just a lot of pieces of the puzzle that I put together.

An assistant superintendent in a Georgia school system responded in a remarkably similar way to the question of how she made sense of the many duties she regularly performed:

> You look over the span of time, and the curriculum guide that we have now is five times better than the curriculum guide that we had in 1980, which is darn better than nothing, which we had in 1975. So you have to figure things over a long period of time, rather than day by day, year by year. We [she and her staff] despise writing monthly board reports, but it helps us assess where we are, what we have accomplished, and all those little fragments begin to come together. . . . By chance, did your newspaper have the same cartoon that ours had in it today? A little guy with "NASA" on his back is shoving these great big pieces of a puzzle, and he only has a few around the edges. Well, that's the way we feel. We're little and the pieces are big and we're shoving them around, but we're getting them together.

Thus, it seems that "understanding the big picture" is not so much a precondition as it is a result of what the supervisor does on the job. The "big picture" emerges as the "puzzle" is solved by fitting together the "pieces" over time. In this way, as Donmoyer and Neff (1983) suggested, the central office supervisor deals with long-term, abstract issues while simultaneously working on immediate and concrete problems. Instead of thinking about understanding the big picture as a necessary precondition to a supervisor's effectiveness, however, it may be more accurate to consider this to be a process in which supervisors are constantly and actively engaged as they perform their jobs. That is, supervisors continuously utilize the "many little things" that they do both to express and construct meaning for others.

The innumerable tasks and conversations in which supervisors engage while performing their jobs may seem unrelated and almost trivial when considered as isolated events, yet their cumulative effect can be powerful, especially when recognized as fulfilling a sensemaking function. Rather than docilely completing disconnected tasks "that have to be done by somebody," in other words, successful supervisors give meaning to the internal school environment as they act upon it to help make events, processes, and policies meaningful to teachers and principals in terms of implications for working with students. As one curriculum director commented:

MAKING SENSE OF DIVERSITY   13

The job represents a vast array of information without a clear-cut sense of sequence or organization and, therefore, finding a focus becomes the first step toward solving the puzzle.

Some authors have suggested that the process of making sense of one's environment as described here is analogous to the problem of solving an anagram from a meaningless sequence of letters or constructing a sentence from a collection of words (Campbell, 1982). For example, the nonsensical sequence of letters O-T-P-S can be arranged to spell "POTS" or rearranged to spell "SPOT" or "TOPS." With each configuration, a new idea is expressed. An advantage to thinking in terms of solving an anagram or constructing a sentence when considering how supervisors of instruction or curriculum make sense of what they do is the likelihood of finding multiple and original solutions or interpretations ("STOP").

A central office curriculum coordinator from a Midwestern state, when asked how someone in his position makes sense of the role, responded as follows:

> I believe at times you make sense out of the role by trying to create it. I mean that in many cases the position is not clearly defined and it takes on meaning through the individual supervisor's past experiences, continued professional growth, personality, and beliefs about education.

When asked if solving a puzzle or an anagram (O-S-E-H-R) was anything like the process of making sense of the role of supervisor, he observed:

> In one sense this is a very good analogy because in the beginning [of one's career] you are learning what pieces make up the puzzle, and little by little you begin to see how they fit together. However, as you gain more experience you begin to realize that the pieces of the puzzle themselves are living and growing entities that must be constantly reanalyzed and reshaped to fit the unique characteristics of a given situation. Thus, "HORSE" may become "SHORE," "HORSES," "HOSE," "HEROES," and so forth, depending upon what is learned as new ideas are tried out.

This individual obviously took liberties with the strict definition of an anagram by deleting and inserting letters to create additional meanings, but that may be closer to what instructional supervisors actually do. A similar emphasis on inventiveness as an essential factor in making sense of the universe of people, policies, processes, events, and materials that comprise an instructional program is evident in the words of an assistant superintendent for curriculum and instruction who said that while she accepted the analogy of solving a puzzle or an anagram as "true," she found it still a bit too constraining as an accurate description of supervision:

> This metaphor assumes that the puzzle and pieces already exist. I like to think that I and my [supervisory staff] have the opportunity to create new puzzles—or at least new pieces for the existing puzzles.

Thus, it seems that supervisors actively discover and invent new pieces of the instructional puzzle as they go about the process of constructing meaning. The importance of personal interpretation to effective enactment of the role of district level supervisor was highlighted in a study by Floyd (1986) of four recipients of awards for outstanding professional service. The participants in this study were district level supervisors who had been nominated by teachers, peers, or administrators within their systems for special recognition because of contributions they had made to instructional improvement. The awards were presented by two state-level professional associations to which the supervisors belonged.

Floyd's study confirmed Donmoyer and Neff's (1983) suggestion that "fuzzy" characteristics of the supervisory role, such as fragmentation and ambiguity, may actually provide a functional advantage for the supervisor because they allow the role to be interpreted according to personal aptitude and professional judgment of local need. Central office supervisors seem to be able to define the specific nature of their role in many instances—for example, during the actual process of working with others on instructional improvement. They are able to do things that might not otherwise get done, but that are nevertheless necessary for the improvement of instruction. Fragmentation and ambiguity of responsibility, along with other factors, Floyd (1986) suggests, actually seem to contribute to the influence of outstanding supervisors. The ultimate definition of a supervisor's role, therefore, cannot be fixed except to say that it involves constant interpretation, reinterpretation, and counterinterpretation of events, processes, and policies in terms of their relevance to the value of benefiting students through instruction.

The Supervisor as Medium

The construction of meaning by fitting together fragments into coherent patterns around an idea is essentially an information-processing function (Campbell, 1982). What emerges from this view is an understanding of leadership as a process of mediating reality (Weick, 1978, 1985; Fisher, 1985). The central office supervisor, accordingly, may be viewed as a medium who receives information, interprets meaning, and transmits understandings to others. Weick (1978) has identified three variables that determine the relative effectiveness of such a medium:

1. the number of elements comprising the medium;
2. the degree of independence among these elements; and
3. the degree to which the elements are internally or externally constrained.

An example of a relatively good medium for both perception and action, Weick suggests, is the human hand with its multiple, independent, flexible, and sensitive elements (i.e., fingers).

In terms of loose-coupling imagery, a good medium for registering information will be loosely coupled internally but tightly coupled to the environment, as in the case of a hand exploring the contours of a stone. When taking action, however, as in throwing the stone, the hand (medium) must become internally constrained and loosely coupled to the environment. That is, the elements in a system must function in an intentional, coordinated fashion when influencing the object, rather than passively responding to it.

Central to the conception of supervision as a process of information mediation is the principle of "requisite variety." Essentially, this principle—which is derived from systems theory (Buckley, 1968)—states that a medium must be at least as complex as the environment with which it interacts. The more complex the medium, the greater the medium's capacity to register, influence, and shape aspects of the environment. Thus, the human hand, because it is comprised of many elements that operate independently and are sensitive and responsive to characteristics of the environment, is a better medium than the elbow, which lacks these qualities.

Another example of requisite variety is found in the letters of the alphabet, which are the multiple, independent elements used to construct words. The words in a dictionary, in turn, are the multiple and independent elements of a language. Any idea ever conceived can be expressed with the twenty-six English letters because a tremendous variety of combinations of letters and words is possible. In order to express an idea, however, letters and words must be constrained according to the rules of spelling and grammar. Without this combination of variety and constraint, the construction and expression of meaning would be impossible (Campbell, 1982).

An implication of requisite variety for central office supervision is that a supervisor may be more effective as a medium when dealing with the complex, ambiguous, and unstable environment of the school to the extent that he or she is capable of exhibiting a similarly fragmented and flexible psychological configuration that can alternate appropriately in its fragmentation and cohesiveness in conjunction with the needs of the larger social organization. A conclusion of Floyd's (1986) study of outstanding central office supervisors, in fact, was that a high level of cognitive complexity may be a prerequisite to the flexibility identified as associated with supervisory effectiveness. One might reasonably expect an effective supervisor, therefore, to possess personal traits that include a rich variety of experiences, multiple perspectives of reality, an extensive repertoire of skills upon which to draw, and a willingness to listen to other people and take them seriously.

The principle of requisite variety may be even more helpful immediately, however, for understanding the utility of the diversity inherent in the central office supervisor's role. If a major function of supervision is to interpret and give meaning to the complex reality of schools, then a fragmented, ambiguous, and even contradictory job description may be exactly what is required to get the job done.

If one accepts the principle of requisite variety, then diversity is essential to the central office supervisor's role for registering the complexity of the school environment and simultaneously providing both stability and a capacity for change. On the one hand, the various people, events, policies, materials, and ideas with which supervisors have contact are constrained by their configuration into an expression of the core value of benefiting students through instruction. At the same time, however, the constant interpretation and reinterpretation of the reality of schooling through continuous dialogue at all levels permits infinite varieties of change to occur when needed. Attempts to simplify the supervisor's role by rationalizing it or by limiting its scope, therefore, may actually make the role less effective rather than more so.

References

Barthes, R. 1986. *The rustle of language.* New York: Hill & Wang/Farrar, Straus & Giroux.

Blumberg, A. 1984. *Report of the A.S.C.D. Committee on Central Office Supervisors.* Alexandria, Va.: Association for Supervision and Curriculum Development.

Bridges, E. M. 1982. Research on the school administrator: The state of the art, 1967–1980. *Educational Administration Quarterly,* 18 (3): 12–33.

Bruner, J. 1986. *Actual minds, possible worlds.* Cambridge, Mass.: Harvard University Press.

Buckley, W. 1968. Society as a complex adaptive system, In W. Buckley (ed.), *Modern systems theory for the behavioral scientist*, pp. 490–513, Chicago: Aldine.

Burch, B. G. & Danley, W. E. 1980. The instructional leadership role of central office supervisors. *Educational Leadership*, 37 (8): 636–637.

Campbell, J. 1982. *Grammatical man*. New York: Simon & Schuster.

Costa, A. & Guditus, C. 1984. Do district-wide supervisors make a difference? *Educational Leadership*, 41 (5): 84–85.

Cox, P. L. 1983. Complementary roles in successful change. *Educational Leadership*, 41 (3): 10–13.

Donmoyer, R. & Neff, A. R. 1983. The nature of curriculum and instruction administrators' work. Paper presented at the Annual Meeting of the American Educational Research Association, Montreal, Canada. April 11-15, 1983.

Fisher, B. A. 1985. Leadership as medium: Treating complexity in group communication research. *Small Group Behavior*, 16 (2): 167–196.

Floyd, M. K. 1986. Meanings that outstanding central office instructional supervisors associate with their role (Doctoral dissertation, University of Georgia, 1986).

Fullan, M. 1982. *The meaning of educational change*. New York: Teachers College Press.

Harris, B. M. 1967. Roles of supervisors and curriculum workers. In R. P. Wahle (ed.), *Toward professional maturity of supervisors and curriculum workers*, pp. 1–12. Washington, D.C.: Association for Supervision and Curriculum Development, National Educational Association.

Martin, W. J. & Willower, D. J. 1981. The managerial behavior of high school principals. *Educational Administration Quarterly*, 17 (1): 69–90.

Peters, T. J. & Waterman, R. H. 1982. *In search of excellence: Lessons from America's best run companies*. New York: Harper & Row.

Pitner, N. J. 1978. Descriptive study of the everyday activities of suburban school superintendents: The management of information (Doctoral dissertation, The Ohio State University, 1978).

Rowan, B. 1982. Instructional management in historical perspective: Evidence on differentiation in school districts. *Educational Administration Quarterly*, 18 (1): 43–59.

Sergiovanni, T. J. & Starrat, R. J. 1979. *Supervision: Human perspectives*. New York: McGraw-Hill.

Speiker, C. A. 1976. *Curriculum leaders: Improving their influence*. Alexandria, Va.: Association for Supervision and Curriculum Development.

Sullivan, C. G. 1980. The work of the instructional supervisor: A functional analysis (Doctoral dissertation, Emory University, 1980).

Sullivan, C. G. 1982. Supervisory expectations and work realities: The great gulf. *Educational Leadership*, 39 (6): 448–451.

Weick, K. 1978. The spines of leaders. In M. W. Mccall, Jr. & M. M. Lombardo (eds.), *Leadership: Where else can we go?*, pp. 37–61. Durham, N.C.: Duke University Press.

Weick, K. E. 1985. Sources of order in underorganized systems: Themes in recent organizational theory. In Y. S. Lincoln (ed.), *Organizational theory and inquiry: The paradigm revolution*, pp. 106–136. Beverly Hills: Sage Publications.

Wiles, J. & Bondi, J. 1980. *Supervision: A guide to practice.* Columbus, Ohio: Charles E. Merrill.

Wimpelberg, R. K. 1987. The dilemma of instructional leadership and a central role for central office. In W. Greenfield (ed.), *Instructional leadership: Concepts, issues and controversies*, pp. 100–117. Boston: Allyn and Bacon.

2
Problems, Frustrations, Satisfactions, and Solutions

The central office supervisor's position differs in many ways from other professional positions in the school district. An especially important difference noted in Chapter One is that supervisory tasks are less clearly defined than those of teachers, principals, and superintendents. Given this ambiguity, an individual's interpretation of the situation becomes a major factor influencing the enactment of his or her role. An illustration may be found in the varying reactions of supervisors to the diversity, fragmentation, and ambiguity inherent in their position.

The report of the A.S.C.D. Task Force on Research on Central Office Supervision referred to in Chapter One suggests that much work-related frustration experienced by supervisors of curriculum and instruction results from perceptions of not having enough time and having to wear too many hats in fulfilling job responsibilities. Other sources of frustration identified in the report include having to perform trivial functions unrelated to the improvement of instruction, dealing with uncooperative or incompetent principals and apathetic teachers, facing political and bureaucratic constraints, and not having one's contributions understood or recognized by others in the school system.

The Task Force report also states, however, that much of the satisfaction supervisors experience in their work comes from opportunities

> to try new things, the challenge to be creative, job flexibility and the ability to develop one's own work schedule, the diversity of one's work, the opportunity to develop new and creative relationships with principals and teachers, and the opportunity to observe one's colleagues get a new sense of excitement and challenge about their work. (Blumberg, 1984, p. 14)

Paradoxically, the same dimensions of the supervisory position that are identified as causes of frustration, such as diversity of responsibilities and working with principals and teachers, are also major sources of satisfaction. A likely explanation may be that a range of individuals was surveyed by the Task Force, some of whom experience the diversity and ambiguity of the supervisory role as very frustrating and others who derive great satisfaction from it. This chapter focuses on the subjective experience of being a successful central office supervisor of instruction. The problem of social and psychological distance from teachers and classrooms, sources of frustration and satisfaction, possible solutions to supervisory role conflict, and the importance of norms and goals are discussed.

The Problem of Social and Psychological Distance

The potential for a sizable gap to develop between the ideals of the central office and the realities of classroom life is ever present in any district. A major factor contributing to this gap, which supervisors suggest will severely curtail their effectiveness, is the difference in status accorded to teachers and supervisors by the organization.

An associate superintendent for instruction in a very large and quickly growing suburban school system related an incident that had occurred a few years before. He had been meeting with a principal at one of the newer schools in the district when they decided to take a break and have a cup of coffee in the faculty lounge. The principal was soon called out of the lounge by her secretary to deal with some crisis that needed her immediate personal attention, leaving the supervisor alone to fend for himself.

In a few minutes, a teacher who had been hired fairly recently walked into the room, poured herself a cup of coffee, and struck up a light conversation with the associate superintendent. After ten or fifteen minutes, the teacher gathered up her things to leave and casually asked the supervisor which grade he taught. What happened next is illustrative of the social and psychological distance that may develop between teachers and central office staff. As the associate superintendent described it:

> When I told her who I was, she really got in a hurry to leave. That just ended that conversation. You know, I scared her to death.

Barriers can easily arise, as in the incident just described, that prevent free and open communication. A lack of mutual understanding and an absence of trust may result. Reducing psychological and social distance between themselves and teachers is therefore considered absolutely essential by successful central office supervisors of instruction. An associate superintendent in another district, for example, responded as follows to the question "What is most important about working effectively with teachers?":

> I think teachers need to know that we are not sitting up here in an ivory tower—that we know their problems in the classroom, we're interested in the children, we're interested in seeing that their program is a good educational program. But we're not trying to direct this from a distant planet. . . . We're willing to go right out there on the line with them to see what's happening.

The associate superintendent who accidentally frightened the teacher in the coffee room said that the incident had highlighted the necessity of his taking the initiative to make frequent contact with teachers to learn what they are "doing and thinking." He was especially interested in their concerns because he viewed his job as one of helping teachers solve problems. This supervisor believed that it was especially useful to gain access to teachers outside the classroom where they were most "free to talk." He made a point, therefore, to visit faculty lounges often, to have conversations with teachers during their preparation periods and also to personally attend as many teacher in-service sessions as he could in order to have the chance to chat with teachers informally.

Frequent informal contact with teachers develops the trust that is necessary for supervisors to influence instruction. Supervisors admit that, if the psychological and social barriers between teachers and the central office are not moderated, they have little practical way of knowing what is really going on in classrooms as students are taught the curriculum. Not only are they unable to help solve the immediate problems that teachers face, they are also unable to convey accurate information to the superintendent and school board for use in formulating district policy aimed at addressing system-wide instructional problems.

If sufficient rapport has been established, some teachers will feel free to telephone the supervisor with questions or concerns or even stop by the central office to talk. Many teachers inevitably remain reluctant to intrude so boldly on a central office supervisor's time, however, and will ask for needed information only if the supervisor is physically present in their school. Most successful supervisors develop favorite ways of "closing the gap," between themselves and teachers, that can be accomplished as the supervisor goes about performing his or her regular duties.

At times supervisors function as liaison between classrooms and the central office, as well as between teachers and such external agencies as state departments of education, regional staff development centers, universities, and textbook publishers. They convey information to teachers concerning policy changes, opportunities for in-service training, and newly developed resources and materials. Initiating communication to convey such information, however, can also provide opportunities for gathering information as well. A curriculum director explained that she often invented reasons to be in a school—for example, to hand-deliver books or materials. Several teachers inevitably approached her at such times with pressing needs for information, resources, or other assistance, of which she would have been otherwise unaware. "Whenever I go into the schools," she said, "I'll have two, three, or more things to do when I get back."

An assistant superintendent for instruction explained similarly:

> Sometimes you have to put the paperwork aside, even when the report is due, and go to the kindergarten. Just walk around. It's good for your soul and it's good for them to see you there. Carry your appointment book and look like you've got something to do.

This supervisor was asked to explain why it was good for teachers to see her in the schools. She responded:

> Because then they know you support them. They want to be seen doing what they do well. And they want you to say, "Golly, look at that kid! Look what he's doing!" Sure, they want to hear that. And I want to watch them do it, too, so that I know that [making copies of all these curriculum guides], and sitting here struggling over whether we teach it in the first grade or the third grade, counts for something.

Successful central office supervisors, thus, advocate behavior that is closely akin to the strategy of "management by walking around" advocated by Peters and Waterman (1982). Frequent contact with teachers enables supervisors to have a clear sense of what is going on as well as to foster the kinds of relationships with teachers that are needed for making a contribution to district effectiveness.

Classroom observations have become so formalized and closely associated with evaluation in recent years that it is sometimes difficult to convince teachers that a central office supervisor's visit to their classroom can be informal, nonthreatening, and even friendly. Yet most supervisors say that casual visits to classrooms are helpful mainly because they present an opportunity to find out what is really happening "out there" in the schools. Being able to get close enough to teachers to learn what the real instructional problems are, without posing a threat to them, is not easy, but a supervisor can take steps to appear less formidable to teachers.

A district coordinator in a small system, for instance, described something that he did to "open the door" between the teachers and himself. At teachers' requests, he would occasionally teach lessons on "the history of railroading," which was his hobby. By sharing a bit of his personal life with teachers and students in this way, and by "proving" himself in the classroom, he believed a closer rapport with teachers was established. Some supervisors caution, however, that when teaching a model lesson, it is wise to avoid making the regular teacher's performance look shabby in comparison. The resources that supervisors have at their disposal to prepare an occasional lesson make the "contest" unfair and may even cause some resentment.

More relevant to the district-wide issue, a curriculum director reported that when he first began his current job, he decided intentionally to close the gap between teachers and the central office that had developed under his predecessor over an eight-year period. He began by scheduling meetings with small groups of teachers throughout the system to find out "what they liked about the instructional program and what the hang-ups were." Meeting with groups gave the teachers a numerical advantage, he suggested, and made them feel more comfortable. Talking with groups is also more efficient in terms of time and can prepare the way for the involvement of teachers in committee work.

Frustrations

Reality is fraught with constraints and obstacles, and the world of successful supervisors is no exception. Most frustrations reported by instructional supervisors involve limitations of resources, time, and influence to accomplish everything they would like to achieve.

Not having enough money to do all the things they believe ought to be done instructionally for students is a concern mentioned by many supervisors. This seems to hold true almost regardless of the amount of funds actually available. For instance, a supervisor in a district that had been on an austerity budget for two years understandably said that he felt frustrated because "it impedes our progress." An associate superintendent in a more prosperous district, however, said that he was frustrated by not being able to get funding for the development of a new unit on communication skills that he believed would be beneficial to high school students. It was frustrating for him to see an immediate need for skills in the curriculum and then have to "wait two or three years before finally getting the money to do something about it." He acknowledged that no matter how much they gave him for the improvement of instruction, he would "have the feeling and the need for more."

Not having enough time to devote to instructional improvement is probably the most commonly expressed frustration among supervisors. Attending to the various curricular and instructional needs of teachers and students in the local schools could easily take up all of a supervisor's available time. But, as noted in the previous chapter, instructional issues constantly compete for attention with other tasks.

A supervisor in one district said that "curriculum [was his] biggest and most important job," and his greatest frustration was "not being able to devote as much time" to that aspect of his job as he would like. Paperwork is the most common culprit identified by supervisors in smaller districts as robbing them of time. An assistant superintendent said:

> Visiting schools and classrooms frequently is very important. This is one of the hardest things to do because of all these other demands. The paperwork is horrendous.

A curriculum director in another small district said:

> There are days when there's quite a lot of frustration, quite a lot of headaches. The last few days I've been virtually drowning in paperwork. . . . I cannot believe the number of pieces of paper that go across my desk that require a response. As a principal, I would never have believed that there could be so much paperwork anywhere.

The frustration of paperwork comes from not being able to do other things, like work on curriculum or get out into the schools. Federal grants, for example, are viewed by supervisors in smaller districts as mixed blessings because of the amount of paperwork they generate. While grants provide extra funds that are needed to help enhance the instructional program, supervisors often feel that the time required for making applications and writing reports significantly lessens the already scarce time available to them for working with teachers on instructional improvement. The problem of spending inordinate time on paperwork is especially acute when districts lack secretarial help. A curriculum director in one small district said:

> The thing that's probably hardest to understand for anybody who hasn't been in this job is the tremendous amount of paperwork that requires some sort of a response. . . . A lot of that paperwork is in response to state mandates, documenting things that you've done. . . . There are a lot of times when I think my time could better be spent in classrooms, helping teachers improve teaching skills, than sitting here pushing [a pencil] across paper to document something. . . .

A supervisor in another district similarly observed:

> I'm sure the watchword of the 1980s and 1990s is going to be "accountability." And that in itself causes problems, because in my job now there are just so many forms . . . to fill out. It takes me away from actually being in the trenches with the teachers and the kids.

Supervisors in smaller systems often express negative opinions about the "red tape" and "paper trails" in which they are caught up. In some cases supervisors consider the information requested by state and federal bureaucracies to be simply a nuisance. One district coordinator related, for example, how an official from Washington, D.C., had called him long-distance one day to determine whether a student who had been tested for hearing was a boy or a girl. The child had an androgynous first name, and whoever had done the paperwork originally had neglected to record the student's gender. Because the call came during the summer, the child, the child's teacher, and the school nurse were all unavailable, and it took over thirty minutes to locate the information. The federal official, at his own insistence, waited on hold the entire time. While the supervisor said that he "supposed [the information served] some useful purpose," he resented the intrusion on his own schedule and wondered whether local and federal tax dollars were being spent wisely in tracking down such details.

In contrast, central office supervisors in larger school districts who have adequate secretarial help (and sometimes staff assistants as well) do not usually consider paperwork as presenting a problem of any kind. One associate superintendent went so far as to say that in his opinion the issue of paperwork was simply an excuse that some supervisors used because they really did not want to visit schools and classrooms. Ironically, opportunities for central office supervisors in larger districts to visit and work with teachers seem no greater, because of their involvement in staff meetings and the sheer number of classrooms and schools for which they are responsible. As one supervisor who had worked in several districts observed:

26 CURRICULUM AND INSTRUCTION

I think that the setting in which you work makes a lot of difference in the perspective you have about supervision. . . . I think the size of the school district has a lot to do with it, because that determines the structure—you know: to whom you report, the number of channels things go through in order to effect change, and how often you're able to get into the schools to work with individual teachers or with principals.

An associate superintendent in a fairly large district explained:

There's little time for classroom observation, except when necessary. We're too big a system; we just don't have time to get out there. . . . If we are specifically invited at a specific time, we do go if we can manage it. But to try to get out there every day is just an impossible task. If it were a smaller school district, I think, yes [I could do it].

Another frustration expressed by supervisors is their limited influence over individual teachers and classrooms. Supervisors suggest that in cases where teachers simply choose to do the minimum required by the job, the only means available to improve instruction is by working indirectly through the principal. A supervisor in one district observed:

I have been in classrooms and have seen some very poor teaching that just hurts. And yet, the principal is the one who has to get in there and make the difference.

This supervisor felt that teacher tenure and a tendency by some principals to "protect" veteran teachers who were doing an inadequate job severely limited her ability to improve the performance of teachers.

An issue related to limited influence is the frustration of having a project suddenly curtailed by either the superintendent or the state department of education after the supervisor and others have devoted considerable time and effort to it. When asked what the most frustrating part of the job is, one curriculum coordinator responded:

Sometimes, working with the superintendent . . . because it is their school [district]. They are the ones who are ultimately held responsible. And sometimes it's frustrating to spend a lot of time on something and then be told that you can't do it. They do have the right to tell you no.

Sudden changes in direction can undermine the supervisor's

credibility with teachers and principals. Their frustration grows as it becomes more difficult for the supervisor to rally people behind the next improvement effort. An assistant superintendent related a recent case where teachers and parents in her district, despite initial misgivings, had invested "hours upon hours" on the development of a "life-skills" curriculum in response to a policy directive from the state education department. The recent series of national studies that criticized the public schools, however, resulted in a sudden shift by the state toward an emphasis on academics. The state department never officially rescinded the original directive; it was simply conveniently "forgotten." "All of that just died down," the supervisor explained, "and no one's mentioned it again." The experience for her was clearly unpleasant:

> Those things are frustrating because you spend hours involving teachers, doing staff development, and writing curriculum guides. But this is what the state says to do, and you've got to do it. Teachers were frustrated and parents were frustrated. . . . I'm certainly not against trying something new, trying new ideas and making adjustments as you go along, but getting teachers involved in a new project is difficult. If you're not committed to some real follow-up, long-term follow-up, new ideas come and go. . . . You know the open-space classroom? I'm so glad we didn't knock out any walls.

A final source of frustration identified by some supervisors is that as curriculum generalists there is simply too much going on in the various content areas and grade levels for one person to keep up with. An associate superintendent explained that staying abreast of the latest innovations in every area and grade level was virtually impossible. "There's just not enough time [to stay on] the cutting edge" of everything. And in some areas, he acknowledged, he simply didn't "have the background."

> That's frustrating to me. . . . People see you as all-knowing, and you try to know as much as you can, but you can't possibly know everything.

A district coordinator expressed much the same experience and said that he sometimes felt embarrassed when he could not immediately answer a question concerning some obscure or highly specialized aspect of the curriculum. "I know a little bit about everything," he said, "but I'm really not an expert on anything." He went on to say in mock self-deprecation that at such times he sometimes felt "like a jack-of-all-trades but a master of none."

Satisfaction

The satisfaction for successful central office instructional supervisors, on the other hand, apparently arises from simply doing and accomplishing many of the activities involved in the supervisory position. Working with people, initiating change, and staying informed about the latest ideas and developments in education are things that successful supervisors say they find intrinsically enjoyable.

The complexity and diversity that stymie easy understanding of the role of central office supervisor apparently are experienced by successful practitioners as stimulating. For many, the job is described as perpetually novel and self-renewing; it represents a chance to work with new people and new programs, with "no two years exactly alike." The following, quite typical response to the question of what the experience of being a supervisor is like came from an assistant superintendent with ten years' experience:

> It's fascinating because every day is a new day and there's something new happening all the time.

Another supervisor—whose extensive experience included being a classroom teacher, a principal, a subject area specialist, and acting superintendent—summed up the feelings of many of his colleagues when asked what his job is like:

> I look upon it as the single most interesting and satisfying job in the school district, the greatest opportunity to have an impact on what happens in the classroom, where the action is. I'll happily finish out my career this way.

A curriculum coordinator responded to the same question similarly:

> It's a very exciting job because you're always working with the teachers, who are working with the students, and you're making the changes and the differences that go into making a school dynamic. It means having a thousand things going on at once. You can never sit back and wait to finish one experience, because you have something else happening at the same time.

"Interesting," "satisfying," and "exciting" are terms that successful central office supervisors almost universally use to describe their work. They enthusiastically portray their jobs as being dynamic and ever changing, as one of the most stimulating and fascinating in education, and as providing constant opportunity for personal growth and expression of creativity. Excitement, novelty, and change do not imply in any sense, however, that there is a lack of direction or purpose. Descriptions of supervisors' experiences of the role suggest a constant and almost organic growth process. The words used by a director of instruction convey this idea well:

> Something that is very pleasing is that we'll finish one job, and it automatically opens into another job that is very relevant. We're not just sporadically hitting trouble spots; everything is like a continuous unfolding of different types of activities leading to the same overall goal of effectiveness for the school system.

The variety and novelty of events that central office supervisors contend with provide numerous opportunities for creative expression. Effective supervisors seem to develop an interactive, rather than simply reactive, relationship with their environments, and they enjoy being able to "generate a lot of new ideas" and see them introduced in the schools. Although supervisors certainly are influenced by the nature of the job and the particular situational context of their work, as noted earlier, they seem in many ways to have more latitude than those in other positions in the school to influence the reality of their work environment (Donmoyer and Neff, 1983).

The most constant characteristic of the role of supervisor, it seems, is that it is forever changing. Rather than presenting a problem, however, this mutability can be an exciting challenge. One curriculum director described her job as "dynamic," and she most enjoyed being a part of changes that she saw as benefiting students:

> You see teachers get excited, you see students get excited, you see change coming about, and you see that you're making a difference with kids.

Deriving pleasure from the intrinsic satisfactions of doing the job and doing it well is seen by some supervisors as especially important because recognition and praise and other types of verbal encouragement are relatively infrequent. "One better get personal satisfaction from doing the job," a supervisor said, "because no one else knows how hard you work." The instructional program is supposed to receive the recognition, supervisors explain, not the supervisor. According to an assistant superintendent, the success of everyone

> reflects on the program as a whole, and that's your job. So you get your jollies through that, not through blaring name-recognition. It has to be that way. If it's not, you're in the wrong job.

Thus, central office supervisors have to remain aware of the progress achieved within their districts in the area of instruction in order to derive satisfaction from knowing that they contributed to that success.

For some district level supervisors of instruction, prestige and higher pay compensate in part for the absence of external praise and recognition for specific accomplishments. Having a strong, positive sense of one's abilities and personal worth, however, appears to be more important to a supervisor's psychological well-being. "You get personal satisfaction knowing that you've done a good job and that you're being paid a decent salary for what you're doing," one supervisor observed, "but you'd better be personally secure or you're going to have problems." Conferred status alone, this supervisor suggested, is no protection against the moments of uncertainty and self-doubt that must be faced.

In addition to intrinsic and extrinsic satisfactions available to supervisors, a third source of satisfaction might be termed "altruistic rewards." In this case, enjoyment is said to be derived from the ability to influence students and teachers in positive ways by satisfying their needs and contributing to their personal and professional development. "I get a lot of personal satisfacton," one supervisor commented, "in being able to affect the lives of all the students in our schools."

An associate superintendent said that he thought he would eventually look back with the "greatest satisfaction" on the recently completed large-scale introduction of computers into the curriculum of his district. The change had been initiated by teachers and was accomplished despite severe financial difficulties and initial resistance from some building administrators. When asked what in particular made this satisfying, he responded:

> Because we've affected something that's happening in the classroom, and it was a desire and a recommendation made by the teachers.

A district coordinator said that he felt satisfied when teachers commented upon an in-service session he had planned, saying that it was "worthwhile" and they "got something useful out of it." In the words of an assistant superintendent:

> I like the recognition. But if I, or one of my staff, can come up with a new or better way of doing something [in instruction], that's the real joy. And I guess that's the reward: seeing that thing tried and working in the classroom and seeing [teachers and students] excited about it.

Supervisors tend to define their own success, it seems, more in terms of the success of classroom teachers and student accomplishments than in their own achievements. An important dimension of supervisory success is the introduction of new materials, techniques, and ideas that teachers find useful in the classroom. For example, one assistant superintendent responded to the question of how she could tell when she had been successful by saying:

> When people tell you that they are seeing success in what they're doing with programs and with children, and when people ask you for your advice, you feel good about what you've done.

Supervisors appear to rely heavily on anecdotal evidence from teachers and principals as relevant feedback for guiding their practice. Although many report that they are also sensitive to student test scores as indicators of personal success, such objective measures are seen as too gross and infrequent for making the fine adjustments needed for doing the job well. In contrast, anecdotal evidence is considered more helpful on a day-to-day basis because it is immediate and readily available. Analyses of standardized test results in some districts influence the curriculum and instructional emphasis of teachers, but such results seem to be used more often for long-range planning. Supervisors generally claim to be neither highly encouraged nor overly discouraged by a single test result. They look instead for larger patterns of success and are reluctant to rely on any single measure of progress, which they know can fluctuate considerably from year to year.

Supervisors speak of working toward broad instructional goals, but they caution that true success comes in small, gradual increments over a long period of time. District goals tend to be used as general guides that orient behavior rather than as outcomes that are actually achieved. An associate superintendent had the following to say about success:

> It's not an event that suddenly happens. It takes years to really be successful in our setting, where you're teaching others. And I think that if you can see consistency and constant movement toward [instructional] goals—whether you're actually there or not—that to me says I'm successful.

This description of success suggests a gradual accumulation over time. Many supervisors say that they think of success, in a related sense, as a process of uniting diverse and seemingly unrelated elements into a cohesive whole. The result represents something new for themselves or for others. An associate superintendent described how she had felt successful after writing a grant that was to benefit special-education students. This task had been especially challenging because special education was not one of her areas of training, expertise, or responsibility:

> There was a feeling of accomplishment because it was something totally different than I had ever done before, and it took me a great deal of time to get a handle on it and pull it together.

The "pulling together" of diverse elements within the district is not limited, however, to information. Nor is it something the supervisor typically does alone. In most cases it involves a consensual agreement and mobilization of many people and processes toward a common purpose. When asked for an example of when she felt successful, an assistant superintendent responded:

> I feel good each spring, when we select a textbook committee and have teachers come in to examine books and then reach a conclusion that's agreeable to everybody.

When asked what in particular made her feel good about the textbook selection process, she answered:

> Well, we are all with the same system. We're all working toward the same goal of doing good things for kids. If the teachers are happy, are pleased with what they're doing, then I'm pleased somehow at the same time. . . . The way people react is the bottom line.

Reducing Role Conflict

Roles in any social system are obviously influenced by the tasks required of them and can even be defined simply in terms of executed behaviors (Thibaut & Kelley, 1959; Sztompka, 1986). Proponents of management by objectives or merit pay schemes are especially fond of such task-based definitions for the purposes of measuring and evaluating the performance of individuals. However, it is difficult if not impossible to describe the central office supervisory position behaviorally without referring directly to tasks performed by others. This is because district level supervisors primarily support and facilitate the activities of teachers, principals, and the superintendent. Fortunately for the sake of our understanding of the work of central office supervisors, it is possible to define a position in an organization other than in behavioral terms.

Sociologists define a role, for example, in terms of norms or expectations for behavior that are associated with a particular position within a social system (Homans, 1950). These norms apply especially to the relationships that a person establishes and maintains with other people. Any given position within a school, such as that of supervisor, may be described as being comprised of a number of roles, each of which relates to another status or position within the social structure of the school. Thus, a central office supervisor enacts different roles, depending upon whether he or she is interacting with a teacher, a principal, a superintendent, a student, or a member of the school board. This collection of associated roles is referred to as a "role set" (Merton, 1968).

When the expectations that are held by the various people with whom an individual interacts are inconsistent or contradict one another, role conflict is the result. For example, teachers may hold the expectation that a supervisor or curriculum director should be readily available in the schools to help solve instructional problems as they arise. The superintendent, on the other hand, may hold the expectation that the supervisor should spend time applying for state and federal funds to finance innovative instructional programs. "If the superintendent has certain expectations for the job that prohibit you from doing something that a teacher expects you to do," a curriculum director explained, "then you've either got to explain to that teacher why you can't do what they want, or you're going to have a teacher thinking that you're not doing your job."

Individuals can respond to role conflict in a number of ways. In any hierarchical organization there is considerable pressure on a role occupant to conform to the preferences of the person who holds the most power. For a district level supervisor, this person is the superintendent. Completing paperwork in the central office can thus take on a disproportionate urgency because it has a tangible outcome that is very visible to influential persons, such as the superintendent and state and federal officials. There is also a tendency in social settings, however, for individuals to conform to the expectations of those with whom they have the most frequent contact or to whom they are most visible. If a supervisor frequently gets out of the central office and into the schools, teachers and principals may become a potent source of expectations as well.

Conforming to the expectations of one individual at the expense of others is an unsatisfactory solution to role conflict for central office supervisors of curriculum and instruction. The neglect of one or more roles that comprise the position will inevitably impair the organization unless someone else assumes responsibility for them. Even additional help may not solve the problem permanently.

In an attempt to resolve the dilemmas posed by role conflict for instructional supervisors, Sturges (1979) once called for a redistribution of supervisory responsibilities into two separate positions, one to be called "administrative" and the other "consultative." This proposal would, in effect, simply eliminate some of the role demands by assigning them to another position. While this solution might temporarily ease the problem of role conflict for district level supervisors, the administrative position probably would be in jeopardy before too long because most of its tasks could be handled fairly easily by a competent secretary. The consultative position would probably eventually drift back into the administrative realm due to the inherent pressures on people within organizations to please superordinates and to produce visible outcomes.

Some degree of role conflict is inevitable because of the competing demands from the variety of people who comprise a district level supervisor's role set. However, two practical solutions to the problem of role conflict exist that also happen to be consistent with fulfilling the requirements of the central office position effectively.

One alternative for dealing with role conflict that does not require sacrificing one set of role expectations to fulfill another involves seeking "mutual support" from others who hold the same position as oneself (Sztompka, 1986). A national professional organization—the Association for Supervision and Curriculum Development, for example—along with its state and local affiliates, might effectively neutralize conflicting and seemingly irreconcilable forces operating within local school districts by establishing external professional standards for the position of central office supervisor. A bonus accompanying this solution, of course, is that interaction with colleagues in a professional organization also provides opportunities for personal and professional development, which may enhance one's effectiveness.

Another alternative, which may help to resolve role conflict without sacrificing role expectations, involves heightening awareness among the members of one's role set of the contradictions that are inherent in one's position. By openly acknowledging that some of the demands of one's position contradict others, the burden of resolving role conflict shifts from the individual to the group (Sztompka, 1986). The advantage of this approach is that in the process of resolving one's own role conflicts, the central office supervisor is able to help others clarify ambiguities in the broader social system. Through an open dialogue, normative expectations can be made explicit.

Importance of Norms and Goals

Homans (1950, p. 126) suggests that a norm can be thought of as a kind of retrospective goal that helps people to make sense of what they are doing:

> If we think of a norm as a goal that a group wishes to reach, we can see that the goal is not set up, like the finish line of a race, before the race starts, but rather that the group decides, after it starts running, what the finish line shall be. Once the norm is established, it exerts a back effect on the group. It may act as an incentive in the sense that a man may try to bring his behavior closer to the norm. But the norm can be a mark to shoot for only if it is not too far away from what can be achieved in everyday life. If it gets impossibly remote—and just how far that is no one can say—it will be abandoned in favor of some more nearly attainable norm. Society's preaching and its practice are elastically linked. Each pulls the other, and they can never separate altogether.

Coincidentally, one of the Latin meanings of "curriculum" is "racetrack." Consistent with Homans's analogy, the curriculum of a district may be thought of as a goal that is both pursued as an ideal and enacted in practice—but a goal that is continuously adjusted by the members of the group. An effective curriculum is dynamic in the sense that it is negotiated between the two poles represented by central office idealism and classroom reality through an ongoing discussion among teachers, administrators, and central office staff. The curriculum may therefore be thought of as an instructional norm, derived from the core value of benefiting students through instruction, which guides and influences the behavior of educators within the district. From this general norm and ongoing dialogue, more specific instructional goals can be formulated.

The pursuit and achievement of specific instructional goals provides supervisors with feelings of completion and evidence that progress is being made. It was noted in the first chapter that supervisors seem to make sense of what they do for themselves by looking both forward and backward in time. District-wide instructional goals seem to be a part of this process of sense-making for supervisors. One curriculum director commented that goals were important for her knowing when she is successful:

> By looking back over time, I know what the goals are, and I know where we are trying to go. If I can look back and see that we are

closer and I can say, "this happened because of something that I facilitated"—that feels good.

District-wide instructional goals can also give a supervisor a sense of ongoing purpose and direction while engaged in the diverse responsibilities of the position. One supervisor reflected, after recounting the numerous and varied events that had comprised his previous workday, that it might appear fragmented to an outside observer, who would think that he "hopped from one thing to another." He explained, however, that the things he did each day usually did not "arise haphazardly." Although the tasks he engaged in were certainly different from each other, he emphasized that they all related in some way to a few major goals that he constantly kept in mind.

Thus, district-wide instructional goals that are derived from a dialogue with teachers and administrators help to provide a focus that maintains consistency and continuity among the wide variety of things a supervisor does each day. These goals help an instructional supervisor comprehend how one activity is related to another, both immediately and over the long run. Any given activity may not be directly related to the activities immediately preceding and following it, but that does not mean that the supervisor's activities are haphazard, purely reactive, or entirely unrelated to one another. General instructional goals, arrived at through a continuous dialogue with others in the supervisor's role set, unify the diverse activities in which supervisors engage by providing a broad-scope and long-term frame of reference. In the process of closing the gap between the idealism of the central office and the realities of the classroom, a social reality is interpreted and reinterpreted, which gives direction and meaning to behavior at both levels of the organization.

References

Blumberg, A. 1984. *Report of the A.S.C.D. Committee on Central Office Supervisors*. Alexandria, Va.: Association for Supervision and Curriculum Development.

Donmoyer R. & Neff, A. R. 1983. The nature of curriculum and instruction administrators' work. Paper presented at the Annual Meeting of the American Educational Research Association, Montreal, Canada. April 11-14, 1983.

Homans, G. C. 1950. *The human group*. New York: Harcourt, Brace & World.

Merton, R. K. 1968. *Social theory and social structure*. New York: Free Press.

Peters, T. J. & Waterman, R. H. 1982. *In search of excellence*. New York: Harper & Row.

Sturges, A. W. 1979. Instructional supervisors: A dichotomy. *Educational Leadership*, 36 (8): 586–589.
Sztompka, P. 1986. *Robert K. Merton: An intellectual profile.* New York: St. Martin's Press.
Thibaut, J. W. & Kelley, H. H. 1959. *The social psychology of groups.* New York: John Wiley & Sons.

3
Organizational Culture and Social Structure

During the last decade, organization theorists have called attention to some unique characteristics of schools that make them less rational and presumably more difficult to manage than other types of organizations. It has been noted, for example, that the goals schools pursue are multiple and shift frequently. Not only are schools expected to be all things to all people, they are also expected to respond immediately whenever society decides to change direction. Although newly rediscovered, this capriciousness on the part of society is by no means a recent development. Over fifty years ago Anna Freud (1935) observed that society's ever-changing and conflicting demands upon schools were equivalent to requiring that a single industry produce featherbeds in times of peace and cannonballs in times of war.

Another complicating factor in the management of schools is that the processes and techniques that educators employ are generally unpredictable in their consequences. A teacher cannot guarantee that all students will learn what is taught, for example, even if they do exactly what is prescribed for them. Too many uncontrollable psychological and environmental factors inevitably intervene. Educators are essentially limited to creating a set of conditions under which learning is more likely to occur among students. The results are never entirely certain.

A school, therefore, is very much *unlike* a steel mill, where certain proportions of iron, coke, and lime, when combined at a predetermined temperature and pressure, can be counted upon to produce a particular grade of steel time after time. A school is more like a brokerage firm, which provides information and advice in the form of general recommendations based upon experience and informed hunches about what clients should do, but which cannot predict specific outcomes with certainty because of the volatility of the marketplace and the fact that investment decisions are ultimately made by the client.

Complicating matters further, to the uncertainties inherent in educational goals and techniques may be added a formal organization that is fragmented and compartmentalized, learning outcomes that defy easy measurement, frequent turnover among students and professional staff, and turbulence originating in the economic, social, and political environments. On the basis of these characteristics, organization theorists have described schools as "loosely coupled" systems (Weick, 1976), a view that contrasts sharply with the more traditional view of schools as "tightly coupled" bureaucracies.

March and Olsen (1976, p. 12) use the term "organized anarchy" to describe the manner in which schools and other public organizations respond to a chronic condition of "ambiguity" that exists due to shifting and poorly defined intentions, an unclear understanding of technologies and environments, difficulty in interpreting the relationship among events, and uncertain and changing patterns of participation. A secondary school principal recently described his job to me as trying to "coordinate bedlam," which seems to capture nicely this view of reality and highlights the urgent practical need in schools to reduce ambiguity and uncertainty.

Behavior loses meaning for people, however, when it is too closely determined, just as quickly as it loses meaning in the presence of chaos. Sentences that are entirely predictable soon become boring, for example, but sentences that are entirely unpredictable cannot be understood at all. The rules of grammar conveniently constrain the use of words in forming sentences, but not the meaning that a combination of words can convey. A certain limitation of uncertainty is necessary for a message to have meaning, it seems, yet a degree of ambiguity is also necessary for creativity and innovation to occur.

Campbell (1982) points out that a balance of freedom within flexible constraints is precisely what governs the orderly transmission of the genetic code from one generation to the next, while permitting the spontaneous proliferation of mutations that potentially contribute to evolutionary progress. In an analogous way, effective central office supervisors facilitate the consensual development of order around the core value of benefiting students through instruction, while simultaneously encouraging multiple expressions and enactments of this value by principals and teachers.

A large part of what central office supervisors and curriculum directors do, therefore, may be understood as being aimed toward the reduction of uncertainty in the ambiguous, unpredictable, and unstable reality of schools. And yet successful supervisors also intentionally strive to retain a fairly high degree of diversity within the system.

An essential function of effective supervision in education, in other words, involves helping people to understand what is happening to them and around them and how it all is related to what other people are doing, without imposing an overly predetermined pattern. The reduction of uncertainty through the construction of meaning in this way prevents the system from regressing toward chaos, yet it maintains the variety needed for adaptation and innovation.

More specifically, supervisors reduce uncertainty in school districts through activities that cluster around the interrelated dimensions of tasks, roles, and norms. Each of these dimensions is important in its own way and will be discussed in detail in a later chapter. Our understanding will be helped at this point, however, by establishing a theoretical frame of reference.

Organizational Culture

Organizational culture has been identified in recent years as a major determinant of organizational effectiveness in both business (Peters and Waterman, 1982; Deal and Kennedy, 1982) and education (Patterson, Purkey, and Parker, 1986; Lewis, 1987). The concept "culture" focuses our attention on social reality rather than on technical or bureaucratic definitions of what goes on in schools. While the concept represents an advance in our thinking about organizations, much of the literature on the subject really does little to inform the reader about what specifically can be done on a day-to-day basis that will contribute to a positive culture or transform an ineffective culture into an exceptional one (Conway, 1985).

Cultures in organizations, as in societies, represent shared understandings and expectations, or common frames of reference, that guide and give meaning to people's actions. Members of the same culture tend to perceive situations, define problems, make judgments, and interpret events in similar ways. Deal and Kennedy (1982) and Schein (1984) suggest that culture acts something like a "glue" that holds an organization together. That is, a culture bonds people and activities through a system of shared meanings and understandings. Although he does not link the process to culture formation, Glickman (1985, p. 4) makes a similar argument that the process of supervision acts like a "glue . . . that draws together the discrete elements of instructional effectiveness into whole-school action."

Cultural linkages may be an effective complement, if not an alternative, to bureaucratic rules and standardized procedures for reducing uncertainty within social systems, such as schools (Firestone and Wilson, 1985). Predictability and coordination are possible through culturally defined social norms that prescribe certain types of conduct considered appropriate by group members under various conditions. The advantage of normative controls over mechanistic controls is that they are less likely to result in some of the dysfunctions commonly associated with bureaucracy, such as feelings of isolation and alienation.

The importance of culture to school effectiveness has been highlighted by Deal (1984), who suggests that the process of improvement in education relies heavily on something akin to the self-fulfilling prophecy, or the Hawthorne effect. Drawing on L. Frank Baum's *The Wizard of Oz*, he makes the point that lasting and effective change cannot be "installed" from outside an organization. He suggests that educators have to learn, like the Scarecrow, Cowardly Lion, and Tinman in the Oz story, that virtues such as wisdom, courage, and heart have to emerge from within. Instead of searching for wizards and relying on technical solutions to problems in education, Deal suggests, educational excellence requires nothing less than an abandonment of rationality and a return to traditional attitudes and behaviors:

> The secret to educational excellence lies in rekindling and revitalizing dormant values, weakened or eroded through a decade of neglect and attack. It requires replacing a culture of technocracy and rationality, and reaffirming a time-tested culture of tradition and moral authority. (1984, p. 64)

In one sense, this view of organizations can be considered a step in the right direction in that it returns our attention to those qualities of social life that are meaningful to people and that the technical and bureaucratic perspectives miss entirely. It suggests that instead of working through the formal organization exclusively, educational practitioners need also to consider cultural values and norms when trying to get things accomplished.

On the other hand, using symbols, rituals, and ceremonies may be objectionable because they impact strongly on unconscious thought processes. Manipulating people in this way could effectively minimize opportunities for exercising rational choice. What is needed, both theoretically and practically, is a perspective of schools as organizations that takes into account the importance of social and cultural reality in people's lives, yet does not abandon consciousness and reason while doing so.

Schein (1984) has introduced the helpful notion that an organizational culture is necessarily comprised of elements that meet both the human need to avoid anxiety *and* the need to solve problems. The anxiety-reduction function of culture, which often is manifested in the form of ritualistic behavior, relates to "the human need for cognitive order and consistency" and motivates people to develop "a common language and shared categories of perception and thought" (p. 8). The discovery of new solutions, on the other hand, arises from these "interactive, shared experiences [at] times when habitual ways of doing things no longer work or when a dramatic change in the environment requires new responses." Such occasions require that leaders play a dual role:

> At those times, leadership must not only insure the invention of new and better solutions, but . . . also provide some security to help the group tolerate the anxiety of giving up old, stable responses, while new ones are learned and tested. (P. 9)

The Four Components of Social Action

Any type of social system can be analyzed in terms of four essential components: values, norms, organized roles, and tasks (Homans, 1950; Thibaut and Kelley, 1959). These components can be viewed as hierarchical in terms of their specificity and their relationships with each other (Parsons, 1960, 1961; Smelser, 1962). Values, for example, represent the most general guide to social behavior. Values influence the pattern of norms, roles, and tasks in an organization, but they do not limit these more specific components entirely. Sergiovanni and Starrat (1971, pp. 27–29) have proposed that "enlightened supervision" attends to these components, which they describe as "four basic needs which all organizations as social systems seek to satisfy."

Smelser (1962, p. 31), who refers to the task level as "facilities," related the four components of social action to education very generally as follows:

> In America we are committed to a *value* of free public education. To implement this value at a *normative* level, we establish rules guaranteeing children of certain ages an opportunity to go to school, specify qualifications for entering and leaving school, enact property laws and float bonds to construct schools, and so on. At the *organizational* level we mobilize human motivation and talent into roles of administrators, teachers, and pupils to realize the goals of education in a concrete social setting. And finally, with regard to *facilities*, we use techniques of instruction, books, musical instruments, etc., to implement the goals of education.

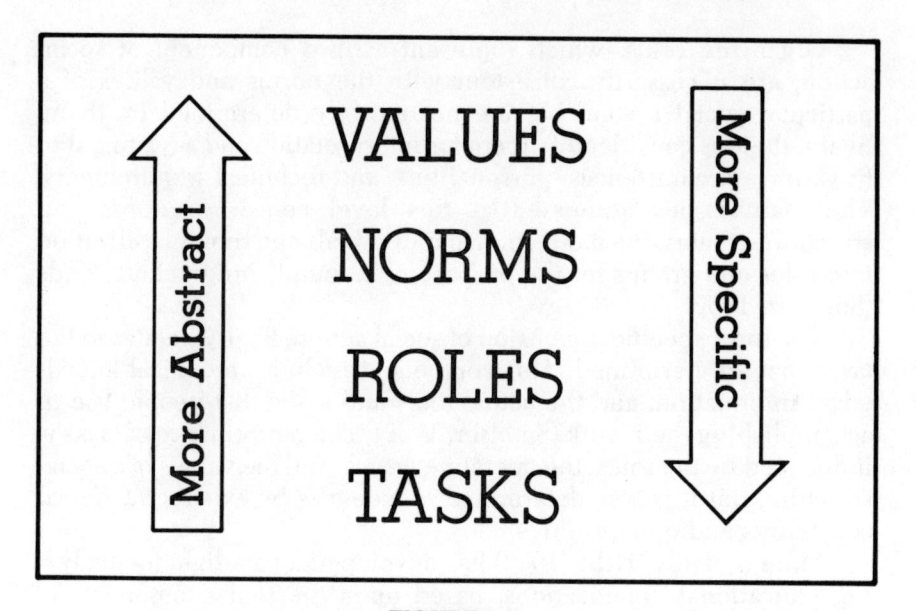

```
┌─────────────────────────────────────────┐
│    ↑                              ↓     │
│    │                              │     │
│  More    VALUES            More         │
│  Abstract                  Specific     │
│          NORMS                          │
│                                         │
│          ROLES                          │
│                                         │
│          TASKS                          │
└─────────────────────────────────────────┘
```

FIGURE 3.1

HIERARCHY: THE FOUR COMPONENTS OF SOCIAL ACTION

The hierarchical arrangement for the four components is depicted in Figure 3.1. The relationship among these social components is such that a change in values requires a reconstitution of the three lower levels. A change in norms, in turn, necessitates a reconfiguration of roles and tasks, but not a change in values. A change in roles only affects the performance of tasks, and a change in tasks is possible without necessarily affecting any of the more general components.

An illustration of the subtle influence of values on the subsequent pattern of social organization is provided by Smelser (1962) with regard to the value "democracy." Though there are many nations that may be called democratic because of their commitment to this core value, he points out, the specific enactment of democracy takes many forms. The constitutions, political processes, laws, economies, means of production, and the freedoms enjoyed by citizens vary enormously among nations. Nevertheless, they may be appropriately classified as democratic because they espouse the same general value.

Norms may be viewed as more specific than values but less specific than organized roles and tasks. Norms serve to specify, integrate, and regulate behavior within a social system and represent broad standards of conduct that apply in the pursuit of valued ends. Norms may be formally stated as laws and regulations or may be unconsciously understood as appropriate by the members of a given culture.

Organized roles, which represent a third component of social action, are necessarily consistent with the norms and values of a particular social system but are not entirely determined by them. Again, there is considerable room for interpretation and adjustment to fit various circumstances, personalities, and technical requirements. The main issues addressed at this level concern rewards and structure—that is, the motivation of individuals and their mobilization into roles and groups for the purpose of accomplishing definite ends (Smelser, 1962).

The most specific dimension of social action, finally, relates to the tasks that are performed. This component includes technical knowledge, information, and the actual tools and skills that people use in accomplishing their work (Smelser, 1962). The performance of tasks is influenced by the roles, the operative norms, and the values of a social structure, but it is also determined to a degree by existing technical constraints and opportunities.

More recently, Hills (1982) has developed a paradigm for analyzing educational organizations, based upon the four components of social action, that emphasizes their symbolic quality and contribution to cultural meaning. Hills proposes that in social systems values function much like DNA molecules, and norms like rules of grammar, in that they pattern and regulate the organization of a system according to predetermined principles, while permitting an infinite variety of expression, which allows the system to adapt to specific situations.

Values, according to Hills, operate as "master blueprints" or "symbolic cultural codes" that "program" but do not entirely restrict patterns of action and meaning at the progressively less general lower levels. Thus, the primary function of values in schools is overall pattern maintenance within the social system, and the purpose of norms is a more specific integration of elements. Organized roles, in turn, are mobilized to attain specific outcomes, and the performance of tasks serves the purpose of adaptation. "Action," according to this perspective, "is conceived as the control of the expenditure of effort to realize symbolically defined intentions in symbolically defined situations" (Hills, 1982, p. 39).

The Social Components, Collective Behavior, and Schools

Smelser (1962) applied the four components of social action in a classic analysis of uninstitutionalized episodes of collective behavior, including such phenomena as panics, crazes, hostile outbursts, social and political movements, and religious revivals. The relevance of this work for understanding and functioning of schools as organizations comes from the observation that these phenomena occur as a reaction to "strain" originating from ambiguity at the various social-component levels; they represent an attempt by people to reconstruct the social order or one or more of its components in order to resolve the ambiguity. If the loose-coupling theorists are correct in their assertions, public education should be rampant with structural strain and attempts to resolve it. Lortie (1986), in fact, has recently suggested that declines in teacher satisfaction over the last twenty years may be the result of unresolved structural strain in schools.

The sources of structural strain in an existing social order, according to Smelser (1962), differ somewhat at each level. At the task level, for example, ambiguity concerning the relationship between means and ends raises the question of whether existing knowledge and skills are adequate for getting the job done. At the level of organized roles, an imbalance between responsible performance and the rewards available may cause problems of motivation. Conflicting expectations at the normative level, in turn, can negatively affect the degree of integration of elements and efforts within the system. The existence of competing values at the most general level, finally, raises fundamental issues of personal commitment.

Structural strain arising from ambiguities within a social system at any level results in feelings of uncertainty and dissatisfaction among individual members. Collective behavior, including crazes and social movements, can be viewed as an attempt by people to resolve this psychological uncertainty by restructuring one or more social components. Following Smelser's reasoning, therefore, the ambiguity and uncertainty inherent in schools as organizations may be precisely what makes them so susceptible to fads and crazes and may also help explain why schools are so often targeted for reforms.

The particular type of collective behavior manifested within a group, according to Smelser (1962), depends largely upon which social component is the focus of strain. At the level of facilities, for example, uncertainty concerning the relationship between means and ends may result in either a "panic" or a "craze." The former is a sudden collective flight away from existing patterns of interaction based on a negative definition of the situation, while the latter represents a collective rush toward something new. In education, the periodic denigration and abandonment of established instructional techniques and subsequent embrace of the latest innovations seem to be excellent examples of the "panic" and "craze" at work in tandem.

Strain in a social system is most likely to be felt first at the level of greatest specificity, that of tasks, where technical knowledge and skill are applied. Rumors typically develop and spread in an environment of ambiguity and uncertainty as individuals flounder around for meaning. These rumors eventually coalesce into a "generalized belief," which represents an attempt by the group to provide a degree of structure and constitutes "a 'common culture' within which leadership, mobilization, and concerted action can take place" (Smelser, 1962, p. 82). These generalized beliefs frequently are characterized by "hysterical" or "wishful" thinking as exemplified in miracle cures, panaceas, fads, crazes, hero worship, and scapegoating.

Successful central office supervisors are sensitive to the ambiguity and resulting uncertainty that can exist among teachers and principals in the local schools. As an associate superintendent remarked, "You need to be constantly aware that there is a certain amount of uncertainty out there." Scarcity of information concerning means and ends at the level where tasks are accomplished is compounded by the fragmented structure of the organization, as evidenced by the isolation of teachers in their classrooms and of principals in their schools. Indeed, the void is often filled by rumor and speculation that are often inaccurate and sometimes actually undermine effective performance. A curriculum director explained how "having to quell rumors" sometimes interfered with her instructional responsibilities:

> As I work in the schools, sometimes the problems that I run into are where people are not certain about what's happening or why. They ask me: "I heard this; is it true? So and so did this, and I hear the system is going to do thus and such." It's little, naggy, sometimes picky kinds of things. And a part of me wants to say, "Hey, that's not important. Let's get back to other things."

One way the central office supervisor can help to resolve structural strain is to recognize that rumors are important to the process of collectively defining the situation in schools. By translating and interpreting rumors in positive ways, supervisors help shape social reality so that people make sense of it in ways that are most beneficial to students.

If strain is not resolved at the level at which tasks are performed, people's attention shifts to the next higher-level component, that of organized roles, where the attempt to restructure continues (Smelser, 1962). In this way, a call for "career ladders" or "merit pay" for teachers logically follows a prolonged period of educational fads and panaceas relating to instructional technique. If ambiguity is not successfully resolved at the level of organized roles, the components of norms and values may in turn become activated, which tends to result in more comprehensive social, political, or religious movements and typically leads to more permanent changes. Adherents of a norm-oriented movement are likely to promote new legislation, rules, or customs, for example, while participants in a value-oriented movement seek nothing less than a redefinition of the moral and social orders.

There is a strong element in all social movements of what Smelser (1962) calls "magical thinking," or an unrealistic "if-only" mentality. Significantly, a recent publication by Patterson, Purkey, and Parker (1986, p. 27) makes the same point in criticizing the application of technical rationality to district level instructional-improvement efforts:

> Proponents of the rational model believe that a change in procedures will lead to improvement in educational practice. In short, the rational model begins with an "if-then" philosophy. If A happens, then B will logically follow. When reality fails to validate this "if-then" perspective (i.e., when B doesn't happen), the argument shifts to an "if-only" position. If only schools will tighten up rules and regulations, improved discipline will follow. If only teachers are given clear directives, then improved teaching will follow. Advocates of the nonrational model claim that the "if-then and if-only" model is wishful thinking; organizations do not always behave in a logical, predictable manner.

By extension, one might characterize most attempts to change schools or reform education as social movements masquerading as rational solutions (Deal, 1984). Though at some point the "generalized belief" held by individuals is transformed into a "more specific belief" that suggests that a particular behavior, goal, or rule will resolve structural ambiguity and strain, this specific belief is described by Smelser as "a general wish-fulfillment fantasy" (1962, p. 205). What seems to occur in social movements is that once a component of social reality is redefined,

> people do not proceed to respecify, step by step, down the line to reconstitute social action. Rather, they develop a belief which "short-circuits" from a very generalized component *directly* to the focus of strain. (P. 71)

An example of a generalized belief of this kind among educational policymakers might be that "academic standards are too low." This shared belief provides the "culture" within which more-specific beliefs develop—for instance, "athletes are not good scholars." No sincere attempt is made to determine if the generalized belief or the specific belief are actually true, nor is an attempt made to understand and remedy the underlying causes of poor academic achievement.

Instead, a "magical" solution typically emerges, one which may have clear overtones of scapegoating, such as the simplistic notion "no pass, no play."

Sarason (1971) similarly attributes the failure of new math—which he considers representative of the "modal process of change" in education—to a lack of clarity as to the intended results and a failure to address the question of how the results would be achieved. New math was intended to alter the relationships among administrators, teachers, and pupils, according to Sarason, yet very little attention was given to these interactions. He observes that implicit values underlie our understanding of school culture, and rather than making the appropriate adjustments in our thinking to fit the reality of schools, reformers inappropriately attempt to bring about change by applying their assumptions and beliefs directly to the "engineering aspects" of the educational process. The result is that, while innovations are frequently implemented, they rarely have any lasting impact.

Social Structure and Central Office Supervision

Collective behavior as evidenced in social movements, Smelser (1962, p. 72) notes, "is the action of the impatient," which contrasts sharply with the gradual adjustment of the social structure and purposeful mobilization of resources to the level of specific situations. Even norm-oriented reform movements, which advocate ostensibly rational solutions in the form of legislation, involve a "magical" element by promising extraordinary results. In Smelser's words:

> Those who adhere to normative beliefs endow themselves and the envisioned reconstitution of norms with enormous power, conceived as the ability to overcome that array of threats and obstacles which constitute the negative side of the adherent's world-picture. The proposed reform will render opponents helpless, and will be effective immediately. . . . Because of this exaggerated potency, adherents often see unlimited bliss in the future if only the reforms are adopted. For if they are adopted, they argue, the basis for threat, frustration, and discomfort will disappear. (1962, p. 117)

A Nation at Risk (National Commission on Excellence in Education, 1983) and other comparable documents urging broad, general reforms in education (such as vouchers or merit pay) as ways of dealing with specific classroom problems strongly exemplify such magical thought processes.

During a conversation I had with an instructional supervisor, the subject turned to the state legislature's recent passage of a law that promised to completely restructure public education in the state through a wide variety of reforms. I asked her if she was concerned that despite the law's apparent comprehensiveness, it made absolutely no reference to such positions as curriculum directors or instructional supervisors. Her response was a straightforward "Absolutely not! Somebody's going to have to make the darn thing work!" This, I believe, is a key to understanding the position of the central office supervisor.

Although central office supervisors are often advocates and agents of change, they are heavily involved as well in activities that contribute to stability and continuity (Sullivan, 1980; Harris, 1975). While this may at first seem paradoxical, change and stability are not mutually exclusive if one thinks of change in schools as an *evolutionary* process instead of a revolutionary one. That is, as central office supervisors resolve ambiguity and uncertainty within the school organization, they also promote a process of internal integration and adjustment.

This interpretation is consistent with Schein's (1984) observation that culture should not be thought of as something that is irrevocably fixed, because it is constantly evolving as people interact with one another and learn new ways of relating to the environment and managing internal affairs. Dealing with the fundamental question of whether to enhance diversity or enforce homogeneity, he suggests, probably requires some form of "culture consciousness raising" (p. 14).

Essentially, central office supervisors might be characterized as "patient realists," who facilitate the emergence and development of "institutionalized" social movements within the school, which serve to rejuvenate and gradually modify the internal culture. This requires, on their part, careful attention to stability as well as change. And they must focus their energies on issues relating specifically to the interpretation of norms, organized roles, and the performance of tasks as they go about helping others to interpret behavior, events, and artifacts in terms of the ultimate value of benefiting children. In other words, they must ensure that the many details that lie between a commitment to the welfare of children and the implementation of effective instruction are actively considered and addressed. Specific examples of how central office supervisors resolve structural strain at the social component levels will be presented in the next several chapters, but the process essentially hinges upon the direct involvement of teachers in curriculum and staff development and the maintenance of a positive definition of social reality within the district.

References

Campbell, J. 1982. *Grammatical man.* New York: Simon & Schuster.

Conway, J. A. 1985. A perspective on organizational cultures and organizational belief structure. *Educational Administration Quarterly,* 21 (4): 7–25.

Deal, T. E. 1984. Searching for the wizard: The quest for excellence in education. *Issues in Education,* 2 (1): 56–67.

Deal, T. E. & Kennedy, A. A. 1982. *Corporate cultures: The rites and rituals of corporate life.* Reading, Ma.: Addison-Wesley.

Firestone, W. A. & Wilson, B. L. 1985. Using bureaucratic and cultural linkages to improve instruction: The principal's contribution. *Educational Administration Quarterly,* 21 (2): 7–30.

Freud, A. 1935. Transl. by Barbara Low. *Psychoanalysis for teachers and parents.* New York: Emerson Books.

Glickman, C. D. 1985. *Supervision of instruction: A developmental approach.* Boston: Allyn and Bacon.

Harris, B. M. 1975. *Supervisory behavior in education.* Englewood Cliffs, N. J.: Prentice-Hall.

Hills, R. J. 1982. Functional requirements and the theory of action. *Educational Administration Quarterly,* 18 (4): 36–61.

Homans, G. C. 1950. *The human group.* New York: Harcourt, Brace & World.

Lewis, J. 1987. *Achieving excellence in our schools.* Boston: Allyn and Bacon.

Lortie, D. C. 1986. Teacher status in Dade County: A case of structural strain? *Phi Delta Kappan* 67 (8): 568–575.

March, J. G. & Olsen, J. P. 1976. *Ambiguity and choice in organizations.* Bergen, Norway: Universitetsforlaget.

National Commission on Excellence in Education. 1983. *A nation at risk: The imperative for educational reform.* Washington, D.C.: U.S. Government Printing Office.

Parsons, T. 1960. *Structure and process in modern societies.* Glencoe, Ill.: Free Press.

Parsons, T. 1961. An outline of the social system. In T. Parsons, et al. (eds.), *Theories of society.* New York: Free Press.

Patterson, J. L., Purkey, S. C. & Parker, J. V. 1986. *Productive school systems for a nonrational world.* Alexandria, Va.: Association for Supervision and Curriculum Development.

Peters, T. J. & Waterman, R. H. 1982. *In search of excellence: Lessons from America's best-run companies.* New York: Harper & Row.

Sarason, S. B. 1971. *The culture of the school and the problem of change.* Boston: Allyn and Bacon.

Schein, E. H. 1984. Coming to a new awareness of organizational culture. *Sloan Management Review,* Winter, 3–15.

Sergiovanni, T. J. & Starratt, R. J. 1971. *Emerging patterns of supervision: Human perspectives.* New York: McGraw-Hill.

Smelser, N. J. 1962. *Theory of collective behavior.* New York: Free Press.

Sullivan, C. G. 1980. The work of the instructional supervisor: A functional analysis (Doctoral dissertation, Emory University, 1980).

Thibaut, J. W. & Kelley, H. H. 1959. *The social psychology of groups.* New York: John Wiley & Sons.

Weick, K. E. 1976. Educational organizations as loosely coupled systems. *Administrative Science Quarterly,* 21, 1–19.

4
Promoting and Maintaining Norms of Organizational Effectiveness

The difficulty of successfully introducing change into schools and overcoming the momentum of established practice is well documented in the education literature. Resistance to change and improvement is far more complex, however, than simple dedication to an outmoded way of doing things (Sarason, 1971; Deal, 1987). It sometimes originates in conflicts and inequities that may have occurred long before the instructional supervisor ever arrived on the scene. These unresolved conflicts and inequities can maintain a definition of the situation in people's minds as one of struggle or injustice. Such normative definitions run counter to the kind of harmonious and positive working relationships among people in the district that supervisors work hard to establish.

One example was described by a curriculum director who had been in the district in which she now worked for only a few years. The school board had shown favoritism, over a fairly long period of time prior to her arrival, toward several schools that were located in more affluent and politically influential neighborhoods within the district. Special treatment, especially in the form of newer and better resources, was accorded to these schools while buildings located in areas of the district with less economic and political clout limped along with inadequate and often second-hand equipment, materials, and supplies. She described the situation she encountered as follows:

> When I came into the school system, I realized that there were a lot of hard feelings about things that had happened in the past.

This system has really suffered in the past. We had schools without materials and resources, and we had teachers with hard feelings toward what had happened. I realized that I really had to work through [those feelings], and I had to bring the teachers up to a point where they felt that they were appreciated, that they were equals, and that they did have rights. They also have to know that they have responsibility in this sort of thing.

The supervisor said that when she first tried to involve the teachers who worked in the neglected schools in the process of selecting textbooks, their response was, "Why bother? There's no money to buy these books." She said that she repeatedly had to reassure them that the new superintendent had promised that money would be provided and that she would "not take them through this for no reason at all." The teachers remained skeptical, however, until the new books actually arrived. The supervisor viewed this event as the turning point in her ability to influence and improve instruction in those schools. The arrival of brand-new textbooks demonstrated to the teachers both tangibly and symbolically that inequitable treatment was no longer the norm, and that a new definition of the situation was clearly in order.

The supervisor in this case emphasized the importance of her taking the time to understand the cause of the teachers' initial unwillingness to cooperate in any type of instructional-improvement effort. They had been taught repeatedly over the years that their needs, opinions, and actions were of little consequence at the district level. The teachers were not going to invest their time in efforts that they believed would not be supported in the end. The supervisor could easily have judged the teachers in these neglected schools to be lazy or uncommitted to instructional improvement and begun a concerted effort to replace them with a more dedicated staff. Rather, she took the time to understand their perspective and demonstrate to them that things were now different and their current definition of reality needed to change. As the supervisor explained:

Instead of being impatient with [the teachers] while they were going through that [book selection] process, I had to be patient and work with them through the conflicts that were going on within the teachers, and within and between the schools.

Another instance where prior events posed an obstacle to instructional improvement was in a district that had experienced a bitter and unsuccessful teachers' strike years before. The conflict continued to negatively influence people's interpretations of events. The central office supervisor described what happened:

We had a very, very serious strike . . . almost ten years ago. It was the longest strike in [our state's] history, as a matter of fact, and it was horrible. It caused a real bad feeling among the community. . . . The strike lasted a month, but we may never get over it. Every so often its ugly head rears up again. It's not as bad as it was when I first came here, though. It was just awful.

The supervisor in this case worked strenuously within the district to resolve differences among various factions and seemed to be unusually preoccupied with publicizing to the community the good things that were happening to children in the system's schools. An event he had recently orchestrated in an attempt to put the decade-old strike to rest was, in effect, a public reconciliation between the former president of the teachers' union and the current school board.

The person who had led the teachers during the strike, and who had actually served time in jail because of it, was described by the supervisor as always having been a good teacher who in the last several years had undergone a "major renaissance." The teacher had become a dedicated advocate of the improvement of instruction in the subject area he taught and headed a committee that had completed a major curriculum project. When it came time to present the first phase of the project to the school board, the supervisor said that he saw an opportunity to "heal some old wounds."

Although the teacher had to be "massaged a bit," in the words of the supervisor, before becoming convinced that appearing before the board of education would be in everyone's best interest, his presentation of the curriculum committee's work was described as "outstanding." Several board members privately made favorable comments to the supervisor, and one long-time incumbent was said to have remarked, "This isn't the same guy I remember a few years ago." The former president of the teachers' union enjoyed the experience so much that when his committee completed the next phase of the project, he matter-of-factly asked the supervisor when he could be "scheduled to give the next report."

The major task of the supervisor, again, was to initiate a new interpretation of the social reality by first understanding the earlier definition of the situation and then by proving to people in a dramatic way that things were now different and a new normative definition of the situation was needed. A new definition seems to require a symbolic gesture of some kind that demonstrates that inequity or conflict are no longer salient issues. This allows a more optimistic and cooperative spirit to emerge, which is then nurtured by the supervisor through a consistent and continued emphasis on fairness, cooperation, and progress for the benefit of students.

Modeling Professional Norms

Norms are broad standards or expectations held by members of a group that specify conduct considered appropriate under certain circumstances (Homans, 1950; Thibaut and Kelley, 1959). They can range from "explicit regulations" to "unconscious understandings" (Smelser, 1962). In either case, norms represent an expression of a group's values and serve to integrate and channel into a unified effort the various elements operating within a social system. However, norms are derived not only from moral abstractions. They are constantly being developed, revised, and abandoned by groups as a result of being tested against reality through the enactment of roles and the performance of tasks.

Leaders, more than other members of a group, must embody the group's norms and promote high standards by example through their actions (Homans, 1950). Successful supervisors of instruction say that they regularly try to reinforce such standards through their own behavior. A supervisor who was very conscious of the impact his behavior had on others said that he always tried to act as a model of professionalism and honesty, two norms that he saw as relating specifically to reducing uncertainty:

> I try to set an example by working hard and by being well read, by getting information and all that kind of stuff, and by being honest and courageous. I'll go out and tilt at windmills if I feel it's worth the effort, but I'll also be very honest. When there are times when we shouldn't do it, I'll let people know.

A curriculum director in another district similarly reported:

> I think that we should be role models. If we want teachers to do a good job, then we should be a role model of being very involved and working very hard. It we don't present ourselves in that way, then something is wrong. How can we expect [other] people to do things if we're not busy and involved? We need to roll up our sleeves and work with the teachers and principals.

Many successful central office supervisors talk about the importance of maintaining consistency in their own behavior, not only as a model for others to follow, but also to promote clear expectations among others. "You have to create patterns of behavior and reactions to behavior," an assistant superintendent observed, "so that people know what to expect." An associate superintendent in another district similarly commented that he tried to avoid sudden changes in his behavior because it caused uncertainty and problems of readjustment for others:

> When someone comes to you and you've consistently reacted in a certain way about a certain problem or project, and then you suddenly switch gears and go in another direction, it causes problems. They expect that because you've done something in the past, it will continue to be your way of thinking in the future. People base what they're doing on what's been tradition with you.

Thus, successful central office supervisors try to model norms of professionalism and honesty that signal to others the kinds of behaviors that are considered appropriate. The consistent enactment of such behaviors serves to clarify social reality for others still further by making the expectations of the supervisor predictable as well as visible.

It is easy to overemphasize the part that leaders play in establishing and reinforcing norms, however, and thus lose sight of the fact that norms by definition belong to the group, not to any single individual. Group and organizational norms are enacted, developed, tested, and revised by teachers and administrators, of course, at times when the central office instructional supervisor is not around. Not all of these norms are necessarily relevant or beneficial to the instructional program.

There are certain norms governing the interactions of people within schools, however, that district level instructional supervisors intentionally and vigorously cultivate. These norms are essential to the positive collective definition of social reality needed for maintaining and improving the quality of instruction district-wide.

Cooperation, Fairness, and Reciprocity

Three general categories of norms are frequently mentioned by supervisors as being especially important for the effective operation of the school district as an organization: cooperation and teamwork, fairness and equity, and reciprocity. The three are interrelated and mutually reinforcing.

The terms "cooperation" and "teamwork" are frequently used almost interchangeably by central office supervisors when they talk about district effectiveness, but it is worth noting an important difference that sometimes appears in the meaning of the two words. Teamwork is almost always associated with a feeling of belonging and a sense of being a part of the whole. "Cooperation" refers more often to the process of people actually working together in the schools, "interacting, and sharing ideas, and using materials that teachers have found work well." Thus, "teamwork" seems to imply the working spirit of the group, while "cooperation" more often refers to the activities in which a group is involved. In practice, it is difficult to separate the vitality of the group from its actions, but it is important to recognize that successful supervisors attend to both dimensions.

"Fairness" and "equity" are two terms that are also sometimes used interchangeably by supervisors, but again there is an important distinction of meaning that is worth noting. "Equity" refers more often to the supervisor's trying to ensure that no teacher, content area, or school building receives more favorable treatment than any other. The term "fairness" is sometimes used in this way, but it is also used in relation to the allocation of resources and support on the basis of where the need is greatest. Supervisors often say, for example, that if a particular school has a large proportion of low-achieving students, then it "deserves" additional supplemental materials or that it is "only fair" for a new teacher to receive greater support and encouragement than more-experienced colleagues. While it appears that supervisors are the arbiters of what is fair and equitable in the district, they emphasize that they can never be capricious. The perceptions and opinions of others with regard to what comprises fairness and equity are very closely considered by supervisors, both as antecedents to action and as outcomes.

Finally, supervisors frequently mention a norm of reciprocity as being important when they talk about effectiveness in a school district. Reciprocity apparently pervades the school organization at all levels of interaction and reinforces the norms of teamwork and fairness. Reciprocity is evidenced in various ways among individuals as they work together, including exchanges of support for influence or of information for trust. In terms of the organization as a whole, however, the willingness of people to engage in such types of mutually beneficial exchanges appears to be based upon a more fundamental ritualistic exchange of credit, or recognition for one's contribution to the group's success.

Managing Conflict

The norms of cooperation, fairness, and reciprocity are important to the effectiveness of school districts because these norms define the situation in a way that enables people to work together harmoniously in pursuit of the shared goal of benefiting students through instruction. However, effective supervisors are also very aware that diversity of opinion is valuable as a source of innovation and should be cultivated in a district as a strength. Conflict is inevitable among professionals who openly and honestly express their opinions to one another. A certain degree of conflict among people who work in schools, as in any type of social relationship, may be beneficial in the long run for establishing trust and strengthening norms of cooperation. Most supervisors believe that conflict is necessary at times for earning mutual respect and for reaching the best solution to a problem. As an associate superintendent explained:

> When working with a group of people, each person may believe in something which I personally don't agree with. But I don't ever hold it against them. That's a real strength, because it involves a lot of discussion and a lot of searching and coming up with answers. I don't ever want us all to agree all of the time.

Many supervisors say that they feel somewhat uncomfortable with conflict and that controversy is inconsistent with their role, but that they sometimes intentionally instigate a confrontation and work it through, rather than allowing a stalemate to continue. A thick skin, patience, and consistency are characteristics that are said to help one deal with conflict when it occurs, along with a readiness to forgive and forget after a disagreement has been resolved. Vindictiveness is considered by supervisors to be entirely antithetical to what they do. The same associate superintendent continued:

> You have to learn that even though somebody gets all over you, or their ideas are opposed to what you believe in, you cannot hold grudges. You cannot be vindictive and be an effective manager. When you leave the room [after a meeting] and you've had a knock-down drag-out session, you leave it all behind you. But when you leave, everybody should leave with some kind of consensus or agreement that we're all going to live with the decision that's made when we go out of here.

Of course, conflict can be more than a temporary phase in the process of ironing out differences of opinion. It may reflect ongoing and deep-seated animosity. For example, a supervisor in one district described a situation where two people who worked in the central office refused to talk to each other for years. When the feuding parties absolutely had to communicate, they did so by memo or through the mediation of secretaries or other persons. In similar cases involving parents, teachers, principals, supervisors, central office staff, or school board members, conflict becomes a problem because it interferes with the flow of communication within the organization. The energies of people who should be working cooperatively are channeled away from the improvement of instruction and into counterproductive efforts to avoid one another. Although trying to deal with such conflicts is not a daily part of the job for most supervisors, the devastating impact of long-term conflict on the instructional program makes it necessary to take some action.

Language suggesting an image of a deep body of water is prevalent when supervisors talk about conflict: They speak of "turbulence," "undercurrents," and "breaking the ice," as well as of conflict "resurfacing" from time to time and "rearing its ugly head" like some long-forgotten sea monster. The supervisor's role in dealing with conflict, it seems, is to quell disturbances beneath the surface that threaten the preferred situation, one of cooperation and harmony.

One way supervisors of instruction help to reduce such turbulence within the organization is simply by listening to teachers, principals, parents, and even the superintendent, when they have complaints. The absence of line authority prevents many supervisors from being able to take direct, substantive action to resolve the problem in many cases, so they often just listen sympathetically. While some might regard this as a sign of impotence, the fact that supervisors can do little more than listen seems actually to serve the function of reducing turbulence within the district quite well.

One supervisor spoke candidly of acting as a "bullet catcher" for the organization. Thus, others with whom she worked felt safe in openly venting their anger in her presence. When plans go awry anywhere in the school district or someone infringes on someone else's autonomy or sphere of influence, the supervisor is very often the first to be told. The supervisor represents a safe authority figure, in effect, before whom people can speak their minds with little or no risk of retribution. As an assistant superintendent for instruction explained:

> Sometimes principals will tell you things or complain to you rather than go directly to the superintendent. That way they know it gets back to the superintendent, but they don't have to face him and seem insubordinate.

The frank information that the supervisor receives, which is often both factual and emotional, can be useful feedback to the central office staff in setting and adjusting policy. The supervisor, thus, seems to act at times as an internal buffer of conflict and a barometer for the organization, permitting the expression of legitimate dissension yet protecting the collective definition of the situation. Part of this function involves simply letting people blow off steam. An associate superintendent said:

> You become a good listener. I have a soft, green couch over here that I let people come in and sit on. Or they call me on the telephone, and its "blow, man, blow!" . . . And I listen. That's important. You need somebody, you might say, to shake it all out, then start over again. It's sort of like they blow off steam on Friday, we put it in the drawer, and then we come in on Monday and talk about it again.

The same phenomenon occurs collectively as well. A curriculum coordinator noted:

> Principals' meetings are used as a forum to vent anger or frustrations. You have to sit there and just listen to it and accept it with a grain of salt and consider where they're coming from. Then, eventually, after they get this wrath out, they come back and are ready to get to work.

Although supervisors lack authority in many cases to take action that will solve an existing problem for someone, effective supervisors become skilled at active listening and helping others to resolve problems for themselves, which reinforces a norm of professional autonomy. One supervisor, for example, made specific reference to Thomas Gordon's "win/win" method of resolving conflict:

> When folks don't communicate, and they misunderstand, and they're emotional, a lot of it is trying to help work those sorts of things out. Generally speaking, all a parent wants, for example, is somebody to listen. After they get a chance to vent all their rage, you can play win/win. It's not a bad idea at all.

When it is not possible for an individual or a group to resolve a problem independently, supervisors occasionally may serve as mediators of conflict between the two parties. "There are always two sides to every situation," one supervisor remarked, adding that it is far better to encourage individuals to resolve their own differences than to become involved oneself, "because that's where the peacemaking needs to take place."

Getting people to start talking to one another, according to a curriculum director, is best done unobtrusively. She observed:

> There are a lot of conflicts that you have to mediate, between principals and superintendents or between teachers and prin-

cipals. And you have to do it without the people involved really realizing that you're doing it.

In relatively rare cases supervisors take a more active stance and try to schedule a meeting betwen a parent and a teacher, for example, or between a teacher and a principal, offering to serve as an unbiased mediator of the conflict. This is not a common event, but supervisors report that it does occasionally occur. The first step is usually simply listening attentively to both sides, followed by encouraging both parties to devise some mutually satisfactory solution.

Sometimes a situation calls for the supervisor to go out and gather additional information so that a rational approach can be taken toward the resolution of the problem. A curriculum director noted that when a superintendent is confronted with a complaint about the instructional program, the supervisor is usually the next person to hear the complaint, often by way of a phone call or visit from the superintendent. In such situations:

> You have to remember that the superintendent is likely to overreact at the moment [he hears] the complaint. So you stay very calm, and you do the necessary legwork to find out exactly what led up to the complaint.

The superintendent's preference for action may lead to a rash decision, which can have a negative impact on morale and the instructional program. Getting an accurate account of the facts behind a complaint helps to delay and moderate any action that is taken.

A curriculum director described an unfortunate situation of this sort. The problem began when a parent called two school board members to complain about the content of a book that had been assigned to his child in the high school. Although this was apparently the first complaint about the book, recent publicity in the newspaper about a group of parents in a neighboring county who were trying to ban certain books from that district's school libraries may have made the board members especially uneasy. They decided to call the superintendent. Upon receiving word from the two board members about the complaint, the superintendent unilaterally had all copies of the book removed from the teacher's classroom over the weekend.

On Monday the curriculum director could do little but listen to the teacher's outrage at this infringement on academic freedom. Beyond immediate anger over what the superintendent had done, what seemed to bother the teacher especially was that she felt she could never be certain that a similar thing might not happen in the future. After informally determining that the school board would be unsympathetic to the teacher's specific complaint and was actually supportive of the superintendent's "decisiveness," the supervisor took a different, creative tack, both to mollify the teacher's anger and improve predictability within the organization. In the curriculum director's words:

> I told her that I understood how she felt and that she was concerned that every book she tried to use might be pulled out. I said, "Instead of going to the board of education, why don't we work through something that will help you to get what you want done." I said, "Your objective is to have a list of books that have gone through an approval process for use next year.". . . And so, on that very same day we met with the principal and came up with a list of people to serve on a supplementary materials review committee. We've got sixteen members, both teachers and parents. I've already contacted the people and sent follow-up letters. That's what I was doing today. And I've gathered materials from several other school systems. We're just going to meet and go through these books and get them approved. The teacher was satisfied with that.

The teacher's satisfaction with this solution may be attributable in part to the fact that she was invited to serve on the review committee. The teacher was thus given influence on the district level that compensated somewhat for the influence that had been taken away from her in the classroom. While the teacher was pleased to take steps to ensure that what had happened to her would not happen to anyone else, the school board and superintendent were pleased as well. A mechanism was now in place that would help the district avoid criticism from the public in the future about the content of materials being used by teachers. This particular response by the supervisor seemed to go beyond compromise to the level of actually integrating the interests of everyone involved in resolving the conflict, including parents, teachers, and board members.

Exchanging Credit

Central office supervisors often use the term "credit" when talking about what they do and how their role relates to others. The meaning of "credit," when used by supervisors in this way, is somewhat similar to the meaning found in the everyday phrase "you really have to give her credit for our success" or in the adage "giving credit where credit is due." Used in this sense, "credit" refers to a form of acknowledgment or recognition. As a working concept that supervisors use in making sense of what they do, however, the term "credit" takes on some specific meanings that shed light on the dynamics of the supervisor's influence and how they relate to other roles in the school, including those of teacher, principal, and superintendent.

Among educators, it seems, a common expectation is that credit is something that should be shared with others rather than accumulated for oneself. This seems contrary to norms prevalent in endeavors such as business, where people more often strive and expect to take credit for success whenever they can. The difference between educators and those involved in at least some business enterprises may be due in part to traditionally limited opportunities in education for individual career advancement and minimal financial incentives. Little practical reason exists in schools for trying to build up one's personal reputation at the expense of others. More is to be gained by sharing credit in exchange for mutual support and cooperation. In fact, giving credit may be a symbolic substitute in schools for more-tangible rewards.

Cash rewards, recognition banquets, and teacher-of-the-year awards have become widespread lately as part of the current education "reform" movement. Such public displays formally recognize individual teachers for their accomplishments. When central office supervisors use the term "credit," however, they seem to be referring to a more private and informal acknowledgment among professional colleagues of someone's contribution to the collective effort.

Credit is something that central office supervisors try to give to others and, they say, scrupulously try to avoid taking. One reason for this apparent unselfishness seems to be that credit is exchanged among educators almost like a commodity. Generally it is exchanged for support and cooperation. An associate superintendent explained that in working with teachers, principals, and subject area specialists:

> You give them credit and you recognize them. I feel they'll just push harder . . . on their next project. I don't get overly concerned about looking good myself. I know that that will come if I am getting the job done.

A curriculum director in another district similarly said that personal recognition was not a major concern:

> Whether it has my name on it or not is unimportant to me. As long as the job gets done, I don't care who gets the credit for it.

A curriculum coordinator, however, described the pitfalls of someone in her position trying to take credit, saying pointedly, "What will kill you is if you take all the credit yourself." When asked to explain what she meant by this statement, she said:

> Because you can't do a thing if the teachers don't cooperate and do it. So if you get a reputation for being a person who is always taking the credit for everything that's done, you won't get people to do anything for you. If you give them the credit, in the long run you get the credit anyway. Because they always go back and say, "You know, if it hadn't been for this and this, then we wouldn't have gotten it done." So you really can kill yourself by trying to play the role of, "Gee, look what I did!"

Teachers, principals, and the superintendent are all recipients of "credit" from the central office supervisor, each for slightly different reasons, but all relating to the fact that the supervisor can accomplish little without their cooperation. The superintendent, for example, has to be depended upon for constant support of the supervisor's efforts. One supervisor explained:

> I think it's important that the superintendent get a lot of credit for things that happen in this system. I might be the one who did the paperwork or the one who did the legwork. But he's the one who gave the permission, gave the incentive, got things going . . . and provided the support, whether it was financial, or encouragement, or directives to people in the field. Whatever it was, you know, it couldn't have happened without him. So I feel that it's important that he get credit for a lot of the things that happen.

Due to the political nature of the superintendent's position, some degree of credit for success must be strategically accepted by him in order to maintain the favor of constituents, including the school board and the general public. But in order to maintain the good will of colleagues, as with the central office supervisor, the larger portion of credit is given to others. One district coordinator suggested that his superintendent sets an example for others to follow:

> Our superintendent . . . wants other people to get the credit, and I think that rubs off on everybody. We're interested that the children get credit.

Although supervisors of instruction report that they freely and willingly give credit to others and that personal recognition is less important to them than the success of the instructional program, they view credit as something that is theirs to give voluntarily. One supervisor remarked that he felt personally resentful if anyone else violated the unspoken injunction against taking credit without it being given:

> Sometimes my nose gets out of joint when someone else takes credit for something I've worked [on for years]. . . . You say, "What the hell, I just did all this stuff and someone else took credit for the grant," or "for this curriculum thing," or "for this in-service," or whatever it is.

The expectation that a successful leader in education should share credit seems to be pervasive. The greater an educator's success, in fact, the more it appears he or she tries to give credit. An associate superintendent described the situation and behavior of a secondary principal in his district as follows:

> He and his staff have won every honor, program by program, from athletics to debate team. Whatever it is, they just take them statewide. His school has been selected as a national school of excellence. One of the things he does—he's up here every month before the board for some recognition—is that he never includes himself in any of those things. He's so careful to give credit to the others who have actually carried out the job. Now in doing that, . . . he really is recognized too. But the other people who are doing the job get most of the recognition.

It was noted earlier that supervisors typically have less formal authority over teachers than do principals and little if any formal authority over principals themselves. The fact that supervisors work from the central office, however, confers a special status that allows them to give credit to both teachers and principals. An assistant superintendent noted:

> Even though we do a lot of the work behind the scenes, it's the principals and the teachers who usually get the credit.

By no means was this individual complaining. She said that this was exactly how things ought to work in schools, and she thought it would be ridiculous to try to take credit for the work done by those in the local buildings because:

> It's the final person on the line who does the implementation, who makes it go, who should get the credit.

When individual teachers make an exceptional contribution to the instructional program and receive credit, however, it is usually awarded privately among colleagues. "Letting their principal know," sending the teacher "a letter of thanks," and placing a copy of the letter "into their personnel file" seem to be the most common ways that credit is given to individuals. Less often, a teacher's name may be mentioned within a superintendent's report to the board of education.

In most cases it seems that credit is shared by groups of teachers, such as representatives of a particular committee, grade level, academic department, or school. A consequence of this sharing of credit seems to be that it encourages and reinforces a unified effort. A director of educational services explained this relationship between credit and teamwork:

> I know that I can give people credit. I know that I can encourage them to do things. And I think we work as a team, and that's important.

An assistant superintendent similarly said that it was important that the instructional program ultimately got the credit, instead of any single individual.

Again, successful supervisors emphasize that credit is never given with the explicit intention, or on condition, of receiving something in return. Credit also is never given unless it is legitimately deserved. Supervisors believe that false praise is easily recognized and is probably resented by teachers as being patronizing. A curriculum director noted:

> Giving people credit for what they have done, as a group or individually—I think that's absolutely imperative. . . . But if you do that and you're keeping track—because you're expecting somebody to then give you credit . . . somewhere down the road—I don't agree with that. I think you need to give it with no strings attached.

There is probably an unlimited amount of credit that can be given away or shared in any school district. Because it is intangible, its reserves may be infinite. Yet many supervisors seem to feel that they give more credit than they receive. An associate superintendent expressed a sentiment that is common among supervisors:

> That's a part of our job. If you've got an ego that demands an awful lot of recognition for a job that's done, then maybe you don't belong in supervision. I think that it's important for all of us; we all like to be recognized and rewarded. Anyone would be foolish, of course, to think that's not the case. But you're going to

get less of it when you're in a support role, and that's just a part of the job, [so you should] expect it.

Implicit in many of the examples cited here is the paradox that a supervisor can gain credit by giving it away. A curriculum coordinator in another district said simply:

I firmly believe the more credit you give to other people, the more it comes back to you.

Traditionally, supervisors of instruction have gained credit vicariously through their association and identification with the instructional program. An assistant superintendent explained:

If you publicize the good things principals, teachers, and schools are doing, it reflects upon the program as a whole, which you supervise. So the credit is really there.

An associate superintendent related that in a restaurant or at a Little League game, parents occasionally approached him and expressed gratitude for what the school was doing or had done instructionally for their children.

In essence, "credit" is a concept employed by central office supervisors in thinking about what they do, and it is therefore helpful for understanding the role of supervisor and the source of a supervisor's influence. The exchange of credit among educators, as viewed by supervisors, is a process that helps maintain mutual support and cooperation within a school or district. One supervisor pointed out that once people accept credit for something, they acknowledge ownership as well, which in turn implies commitment:

If I have an idea, the people I share it with know that it is my idea. If I want them to embrace my idea, I must share it with them and find a way for them to get credit for it. Once they accept credit for it, they own the idea and take on responsibility for implementing their ideas.

The transition from my idea to their idea, he added, "is usually pretty easy, because most ideas come as first drafts anyway and can use modification."

A major characteristic of credit is that it must be given unconditionally, without any expectation of reward or return of favors; and it cannot be falsely given or taken by someone who does not deserve credit. It is intangible and limitless in its supply. And it is paradoxical in the sense that the more one gives away, the more one ultimately receives. Equitably sharing and exchanging credit for accomplishments encourages a continued unified effort, while taking credit for oneself quickly undermines the spirit of the collective endeavor and limits the willingness of others to cooperate in the future.

Although the giving and receiving of credit bears some similarity to an economic transaction, the essential purpose of the exchange differs substantially. Unlike an economic exchange, the object of exchanging credit in schools is to give away more credit than one keeps for oneself. In this way, it seems, the giver of credit gains in reputation as someone who is selflessly devoted to the group and its mission. He or she thereby acquires an informal claim on the time and energy of those who receive the credit. This obligation of the recipients to the giver of credit, however, is entirely voluntary. Nothing is actually owed in a financial or legal sense. The existence of credit and the validity of claims upon it are simply understood by those involved in the reciprocal transaction.

The notion that reciprocity forms a basis of social relationships has been recognized by sociologists and organizational theorists for some time (Homans, 1950; Thibaut and Kelley, 1959). According to Gouldner (1966), the concept of reciprocity may be especially useful for understanding stability and instability of relationships among people in social systems. The continuation of a relationship over time, he suggests, may be due either to the coercion of one party by another or to a high degree of mutual dependence between them. In the first case, a "reciprocity imbalance" is likely to occur, which results in less stability over the long run than in the second arrangement, where a mutual exchange of gratification is evidenced.

Gouldner (1966) posits a universal norm of reciprocity based upon the idea that people should help and not injure those who have helped them. A social system's stability depends upon the internalization of the norm of reciprocity, which, he suggests, maintains mutually compatible expectations and contributes to a "beneficent cycle of mutual reinforcement." Feelings of mutual indebtedness and indeterminate prescriptions for repayment, according to Gouldner, are what bind social structures together. Thus, a norm of reciprocity

> is a kind of plastic filler, capable of being poured into the shifting crevices of social structures, and serving as a kind of all-purpose moral cement. (P. 143)

Reciprocal interactions in loosely coupled organizations, such as schools, and especially the giving and receiving of credit for success (as described above) may indeed serve this unifying function well.

References

Deal, T. E. 1987. The culture of schools. In L. T. Sheive & M. B. Schoenheit (eds.), *Leadership: Examining the elusive.* Alexandria, Va.: Association for Supervision and Curriculum Development.

Gouldner, A. W. 1966. The norm of reciprocity: A preliminary statement. In Bruce J. Biddle & Edwin J. Thomas (eds.), *Role theory: Concepts and research*, pp. 136–144. New York: John Wiley & Sons.

Homans, G. C. 1950. *The human group.* New York: Harcourt, Brace & World.

Sarason, S. 1971. *The culture of the school and the problem of change.* Boston: Allyn and Bacon.

Smelser, N. J. 1962. *Theory of collective behavior.* New York: Free Press.

Thibaut, J. W. & Kelley, H. H. 1959. *The social psychology of groups.* New York: John Wiley & Sons.

5

Mobilizing Effort and Coordinating Roles

A problem of uncertainty exists at the level of organized roles when individuals do not understand what others in the organization expect from them. Their uncertainty is different from the ambiguity that arises from an unclear understanding of the technical relationship between means and ends at the more concrete level where tasks are performed. A curriculum coordinator explained that helping individuals clarify their roles was an important function that she occasionally fulfilled. People sometimes approached her and said something along these lines:

> "Well, I really don't know what they expect of me as a teacher" [or] "I don't know what somebody expects of me as a principal."

She then observed:

> Now if you're not certain about what people expect of you, then you're never sure whether you're on the right track or whether you're going to be backed up when you do take action. So I think it's important [for me] to reduce that uncertainty for people.

Job descriptions, no matter how detailed, are of little assistance in this regard. They do let individuals know the general expectations of the formal organization so that they can judge for themselves how well their behavior conforms to expectations concerning tasks. But job descriptions usually are vague about priorities and how they change as conditions change, so they are of little use in guiding daily practice. More importantly, in terms of resolving uncertainty surrounding roles, job descriptions provide no information regarding the adequacy of one's performance as it is perceived by others. Job descriptions focus on the specific tasks that an individual is expected to perform, not on the informal norms that govern the performance of those tasks.

Uncertainty concerning roles is due in part to the fact that few rewards are regularly dispensed in schools on the basis of individual effort, so individuals receive limited tangible external confirmation that what they are doing is recognized as worthwhile by the organization. Also, there are few opportunities for teachers and principals to receive specific information concerning the adequacy of their contributions to the collective effort. The difficulty of measuring educational outcomes and the relative contribution made by individuals makes a more direct relationship between effort and reward in schools unlikely to occur. The central office instructional supervisor can reduce uncertainty at the level of organized roles, however, by simplifying and supplementing the amount of information available to people within the district in several ways.

Clarifying expectations concerning roles can imply, of course, simply providing "the rationale behind a written policy or procedure" that people are expected to follow. This type of administrative clarification is sometimes necessary and appropriate. But in successful and improving districts, clarifying expectations regarding instructional issues more often involves reducing uncertainty by encouraging a social consensus through a dialogue among teachers and administrators "concerning what we are about" and "where we are going." An associate superintendent for instruction described the process, which he called "establishing direction," in this way:

> You do your work empathically, in an understanding manner. You lay the groundwork for what you want to achieve, rather than laying something on people.

The direction that is established by a supervisor of instruction, in other words, is very much a product of an ongoing process of negotiation with and among others. A curriculum coordinator described how expectations for roles are negotiated, for example, when working with the superintendent. It is interesting to note that the expectations of various groups are taken into account:

> It's really a team, you know. There's a lot of informal back-and-forth talking, discussing, assessing where we are and where we need to be going. We talk about what his goals are, what my goals are, what his expectations are, what mine are, what the parents' expectations are, what the board's are, and what the community expects.

A successful supervisor's duties are negotiated as well, though less formally, among the diverse constituencies that comprise a school district. This is obviously appropriate when one considers that the position of instructional supervisor is primarily service oriented. A somewhat sticky situation can develop for supervisors, however, when the expectations of others conflict with their own sense of purpose. The same curriculum coordinator quoted above reported that she had little trouble identifying what her role in the school should be or what she should be doing, but meeting everyone else's expectations was sometimes difficult. She also noted, "What you think you're doing and what somebody else perceives you to be doing are not always the same." It is beneficial for the supervisor, therefore, to let others in the district know what his or her own expectations are for the position of instructional supervisor as well.

Clarifying expectations for individuals, however, is not usually something to which central office instructional supervisors purposefully devote much time or attention. Although considered important, it is typically a by-product of broader processes aimed at reducing uncertainty regarding how the efforts of various positions and groups can be integrated. Most supervisors refer to this facilitation of integration as "coordination."

Coordination and Communication

Central office supervisors often use the term "coordination" when describing their jobs. Coordination involves "pulling together" people, ideas, events, information, and resources. This mobilization of roles and resources is guided by the norms of the organization and represents an enactment of the value of working toward the improvement of instruction in order to benefit students. Coordination seems to be a broad concept that comprises three related processes: (a) standardizing and routinizing, (b) planning and goal setting, and (c) organizing an overlapping network of committees.

Supervisors speak of a need for coordination when referring to curriculum, resources, and the expertise of others. Coordination is dependent on the supervisor and others who have a broad, long-term perspective of district events and issues, and it is seen as complementing instructional-improvement efforts at the building level. Essentially, coordination involves pulling together ideas, resources, and people to establish a unified purpose and direction. It is viewed as contributing to a team identity and as serving the purposes of both equity and efficiency. Thus, after "first figuring things out," a curriculum director described her job as follows:

It's keeping everything straight. It's keeping everything moving. Making things work. Making sure that the program and the students are getting the best that you can give them.

Coordination involves assembling the independent perspectives and efforts of various people, positions, and schools within the district into a meaningful larger whole. In the words of one supervisor, coordination is "working together" toward common goals, and it means that the jobs "people are doing fit together" and that everyone "pulls together." Close communication among teachers, administrators, and supervisors within the district organization is obviously essential to such coordination. As an assistant superintendent in a small city described it:

> We have a fairly large instructional staff for a system our size, a number of director positions and people who are assistants or members of staff beyond that. So I find that I spend a good deal of time just trying to make sure that everybody knows what's going on, that the elementary folks know what the secondary folks are working on and vice versa.

This supervisor explained that communication was important because services could be delivered to students more efficiently and effectively when the job of each of the instructional staff members complemented the others.

Coordination of effort in schools does not occur spontaneously. It needs encouragement from somewhere. Due to the large number of roles in school districts that relate to instruction or that provide a service of some kind to children, central office supervisors work with people who represent a wide array of experiences and perspectives. Partly because schools as organizations are so highly segmented, direct channels of communication and feedback are difficult to maintain. The contribution made by the supervisor is to both simplify and supplement information available to people within the organization. This is accomplished by encouraging an ongoing district-wide dialogue that integrates different perspectives and interests into a shared understanding of what each individual does and how that fits into the larger whole and overall effort.

Standardization

One dimension of meaning evident in the term "coordination" relates to the standardization of curricular offerings and the routinization of processes, such as purchasing instructional resources and textbooks.

Standardization inevitably has the effect of eliminating diversity of both courses and materials. Nevertheless, it is viewed as beneficial by successful supervisors for two reasons.

First, standardization of curricula and procedures is seen as contributing to the sense of unified effort within the district. Less variety obviously simplifies the problem of understanding for people. But successful supervisors emphasize that the active participation of teachers in deciding upon procedures and curricula is even more important in advancing this sense of cohesiveness. Second, standardization is considered essential for helping to ensure equitable learning experiences for youngsters regardless of which school and classroom in the district they happen to be placed. As a curriculum coordinator in a small rural district explained:

> Before I came into this office, we had no method at all for selecting textbooks. Each principal would just buy what he wanted for his school. The primary school reading program was different from the middle school reading program and every other program. But now we have coordination between the two levels and between the middle school and high school. And I think it makes teachers feel good to have some input into the selection of books, something they did not have in any organized way before.

Another curriculum director suggested similarly:

> Without careful planning in the purchase of supplementary types of materials, without close coordination within the system, materials could be bought in inappropriate areas—in terms of favoritism, you know, or spur-of-the-moment spending.

Locating, selecting, and purchasing instructional materials and textbooks in different content areas and at various grade levels are viewed by supervisors as "different aspects of the total thing" and not as unconnected tasks. By setting up routine but collaborative procedures for selecting and purchasing instructional materials, they believe that decisions can be made in a more purposeful and concerted manner.

The instructional program is therefore coordinated in part by organizing people to make decisions regarding materials and curriculum. An associate superintendent in a large district described how, when he had first accepted his current position, he found that there were some seven hundred different course offerings in the district:

> Many of them were so frivolous that they were almost totally worthless. You know, we had minicourses in about anything that

any kid expressed an interest in or [when] any teacher said, "Hey, I think students need this, I want to teach it."

One of the first things this supervisor did was to work with teachers to cut the number of courses in half. Although this reduced diversity, it left over three hundred courses. The effect on the overall program was seen as highly positive. According to the supervisor:

> Working with teachers to streamline the curriculum and maintain the curriculum that was really needed, helped us to reach the goals that we had set and eliminated some of the things that got in the way.

Concerted, purposeful action became possible, in other words, only after limiting the variety of courses to a level that had some meaning.

The responsibility for maintaining and improving the district-wide instructional program requires that the supervisor be a curriculum generalist. The supervisors who participated in the interviews reported here had all previously taught at a particular grade level or in a particular content area, yet they unanimously saw their current positions as lacking in specialization. Their jobs involved meeting with teacher representatives of departments and grade levels to develop general goals and guidelines. But the classroom practitioners acted as the specialists who contributed the expertise necessary for selecting materials and writing curriculum. The needs, wants, and demands of various constituencies are thereby addressed. As an assistant superintendent described the process:

> Teachers have input and administrators have input. We try to pull it all together and make it something that we can all live with, and which will still meet the requirements of our state [curriculum] guide and meet the children's needs.

Standardization and routinization contribute heavily to the reduction of uncertainty and the improvement of predictability within the district. The most important outcome of standardization from the perspective of central office supervisors is that the quality of learning experiences for children is not left up to chance or to political favoritism. A curriculum director stressed that coordination of instructional materials, textbooks, and procedures is essential

> so that everyone has an equal opportunity. . . . In any school system, some schools have more instructional supplies or a better teaching staff than some of the other schools. I don't know how it

happens, but many times it does. And you need some way to create a balance.

Schools within the same district may differ in the resources available to them for a number of reasons, such as political advantage or as a result of having an especially enterprising principal. At other times differences are due solely to chance. In one district changes in enrollment patterns and an unexpected financial crisis threatened to leave some school buildings with a surplus of textbooks and others with shortages. Working with a principal during the summer months, the curriculum director developed a creative procedure for issuing books from one school to another without violating state regulations.

As another example, in a middle-class suburban district, high school teachers' expectations concerning the likelihood of academic success for entering freshmen depended largely on which of two middle school tracks a student had been placed in. The supervisor in this case believed that the problem originated with different expectations among teachers for students in the middle schools. So he pushed for a revision and standardization of the district's curriculum through the mechanism of a curriculum council to try to ensure that students in both academic tracks had comparable learning experiences when they entered high school. In his words:

> I said to the teachers, "We're looking to help kids out. They can't have voids, they've got to have the basics no matter where they're coming from." And we worked very, very hard at trying to make sure that everyone always thought in terms of k through 12. It's not just one school or just the seventh and eighth grades, and it's not just eleventh-grade English or fourth-grade spelling—because we owe it to the kids to have as smooth and as fair a program as possible. And I really emphasize that.

Thus, the intended outcome of promoting equity through standardization was accomplished through an involvement of teachers in a revision of the curriculum, which resulted in a more inclusive view of the curriculum among teachers.

The standardization and routinization of processes and procedures into formal policies admittedly reduce variety and opportunities for creative adaptation to some extent. Standardization and routinization, however, are not pursued by supervisors as matters of administrative expediency. An example was cited in the previous chapter, where a superintendent arbitrarily pulled a set of books out of a teacher's classroom. In that instance, standardization of the procedures for selecting and purchasing textbooks did have the effect of limiting the freedom of individual teachers to choose their own classroom materials. But on the other hand, academic freedom was expanded for teachers collectively because a formal mechanism was established that legitimated the textbook selection process and thereby precluded further capricious intrusions into instructional matters by the superintendent and school board.

In summary, the standardization of instructional materials and curricula and the routinization of processes for making decisions improve coordination within school districts. The reduction of variety and randomness enhances people's understanding of "the big picture" by simplifying it. Both equity and predictability are improved through standardization, but successful supervisors emphasize that the greatest advantage is obtained by involving teachers in making decisions about standardization. Two additional meanings of coordination—"planning" and "establishing networks"—illustrate more clearly how this is accomplished.

Planning and Goal Setting

The "real planners" in a school district, an associate superintendent affirmed, are teachers, principals, and the superintendent, whose efforts lead directly to goal attainment. Successful instructional supervisors, in comparison, see themselves as more involved in facilitating the selection and pursuit of district goals by others. The supervisor's involvement in planning and goal setting at multiple levels of the organization helps guarantee that the various goals pursued are in accord with one another.

An associate superintendent explained that he learned early in his career that although he freely contributed ideas to plans developed by the superintendent and school board, he was more an implementer and facilitator of those plans than a planner. He did not express regret over this situation; he simply viewed it as a fact. He further explained that his work with principals was of a similar nature:

> Principals need to know the goals of the district so that they can develop their school goals in support of the system-wide goals. And yet principals have to be able to modify those goals to meet the needs of their local community. We all ought to know pretty much where we're going, and my role is to support the principals in accomplishing both system-wide goals and their own goals, while helping them understand how it all fits.

When talking about their work with teachers, supervisors often emphasize that a sense of ownership of the goal by the people who will be pursuing it is essential to its achievement. A curriculum coordinator warned that "you can be working very hard and really fail" when trying to improve district-wide instruction or curriculum. "That's probably because you set your own goal," she suggested, "instead of involving teachers in the selection of the goal and the means by which it is to be accomplished." A district coordinator similarly explained that instructional goals quickly become "dust collectors" unless a supervisor regularly sits down with teachers to review and revise them.

Supervisors of instruction use the terms "planning" and "goal setting" in different ways. Planning involves breaking a situation down into its component parts and then sequencing events and processes in a rational way to make possible the step-by-step accomplishment of a long-term goal. It requires an awareness of the multiple elements and issues that constitute a situation. Planning isn't always done formally, but it involves an awareness of which steps to follow in order to get something done. In the words of an assistant superintendent:

> One of the critical skills in this job is the ability to plan and to know what's involved in planning. You don't have to draw PERT charts for everything you do, . . . but you've got to know how to get from here to there and what the process is in between. . . . It's the ability to look at a situation and break it down into its component parts so that you know what you're dealing with.

The ability to facilitate planning seems to be mentioned more frequently as an essential skill by supervisors in larger districts than in smaller ones. The relative importance that is placed upon formal planning in a school system, therefore, may be a function of the size and complexity of a district's organization. An associate superintendent for instruction in a district comprised of over fifty schools commented:

> We operate with a lot of long-range planning. Most of what we do is on a long-range basis. It's spelled out on a management plan year by year. We'll work on something this year, we'll request funding for something else, and when that's granted, then we'll go to the next step, and the next, and so on.

In a highly complex environment, planning may serve the very practical outcome of allowing the supervisor and others to concentrate on one thing at a time and thus channel their energies in a particular direction. An assistant superintendent for instruction observed:

> If you understand the situation, and you know where you want to go, then someone has to plot those little steps in between and determine how you're going to get there. . . . Planning skills are critical. . . . So many people are scattered, they're hit or miss. They've got something to do, they try to do it, but they don't plan it, and so they don't succeed.

Despite the different emphasis given to planning in districts of various sizes, central office supervisors in both large and small districts view the purposeful selection and pursuit of goals as contributing to consistency and clarity of expectations. Instructional supervisors suggest that it is helpful to be a goal-oriented person in fulfilling the requirements of their positions. For example, "we start with goal setting," an assistant superintendent for instruction commented, "when planning curriculum or any type of instructional program." Being goal oriented, a curriculum director in a smaller district believed, helped her to be more organized, consistent, and fair.

When talking about goals, supervisors distinguish between those that are attainable and those that are ongoing. As a curriculum director observed:

> Some goals go on forever. A goal of improving student–teacher interaction, for instance; that's a goal that will go on forever. Things get better as we go along, but that is something we'll be working toward forever, and ever, and ever.

Although supervisors emphasize the importance that goals have for their work, they seem to be more involved in facilitating the attainment of goals by others in the organization. When asked for examples of the kinds of goals they strive toward, central office supervisors almost invariably mention curricular, instructional, and programmatic goals. But these goals typically relate more closely to tasks at the classroom, building, and district levels that are performed by teachers and administrators. That is to say, the work of supervisors is tied to—one might say, is driven by—the work of teachers, principals, and the superintendent.

For example, the superintendent and the board of education in many districts draw up a set of instructional goals in consultation with the central office supervisor. It works best, from the perspective of supervisors and curriculum directors, when there are relatively few goals and they are stated broadly. Several general goals are better than many specific ones, according to supervisors, because everyone can more easily keep them in mind as they go about their daily activities.

Another advantage of general goal statements is that they can be interpreted to fit many situations, which means that the scope of their applicability is enhanced. In larger districts, however, specific short-term and long-term subgoals are more often derived from the overall district goals. These subgoals are then applied at the building level and in the various content areas.

The goals of a school district, according to the perceptions of supervisors, serve the important function of helping to provide a fairly specific focus that maintains consistency and continuity among the activities of the many people who work in the organization, thus improving the effectiveness of the overall effort. One supervisor reported that "a big part" of his job involved helping people to understand "that there are other jobs to be done" and that everyone has "to work together for the system as a whole." He elaborated on this point, describing it as being a matter of "getting away from the idea of fragmented pieces in the district," such as individual buildings, grade levels, and content areas. Developing in others a more inclusive and integrated perspective of what is happening is the focus of his job.

Instructional, curricular, and programmatic goals obviously cannot be selected and pursued haphazardly. They are consciously screened for consistency with the district's guiding values and norms. Central office supervisors are charged with the responsibility of overseeing the accomplishment of the goals that are developed at different grade levels and within various content areas. Supervisors report that this facet of their work requires a paradoxical combination of firmness and flexibility.

Although teachers and principals in the district have considerable autonomy to choose the specific goals they want to pursue, once a selection has been made, supervisors try to hold them closely to their word. The central office supervisor acts as an organizational conscience, of sorts, by reminding people of what they have agreed to do. At the same time, however, instructional supervisors recognize and emphasize that a considerable degree of flexibility is necessary "on anything you set out to do because some things just aren't going to work like you thought they would." In such cases, an associate superintendent said, "You've got to provide some freedom to try something a little different, or go at it from a slightly different direction."

Holding others to their word is not something that central office supervisors necessarily reserve for organizational subordinates. The existence of published goals can also give the supervisor some leverage in influencing the actions of the superintendent and the board of education. An associate superintendent, for example, explained that a school board member in the district was openly critical of a particular subject area specialist's "casual attitude" and style of dress. The associate superintendent said that he responded to the board member in this case first by calling attention to the district goals that the school board had drawn up and, second, by pointing out the kinds of successes that were being accomplished in the subject area for which the specialist had responsibility. In the words of the associate superintendent:

> It really involved saying to the board member: "You know your goal number five over here? Do you remember what it says? This person is in charge of this aspect of that goal. I want you to look at what has been happening out there. The kids in math are performing at the eightieth percentile nationally. This relates back to that goal. Now there are some other exciting things, and maybe some problems out there, but we're getting at the goal that you have asked us to go after and we've been successful. So maybe some of these personal things that you don't like about this individual are things that we just ought to overlook."

Instead of being restrictive, as with standardization, goals can actually protect the professional autonomy that teachers and administrators need in order to get their jobs done. When the emphasis is placed on goals and outcomes, there is less room for petty criticisms relating to style or technique. The associate superintendent quoted above continued with the more general observation:

> You always call attention back to the product and say, "Here's where we're supposed to be heading." You may disagree with some of the ways a person is going about it or with the person himself. But the job is being done, and that's the important thing to remember.

Organizing Networks

Perhaps the most significant avenue by which central office supervisors help reduce uncertainty at the level of organized roles is by generating and fostering a system of overlapping committees comprised of people from various levels and departments. These committees represent a network by which teachers keep each other informed about what is happening instructionally in other classrooms, departments, grade levels, and schools. This network provides an informal structure in successful districts through which coordinated effort is achieved. The organization's needs for communication and coordination are thus simultaneously addressed. Interestingly, diagrams illustrating these connections are not readily available, though this network of overlapping committees may be more crucial to instructional effectiveness in a district than the formal organizational chart that depicts line and staff relationships.

Not surprisingly, two general types of committees are evident in school districts: standing committees and ad hoc committees. The largest number of standing committees relate directly to curriculum and instruction. The members of these standing committees are usually classroom teachers, but in many cases building administrators and subject area specialists also participate. At the district level especially, parents are also often included. Central office supervisors tend to be ex officio members of standing committees and meet with them on occasion.

Curriculum committees tend to overlap considerably with one another because their members often serve on grade level and content area committees simultaneously. Thus, one teacher may participate on a fourth-grade curriculum committee, an elementary school curriculum committee, and a reading curriculum committee. Each committee reviews and revises the curriculum in the area for which it is responsible. Because a change in one component of the curriculum potentially affects or determines what is taught on other grade levels, close communication among committees is absolutely essential. This overlapping membership encourages coordination of effort by making communication among different committees possible.

Special task-force, or ad hoc, committees, as the name implies, are formed temporarily to address a particular issue, solve a specific problem, or plan a one-time event. The membership of these committees usually includes more administrators than are typically represented on the standing curriculum committees. The reason for this difference in composition probably relates to the difference in function between the two.

Rather than communication and coordination, the purpose of a task force committee is to formulate and take action. It is necessary for these special committees to include people who have authority, access to resources, and time at their disposal to implement decisions that are made by their group. However, these committees usually do include teachers from grade levels or content areas that are likely to be affected by the decisions to be made. The central office supervisor is also more likely to serve as a regular participant on task force committees, representing the interests of instruction throughout the district.

As an example of a task force, an instructional supervisor may work with media specialists, teachers, guidance counselors, and principals in coordinating the federal government's Chapter 2 program, which provides funds for the purchase of library media. Or a supervisor may call together a physical education teacher, a school nurse, a speech pathologist, and an audiologist when responding to a new state requirement that entering students be screened for problems with their motor skills. A committee that approves purchases of supplementary learning materials is similarly likely to be comprised of teachers from various grade levels, departments, and buildings, and may also include parents. Obviously, the membership of ad hoc committees usually overlaps to some extent with the membership of standing committees in the district.

An assistant superintendent described the job of organizing committees as resulting in "meetings, millions of meetings." He immediately added:

> But they're all interacting with other committees, consisting of teachers, administrators, supervisors, and parents.

Sometimes the involvement of certain roles and individuals, such as physicians or parents, is required by state or federal regulations. A beneficial outcome of this involvement of diverse perspectives is that it brings together expertise that is needed for making sound decisions. Another reason for ensuring that a variety of interests is represented from the beginning, however, is so objections are not voiced or support withheld at the time of implementation by those who might feel that they were unfairly excluded. The same assistant superintendent who was quoted above explained:

> This past year we worked on developing a board policy for homework. It involved subject area specialists, teachers, guidance counselors, principals, and parents. And they came up with a recommendation for board policy. I think that's the most productive way to do it, because then people all have an opportunity to present their views and buy in. And it's much more palatable [for them] than having something laid on them by me.

Supervisors often emphasize the importance of coordinating the expertise of individuals who have special knowledge in some area. By pooling the information that teachers have about a particular area of content or classification of students, supervisors generally believe that the group is likely to come up with a decision, plan, or curriculum that is far better than anything that the supervisor could possibly develop independently. While supervisors tend to downplay their role in getting such groups moving or in contributing to the finished product, an interesting function they sometimes perform involves helping groups to make sense of the diversity they bring.

A district coordinator, for example, said that he usually sat in on a newly formed group at its first meeting and took notes. Before the next meeting he always had the major ideas and points that were raised at the first meeting typed and copied for everyone on the committee. This, he believed, was an important source of direction for the group because its members had a "target" that they could "aim for" or "shoot down" at the second meeting. In addition to facilitating the group's efforts, this practice also gave the supervisor an opportunity to unobtrusively shape the direction of a group's efforts.

Supervisors may also make sense of information at the end of a group's existence. Information contributed by diverse sources is sometimes collected and synthesized by the supervisor into reports for internal or external audiences. While developing a policy recommendation concerning homework requirements for the board of education, for example, the assistant superintendent quoted earlier had several groups of parents, teachers, and administrators working on the project simultaneously. The press of time prevented the various groups from meeting to make a decision before an upcoming school board meeting, so the supervisor finally synthesized the reports himself. He remarked:

> The various reports came in. I combined those reports. I called it the fruit salad report: apples, oranges, and bananas. I got it all together, presented it to the board, and I completed the task. I was successful.

The somewhat irreverent tone used by the supervisor in describing this process reveals a personal preference, which he stated later, that groups have a chance to finish what they begin, rather than his having to impose his own perspective on their work.

The most important reason for getting people to work together on committees, according to supervisors, is that it facilitates the improvement of instruction. When people with different points of view meet and talk, opinions are voiced as to exactly where a district is at present and where people want it to be. This can benefit districts that are doing poorly as much as it can benefit those that are already doing quite well. An assistant superintendent in another district suggested:

> People know what is wrong in so many cases. Even in [academically] poorer districts, generally speaking, people know where their weaknesses are. They just don't do anything about [them].

Meeting in groups and "talking about what we're doing," this supervisor observed, "is the first step toward doing something else." Even in districts that are already successful, a frank assessment of the status of the current instructional program can help tremendously. Such ongoing assessment occurs through the dialogue that a network of overlapping committees makes possible.

A curriculum director in a suburban district that prided itself on sending a high percentage of its graduates to colleges and universities said that he made a conscious decision, when he took the position of director of educational services, to involve everyone in instructional improvement, rather than "govern by fiat," as his predecessor had tried to do.

> So we had many, many more meetings with principals, with assistant principals, and with key groups of teachers than probably happened in the last ten years in this district. We took a positive stance in saying, "Let's go out front. We know these [state curriculum] mandates are coming down. Let's beat everybody to the punch by a year or two. . . . Or let's volunteer to be a pilot project." And it's been a [beehive] of activity ever since.

Establishing networks among educators from all levels within the district, supervisors believe, can make a school system more proactive. When teachers have an opportunity to talk to one another about instruction and curriculum, a shared understanding of the overall pattern of what is being done instructionally at different grade levels and in various subject areas and schools gradually emerges. This common understanding of where a district stands at present is a prerequisite for determining where a district is heading, and it provides a sound basis for subsequent collective action.

Bounded Rationality

In a seminal work on organization theory, Thompson (1967) suggests that organizational structure represents an attempt by people to overcome uncertainty that impedes the efficient accomplishment of tasks. Responsibilities are specified and resources and processes controlled in organizations, he asserts, in order to achieve areas of "bounded rationality" wherein a reasonable expectation of predictability prevails and tasks can be completed efficiently and without undue outside interference.

School districts are segmented into many such areas of bounded rationality. Individual schools, for example, are units where resources, responsibilities, and processes are to some extent internally controlled. Schools are broken down still further into classroom units where teaching and learning occur. However, Thompson observes that when an organization is divided into "numerous spheres of bounded rationality" in this way, the coordination of action among these elements becomes a major concern.

Coordination for the purpose of achieving concerted action can be accomplished, according to Thompson, in several ways. He suggests that organizations typically minimize costs by grouping bounded units in ways that simplify the coordination problem. An example would be the grouping of classrooms into schools and departments according to grade level or subject. The simplest and least costly way to coordinate action among fairly autonomous units, such as classrooms and schools, is through standardization of rules and routines. Because the same rules apply to all, fewer decisions have to be made and less communication among units is required. Standardization is considered most effective as a means of achieving coordination when the organization's environment is comparatively stable (Thompson, 1967).

A second way that organizations accomplish coordination among units is through planning (Thompson, 1967). With planning, committees representing various units, such as classrooms and schools, establish schedules for accomplishing certain agreed-upon ends that govern the actions of the individual units. Planning is less rigid than standardization and is considered more appropriate for changing situations.

The third way of coordinating fairly autonomous units is through a relationship among them that Thompson calls "mutual adjustment" or "reciprocal interdependence." Mutual adjustment relies upon task forces or project groups and requires frequent communication of information between and among the bounded units as they take action. Of the three, "mutual adjustment" is considered most suitable for adapting to variable and unpredictable situations, but it is also the most complex and costly to the organization in terms of time and energy devoted to decision making and communication.

The three methods of accomplishing coordinated effort that are identified by Thompson (1967) closely parallel the ways by which supervisors say they achieve coordination in school districts. Central office supervisors sometimes enforce rules within the district, and they sometimes provide information to teachers and principals concerning such things as state education department policies governing certification or the district's policy on granting teachers credit for in-service activities. However, successful supervisors of instruction seem to consider standardization to be a comparatively minor responsibility. They report spending larger amounts of time and effort facilitating the selection of goals and the formation and efforts of committee networks and task force groups.

Thompson (1967) more closely associates the presence of staff or liaison positions in organizations with standardization, because he notes that staff positions are needed for linking various units and for formulating, interpreting, and applying rules and regulations. He sees less need for staff positions when planning and mutual adjustment are utilized, because these mechanisms rely upon committees and groups to achieve coordination among bounded units. This may partly explain why many successful central office instructional supervisors paradoxically observe that the better they are at doing their jobs, the less their positions appear to be needed.

It would be a serious error to take such statements by supervisors literally. District-wide coordination of instruction and curriculum is unlikely to occur without someone having the responsibility to see that it occurs. Historically, the position of central office supervisor may indeed have been developed to oversee standardization as a way of achieving coordination. The ever-changing nature of modern society suggests, however, that more dynamic forms of coordination in schools will become increasingly important to district-wide effectiveness (Patterson, Purkey, and Parker, 1986). Those central office supervisors of curriculum and instruction who are successful today and in the future will be those who devote their time to empowering and developing the leadership of others by providing them with opportunities for involvement.

References

Patterson, J. L., Purkey, S. C. & Parker, J. V. 1986. *Productive school systems for a nonrational world.* Alexandria, Va.: Association for Supervision and Curriculum Development.

Thompson, J. D. 1967. *Organizations in action.* New York: McGraw-Hill.

6
Clarifying Tasks and Outcomes

When adapting to any situation in which tasks are performed, people try to learn which outcomes result from which activities and which activities lead consistently to positive outcomes. A task is considered ambiguous when relationships between activities and outcomes are unclear. In situations where the connections between actions and outcomes are generally unpredictable, as in classrooms and schools, people tend to look to experts for advice in selecting and applying means to desired ends and to consider the opinions of others when evaluating the outcomes of their own actions (Thibaut and Kelley, 1959, p. 167). Simply stated: When people perform ambiguous tasks, they seek guidance and confirmation from other people.

Central office supervisors of instruction furnish guidance and confirmation of this sort for teachers and administrators by providing them with technical advice and resources, by building their self-confidence, and by confirming the worth of instructional efforts and programs already underway. Reducing technical ambiguity and psychological uncertainty among teachers and principals relieves structural strain at the level of task performance and contributes to a stable definition of reality within the organization. Five distinct activities in which supervisors engage appear to reduce ambiguity and uncertainty related to tasks, namely: (a) securing resources for instructional improvement, (b) supporting improvement efforts with information and materials, (c) providing in-service opportunities, (d) validating worth, and (e) building confidence.

Securing Resources for Instructional Improvement

Providing support for the instructional program is one of the most frequently recognized and readily agreed-upon duties that supervisors of curriculum and instruction are expected to fulfill (Oliva,

1984; Tanner and Tanner, 1987). Instructional support involves providing materials, information, and ideas at the school and classroom levels to assist principals and teachers in their instructional efforts. Supporting teachers with resources and encouragement is seen as especially important by successful supervisors of curriculum and instruction during periods of change. Supervisors know that they cannot unilaterally improve instruction and that they must rely upon teachers and principals to do so largely voluntarily. Supervisory support in the schools throughout the change process is therefore essential to success. A supervisor in one district stressed the point that support for teachers was of utmost importance when introducing change on a large scale:

> I've learned not to apologize for asking [the school board and superintendent] for things that really need to be done, either for the teachers or for the kids, or to ask for things that help me help teachers do a better job, so that instruction is delivered in a better way to youngsters.

In districts where people are accustomed to academic failure, supervisors have to work hard at providing support simply to keep the instructional program from deteriorating any further. A peculiar characteristic of schools, however, is that once success is experienced, teachers and principals begin to become more aware that additional resources are necessary. It seems that success inevitably raises expectations (Stallings, 1987). The more professional the staff becomes and the more they get accustomed to succeeding, the broader their horizons become and the more they begin to recognize that the possibilities for improving instruction are infinite. Unfortunately, the resources required to support improvement are certain to be limited.

Securing additional funds to improve the instructional program is a universal preoccupation of central office supervisors, even though finance is not usually a responsibility associated with the position. Salaries for instructional personnel comprise the largest part of any school system's budget, and instruction competes with more-tangible categories, such as transportation and buildings and grounds. This circumstance makes it difficult, even in fairly wealthy districts, to justify the spending of additional funds needed to go beyond maintaining the current level of instructional quality. As an associate superintendent for instruction in a rapidly growing, affluent suburban district put it:

> You hardly ever get beyond the continuation budget, and it's frustrating. . . . The needs are never met, and that's frustrating. Money holds us back.

In most districts, the consumable materials that teachers need for their classrooms on a daily basis, like chalk and paper, are purchased at the building level with little direct involvement of the central office supervisor. The purchases of textbooks and other instructional supplies and equipment are more likely to be coordinated system-wide. But principals often do the ordering of books and supplies, and teachers enjoy considerable discretion in terms of which materials they actually use. This autonomy at the building level is undoubtedly functional, to an extent, in that it permits rapid adaptation to changing local circumstances and needs.

Two practical benefits of coordinating the purchase of instructional materials from the central office, on the other hand, are that costs may be lowered by eliminating duplication and equity can be assured among schools within the district. The major advantage of coordinating the purchase of materials at the district level for the improvement of instruction, however, is that it makes long-term planning for program improvement possible. Resources can be directed to specific content areas and grade levels in a purposeful manner. A curriculum director in a small suburban district explained as follows:

> We get X amount of dollars per student for textbooks each year. Two years ago we revised the reading program on the elementary level, kindergarten through sixth grade. That was huge: $66,000 the first year, $40,000 the second year. Right now the high school needs more money for textbooks to fit the new English and math curricula. That's a lot of money when you're talking about a whole district. But I can say, "OK, remember when we emphasized reading and the high school went a little light? Well, let's reverse that now."

Needless to say, such planning requires a high degree of cooperation among teachers and principals and a commitment on their part to district-wide effectiveness.

Ideally, instructional supervisors participate in planning the district's budget, so that the banner of instructional improvement is represented when money is allocated. It is also advantageous for categories like "curriculum" and "staff development" to be listed as line items on the district's budget, according to supervisors, instead of being subsumed under a catch-all heading like "general instruction." Although cutbacks still may occur, separate line items are not likely to be eliminated through oversight.

At the very least, a supervisor has to work closely with a superintendent who is committed to supporting improvement efforts financially. Instructional supervisors feel strongly that a large measure of their credibility depends on being able to assure teachers that new programs will be funded. Telling teachers that money is not available, after they have devoted time and energy developing new curricula and selecting materials, is said to be "devastating to morale" and essentially eliminates interest in large-scale improvement efforts for a long time afterward.

Many central office instructional supervisors rely to a large extent on money obtained from federal and state grants, gifts solicited from private businesses, Parent–Teacher Organizations, and even academic booster clubs, to purchase supplemental materials needed by teachers. Major sources of funds for library books and equipment in virtually every school district are federal and state grants. Supervisors often express some resentment about the time and tediousness of record keeping required by governmental agencies because it removes them from their work in the schools. But supervisors also view grants as valuable resources that create a pool of money that can be drawn upon to meet a variety of special instructional needs.

A curriculum coordinator in a small rural district described a case where an elementary art teacher had requested an expensive ($400) collection of slides of classic artworks. For several years the teacher had submitted requests at the building level that were repeatedly turned down by the principal because he would have had to reduce the amount of money available to other teachers. The coordinator learned about this frustrated instructional need during a revision of the art curriculum, and he suggested that the district order the slides through the library's Chapter 2 grant. The curriculum coordinator was thus able to channel money toward the purchase of materials that was not available through the regular instructional budget.

Some supervisors of instruction, but not all, say that they spend a significant portion of their time writing proposals to fund special projects and purchase equipment. The extent to which supervisors devote energy to writing proposals seems to depend on a combination of factors, most notably system need and past success in securing funds in this way. The time spent preparing a proposal that is not funded is viewed as wasted. After only a few such experiences many supervisors prefer to concentrate on other activities. Even supervisors who have successfully funded proposals are conscious of letting other responsibilities slide. A curriculum director in a financially strapped district explained:

> I'm the grant writer for the district. I try to do whatever I can to find money from whatever diverse sources that may be out there.

> Right now we're on a big kick with local industry. I'm trying to get them to help us out, with computers in particular.

It turned out that this individual secured a substantial grant of equipment directly from a well-known manufacturer of business computers. While he was justifiably proud of this achievement, he observed:

> I believe I could write enough proposals to generate more money for us. But curriculum is my number one love, my number one expertise, and number one responsibility.

Locating Materials and Information

Something that supervisors of instruction seem to find particularly enjoyable is a serendipitous instance when they can nurture a "left-handed idea" like "doing more with human relations in the elementary grades." Success in such ventures usually depends on timing and a willingness to take risks. Considerable pleasure is derived from "finding a way to do the unusual." It involves "playing devil's advocate" and, through careful preparation, "carrying off something that might have initially seemed impossible." Extra materials are located and supplied in such instances to individuals or groups of teachers who are involved in creative projects, curriculum planning, or staff development.

Although locating materials to help creative teachers do the "unusual and off-beat" is a major source of satisfaction, the central office supervisor's duty is also to teachers who need assistance. "Coming through this office," one supervisor said, "are all kinds of samples, textbooks, workbooks, goodies that teachers like to get their hands on." This person commented that her main responsibility in distributing these materials was to make them available first to the teachers and schools where improvement was most desperately needed.

Supervisors also help teachers by collecting and distributing information. A supervisor in one district explained that the first step taken in planning a foreign-language program for elementary students was to request information from other districts across the country that already had programs of that type in place. In a very real sense, the supervisor operates as an idea and resource "broker" (Sullivan, 1980), making information available concerning resources and techniques to individuals and groups of teachers who apply them to instruction. In the words of an assistant superintendent for instruction:

I serve as a person who knows where you can get information. In reading and looking around, invariably I find out the sources where things can be located. Then, when something comes along that we need to work on, it's very easy to say, "You need to check so-and-so." So I do a lot of that, referring people to the different sources that are out there.

These sources to which supervisors refer people can be other institutions or outside experts. Teachers may be sent to another site for special training, for example, or consultants can be brought in to provide technical advice on the spot. A director of instruction in a rural district explained in the following words how she helped an elementary teacher by referring her to practitioners in other districts and to experts at a nearby university:

Our teachers are very creative. We had one teacher who wanted a language development center within her classroom in both Spanish and English. And I was able to facilitate her reaching resource people who helped put together units for use in her class. The last time I was in that classroom, the teacher and all the students were speaking Spanish to me and I couldn't understand what they were saying. But I had spent hours going back and forth [in my car and on the telephone] . . . contacting the right people and doing all types of manipulations to get her the materials she needed.

Teachers apparently greatly appreciate a supervisor's fulfilling this resource or information-broker function, and it generates good will between them. A director of educational services described how he and a particular high school department chairman had experienced a series of minor misunderstandings and disagreements over a period of several years. The supervisor said that it seemed the teacher had believed "that central office was a place to go and put your feet up before you retire."

It turned out that this teacher was selected by his colleagues to head a committee charged with revising the mathematics curriculum. Closer contact with the director of instruction as a result of this assignment seemed to give the teacher a greater appreciation for the central office role:

When he headed up this study for the seventh-through-twelfth-grade revision of the math curriculum, he found out the kinds of things I could do for him, people I could put him in contact with, materials that the committee could use, things we could do by brainstorming together.

As a result of this collaborative effort, the director said that he and the teacher now had a "much healthier respect for one another."

Experience is apparently the best way for a supervisor to become effective as a broker of ideas and resources. Useful information is accumulated over time, supervisors report, through professional reading and by attending conferences. Contacts are made by meeting people both within and outside the district and by listening attentively to what they are interested in and what they are doing. Most supervisors say that it is important to have a broad knowledge of curriculum and instructional techniques and that they themselves contribute many original ideas to new programs. But supervisors generally emphasize that it is neither necessary nor possible to be an expert in all the areas for which they are responsible:

> Knowing everything yourself is not important, but knowing where to find answers is important. Knowing who can help with things [is important] so that when teachers identify a problem, either as individuals or as a group, you know where to find some help for them.

Serving as a broker of ideas and resources may easily become a reactive function, because it involves meeting the technical needs of others. But successful supervisors of instruction are more than simply "matchmakers." Rather, they actively promote new ideas and resources through the interest and enthusiasm they convey for the information that is at their disposal.

For example, a supervisor may try in a rather low-keyed way to stimulate interest among teachers and principals by casually working into a conversation a few tidbits about resources that are available to support a particular innovation. Such informal asides are said to often result in a phone call a week or two later with a request for more details. Some supervisors report, however, that they are much more direct. After telling a group of principals about the types of support that were available through the central office for a state-initiated pilot program, one associate superintendent said that he literally challenged them to take advantage of the opportunity to "become instructional leaders."

Improving Skills Through Training

Offering topics that are relevant to teachers' classroom concerns may be the best way of improving instruction through in-service sessions. According to supervisors, many more teachers will attend workshops sponsored by a district if they believe that as a result they will learn something directly applicable to their performance in the classroom. Most teachers want to do their jobs better, supervisors generally believe, and any information that will help them do so is eagerly sought. As a curriculum coordinator noted,"You can get a lot of teachers going to in-service voluntarily, even after hours, if you just offer the right courses."

Needs assessments are widely used for identifying appropriate in-service topics for teachers because they ensure relevance to classroom problems. An assessment of individual needs can lead to some surprising results. A curriculum coordinator, for instance, discovered that an elementary teacher very much wanted to attend a national social studies conference. Special arrangements were made with the superintendent to provide the money to make it possible, although the teacher paid for a portion of the expenses herself. The supervisor said that she felt good about helping to meet the professional needs of an individual teacher because otherwise they could "easily go unnoticed."

In most cases, however, needs assessments are used to determine the extent of knowledge and interest among members of larger groups or an entire faculty about a specific area or topic. In one district the introduction of computers into classrooms was accompanied by a massive staff development effort involving teachers, administrators, aides, and secretaries. The instructional supervisor explained:

> I had my own feelings about what we needed for in-service. But I thought that the only way to know for sure is to find out: one, what people already know about computers; two, what they care about them; and three, where they think their future is with computers.

On the basis of a survey, alternative sessions were planned that matched the various levels of knowledge, interest, and relevance for people in different positions system-wide. Thus, needs assessments can help to ensure that the content made available through in-service is appropriate and applicable to the tasks that people are expected to perform.

As an incentive, many school districts offer teachers staff development units in exchange for attending in-service sessions. These units may be accumulated within the district, much like college course credits, to earn salary increments. Staff development units may be especially attractive to experienced and proficient teachers who want to earn more money as they acquire new information and skills, but who may be reluctant to enroll in university programs. One supervisor commented, "Some of these people haven't been inside the ivy-covered walls of a university for years—and I'm talking *years.*" Attending staff development courses locally within the district, he thought, was less threatening and more convenient for such teachers.

In-service sessions can also be made more attractive to teachers through symbolic gestures. The same instructional supervisor who conducted the district-wide needs assessment on computer utilization, for example, explained that he made a conscious effort to demonstrate how strongly the district was committed to the introduction of computers by making the training more professional than it had been in the past:

> In the past we've run in-service after school, and the teacher had to pay fifteen bucks out of his own pocket to attend. He got staff development credit, true, but working from three-thirty to six o'clock at night is tough. . . . Well, last year, we set up a computer task force in the district and they said: "Listen, let's do it during the school day. Let's have three-hour stints during the day and hire substitutes. Let's take the teachers away from their buildings so there won't be all sorts of interruptions. Let's take them out to lunch!" The board said, "Fine." I think that that's had a good impact.

In summary, effective in-service training is defined from the very beginning as relevant to the task of teaching and professionally rewarding. Needs assessments ensure that training sessions provide the information and skills that teachers believe are pertinent to them. Individual differences in knowledge, interest, and motivation are also taken into account. Both tangible and symbolic reinforcements are provided. By far the most important factor to consider in making staff development worthwhile for teachers, however, is to involve the most knowledgeable and interested members of the faculty in the actual planning and directing of in-service experiences. It is through the participation of teachers that the collective definition of reality is best formulated. (The importance of teacher involvement will be addressed more fully in Chapter Seven.)

Validating Worth

The support for instruction that supervisors provide in the form of resources, materials, information, and training helps to reduce ambiguity in schools with respect to the technical means available for achieving outcomes, but it does not necessarily reduce the psychological uncertainty surrounding instruction. A degree of unpredictability will always remain in teaching despite efforts to specify outcomes and rationalize techniques. A very beneficial related function that supervisors serve is to structure this psychological uncertainty according to positive generalized beliefs.

Under unfavorable conditions a visit by a central office supervisor to a classroom or a school can be a threatening experience for teachers and principals (Blumberg, 1980). But in districts where supervisors are performing their jobs effectively, such a visit can be viewed almost as an honor and a confirmation that something exciting is happening—or at least that things must be going well.

Praise may be the simplest, most direct method by which supervisors personally validate the worth of others' efforts. Among the reasons that supervisors say they rely on praise are the belief that it contributes to better performance and the observation that encouragement is rarely received by adults who work in schools. As a curriculum director explained:

> It's so important for the people you're working with to have a good self-image and to get reinforcement for what they're doing, because if they feel good, they'll work even harder.

When genuine and deserved, praise is seen as contributing to rapport and the ability to work together. A curriculum coordinator in another district said, for example:

> I think that positive reinforcement is important. Success breeds success. And not false praise and that kind of stuff, but the idea that you're working hard, and I'm working hard, and we're doing it together. I think that's important. So I do encourage effort in that way.

Supervisors generally feel that "catching a person doing something right" and complimenting one for it immediately will beneficially affect that individual's future performance as well as the performance of others with whom the individual has contact. Admittedly, it is impossible to predict specific outcomes from so simple a strategy. But the consensus among successful supervisors seems to be that if praise is given often enough and at appropriate times, it can contribute to an almost contagious cycle of successful feelings and satisfactions in schools. An associate superintendent in a district that is highly regarded for its instructional program—a man who has a large staff of specialists working with him—said that he tried his best to "institutionalize an emphasis on the positive":

> I remind my staff all the time, "Let your people know that they're doing a good job!" None of us ever does enough of that.

Supervisors say that they give praise and encouragement not only to subordinates but to people at all levels within the organization. An assistant superintendent said, for example:

> I don't think anyone's immune. And, hey, you get more flies with sugar. . . . I said to the deputy superintendent, who filled in for the superintendent last night at the board meeting, "Hey, you did a nice job last night." He said, "Gee, thanks." I feel that if the guy did a nice job, I should tell him. If the secretary does a nice job on something, it doesn't hurt to let her know either. I'm talking about positive reinforcement. That's it!

One supervisor explained that his reason for giving encouragement to principals was based on the personal experience of not receiving such feedback when he himself held a building-level administrative position. During a recent evaluation conference with the superintendent concerning a principal who had served the district for a number of years and who "ran a tight ship," the supervisor said that he described the degree of success accomplished by the principal as "exemplary" and his style as "commendable." The principal stood up and gleefully exclaimed, "Nobody's ever told me that!" The supervisor then elaborated:

> And I said, "Well, that's the way I feel about it. . . . Nobody ever told me when I was a principal that I was doing a good job. . . ." And I had two of the best schools in the district. I was told that by the president of the school board once, but the superintendent never told me that. Not once. Maybe that's one of the reasons I have strong feelings about letting somebody know if they do a good job.

Although supervisors say that they try to be generous with praise, they are by no means indiscriminate. They are quick to caution that undeserved praise is worthless, that honesty is extremely important when someone's performance is less than adequate. The same individual quoted above also said:

> But on the other hand, if people do a poor job, you've got to let them know that too. One of my colleagues said [to me], "You operate like a pussycat." And I said, "Yeah. Well, don't forget, a pussycat's got claws, and every once in a while you have to use them." So I wear the black hat if I have to. But I . . . don't believe that you have to be hard as nails all the time.

Even in cases where a teacher's or a principal's performance is judged inadequate, however, supervisors still express optimism about their chances of helping them improve to acceptable levels. A curriculum director with eight years' experience in her current position remarked:

> I guess I've learned to appreciate individuals more and more and to value their uniqueness. It's interesting to work with people long enough to begin to find strengths where you may have felt initially there [were] no strengths in [the] individual. But if you look hard enough, there really are some things that you can dig into and build upon.

An associate superintendent tried to explain this process of identifying and building on people's strengths. What seems to be involved is an intentional effort to identify areas where teachers or principals are already successful and then to create further opportunities for them to succeed. This not only boosts their self-confidence, she explained, it calls attention away from inadequacies of which they are often painfully aware and that get in the way of their performing as well as they might. The implicit assumption seems to be that feelings of success in one area of performance are, again, generalizable to other areas and can contribute to improved overall effectiveness. This supervisor continued:

> You don't ask someone to do something where you know he's lacking. You work through [positive experiences] in hopes that once he gets a little more of the positive things, they'll help the negative, the areas where he's lacking. You don't put him in a situation where you know he's going to have problems.

A director of instruction in another district similarly described the process of building on people's strengths. While stating that teachers needed a basic sense of competence, as we all do, she added that problems in the classroom should never be ignored, commenting:

> You should talk about it and get it out in the air, and then when someone makes gains in building up that area, at that point give the reinforcement. I don't believe in artificial self-confidence.

The single exception to this rule, she continued, was when working with beginning teachers, who frequently demonstrate potential, but nevertheless have obvious difficulties. "I may try to reassure somebody like that even if they're not yet up to par," she said, "but in most cases it's important to be truthful and not give people reinforcement if they don't deserve it."

The most formal validation of worth for supervisors of instruction is the process of securing and maintaining accreditation for the district. District level supervisors are invariably involved, it seems, in coordinating the preparations for visiting state inspection committees and accrediting agencies. Committees are formed, meetings are held, data are gathered, and reports are written. Supervisors of instruction are usually responsible, it seems, for everything from initial planning to final editing.

Building Confidence

While "validating worth" lets people know that what they are already doing has value and is appreciated by others, "building confidence" in people prepares them psychologically to take positive action in the future. The former focuses on tasks and outcomes that have been achieved or are currently underway. The latter relates specifically to reducing psychological uncertainty between activities and as-yet-unrealized ends. Validating worth allows teachers and principals to look back with satisfaction at what they have already achieved, while building confidence encourages them to look forward toward future accomplishments with optimism.

District level instructional supervisors tend to view success and the *expectation* of success as being very closely related. Supervisors say that they personally expend a great amount of effort highlighting the successes of others and cheering people on toward ever greater accomplishments. They actively encourage and try to generate enthusiasm and excitement wherever they go in the district for the kinds of things that teachers and principals are doing in classrooms and schools. In other words, supervisors' actions contribute to an optimistic definition of the situation that promotes the kind of culture in which good things can happen. Successful supervisors purposely try to institutionalize a positive self-fulfilling prophecy in their districts.

According to many supervisors of curriculum and instruction, building confidence in people is, or should be, one of the fundamental processes of schooling at all levels. As a district coordinator remarked:

> Building confidence is something that any administrator does or any teacher does. The teacher should be building confidence in the students, and the principals should be building confidence in the teachers, and we ought to be building confidence in the principals and teachers.

A director of instruction offered the insight that teachers are capable of building confidence in students only to the extent that they have confidence in themselves. She saw a large part of her own responsibilities, therefore, as providing psychological support and encouragement to teachers for the work they are doing in order to "build up their self-esteem." This supervisor said that she received the encouragement she needed from the superintendent, and in turn she "tried to be a confidence builder" for everyone else, "from the superintendent down to the students." She cautioned, however, that "it's a responsibility of everybody" and not her's alone. Building confidence, then, is something that everyone in a school needs. Everyone is responsible for generating confidence in others, but this is a process that supervisors both initiate and encourage.

A curriculum director who expressed very strong feelings about the importance of building people's confidence described herself as "of the old school," where it is "believed that you get pretty much out of people what you expect." She observed that building confidence in others basically involved "seeing the good and recognizing and encouraging it." While noting that public recognition of teachers at events like award ceremonies served a useful purpose, she suggested that more often and more importantly a supervisor communicates confidence in a teacher's or a principal's ability to accomplish a task successfully "in very subtle ways" during casual interactions.

Although confidence and success are seen as being closely related, supervisors recognize that the former does not simply and directly result in the latter. The relationship between confidence and success is viewed as being more reciprocal, or cyclical, than linearly causal. A legitimate question with respect to practice is: "Where does one begin if both confidence and success are lacking?"

Supervisors admit that it is difficult to build confidence among teachers in a school if the school is not already successful at some endeavor. Both success and failure seem to be habit forming among groups of people and are capable of being generalized from one activity to another (Vail, 1978). It is helpful if the supervisor can discover some already existing notable achievement by students or teachers to point to as evidence that the school is capable of success in another arena. The absence of such evidence makes the job of confidence building more difficult, but by no means impossible. The evidence of successful achievement in such cases, however, first may have to be generated.

A curriculum coordinator, for example, suggested that the best way to build teachers' confidence is to give them responsibility for some task at which they can succeed that is outside their normal work routine. Once they have experienced success in this way, it "builds their confidence for the next time, and they feel much better about what they're already doing." Supervisors report that under unfavorable circumstances, where people are simply not accustomed to succeeding, it is important to set up situations in which it is highly likely, but not absolutely certain, that success will be achieved. An element of unpredictability should be preserved, they say, but not to the extent that people who lack self-confidence will feel overwhelmed.

One way of building confidence among teachers in the area of instruction, for example, is to establish a committee, comprised of the most dedicated and enthusiastic teachers, to accomplish a challenging but achievable task. The supervisor then works closely with the group, finding resources, answering questions, and generally facilitating their work, in order to guarantee success to as great an extent as possible.

Once success is accomplished, even if it involves a comparatively risk-free activity like writing or revising the curriculum, it should be publicly acknowledged. Many supervisors not only praise teachers for their work, they also are careful to involve teachers in presentations that are made to other teachers and even to the board of education. Larger victories eventually become possible, supervisors suggest, through the accumulation of small successes.

A caveat mentioned by some supervisors, however, is that being honest and realistic with teachers is equally essential. Raising expectations unrealistically or too early is viewed as counterproductive. Teachers and principals need to be aware of the constraints under which they and others operate and the resources that are actually available. They need to recognize as well that real success does not come easily, but requires persistent effort and commitment.

A prerequisite of building confidence in others, according to one associate superintendent, is that the supervisor should have a "clear and strong" personal definition of self. "The important thing," this individual observed, "is not to be insecure, but rather to have a clear sense of who you are and what you're trying to accomplish." Personal doubts and second-guessing one's own decisions and actions make it difficult to inspire confidence in others, she believed.

Developing a System of Support

The impression may have been created in the foregoing presentation that the activities in which supervisors engage, while reducing ambiguity and uncertainty at the level of task performance, are indeed fragmented and performed independently of one another. In fact, all five activities—securing resources for instructional improvement, supporting improvement efforts with information and materials, providing in-service training, validating worth, and building confidence—are all highly related and occur in close association. Often, funds are secured, materials acquired, and information collected, for example, for groups of teachers as they plan in-service training for their colleagues. The participation of teachers in such planning activities also contributes to the processes of validation of worth and confidence building.

Supervisors openly describe themselves as "support persons" because they frequently provide teachers and principals with resources, materials, information, training, and encouragement. But the key to successfully improving a school district seems to be the establishment of an instructional support system rather than personally attending to innumerable details. This involves rallying people at various levels within the organization, locating those who have similar interests, and putting them in touch with one another so that they can provide mutual support by sharing resources, information, and encouragement already at their disposal.

A system of support can assume various manifestations. It often begins with the establishment of an informal network among people with similar interests or concerns; or, as was described in Chapter Five, it can become as formal as agreeing upon and enacting a policy for the equitable and timely selection and purchase of materials and supplies.

A support system among teachers may ultimately result in more-formal endeavors like attempting to secure extra funds for a special curriculum project, planning and developing an in-service program, or arranging for securing materials from an external agency like a public television station or a local university. Supervisors say that they typically use a "hands-off" approach when nurturing the growth of these support systems, but they make themselves readily available whenever they are asked for assistance.

References

Blumberg, A. 1980. *Supervisors and teachers: A private cold war.* Boston: Allyn and Bacon.

Oliva, P. F. 1984. *Supervision for today's schools.* New York: Longman.

Stallings, J. 1987. For whom and how long is the Hunter-based model appropriate? Response to Robbins and Wolfe. *Educational Leadership,* 44 (5): 62–63.

Sullivan, C. G. 1980. The work of the instructional supervisor: A functional analysis (Doctoral dissertation, Emory University, 1980).

Tanner, D. & Tanner, L. 1987. *Supervision in education: Problems and practices.* New York: Macmillan.

Thibaut, J. W. & Kelley, H. H. 1959. *The social psychology of groups.* New York: John Wiley & Sons.

Vail, P. B. 1978. Toward a behavioral description of high performing systems. In M. W. McCall, Jr. and M. M. Lombardo (eds.), *Leadership: Where else can we go?* Durham, N.C.: Duke University Press.

7
Involving Teachers in Change

The term "supervision" in education is increasingly becoming associated with the direct observation of teachers in classrooms. This situation may be partly the result of the popularity of the clinical supervision model and partly due to the importation of conceptual schemes from industry and the military that emphasize conformity over innovation. In these noneducational settings supervisors are commonly viewed as being mainly responsible for watching subordinates closely and monitoring their activities to make sure that they do as they are told.

Some educators seem to be forgetting that the observation of teachers in classrooms is only one part of what supervision in schools is about (Cogan, 1973). What also seems to be getting lost is the understanding, so eloquently stated by pioneers like Goldhammer (1969), that effective instructional supervision is essentially a collaborative venture involving the purposeful construction of meaning in the classroom and school.

Central office instructional supervisors certainly are involved in improving the quality of instruction at the classroom level, but they report spending comparatively little of their time actively engaged in classroom observation for the specific purpose of making suggestions to individual teachers. Successful central office supervisors say they are more heavily involved in the initiation and facilitation of broader organizational processes like instructional support, curriculum development, and staff development. These impact less directly on any single classroom but potentially affect larger numbers of teachers and students. Classroom observations are certainly important to district level supervisors, but usually more as a source of information concerning the operation of the instructional program as a whole than for assessing the performance of particular teachers.

Much current literature in the field of instructional supervision is also focused both explicitly and implicitly on the idea of working with teachers who are either inexperienced or incompetent. The concerns of practicing central office supervisors usually relate much more to improving the performance and enhancing the commitment of the majority of able teachers who are already working satisfactorily and who have enacted their roles successfully for a number of years. As a curriculum coordinator in one district explained:

> I don't think that [a central office supervisor] can make much difference with the really poor teachers. But I think that, for example, with the teachers who are ready to burn out, just to make them feel that you have an interest in them, just to [give them] a spark can make a difference. Whether it be through in-service, or through encouragement, or through giving them materials or ideas that are new and different, it's a way of moving them along.

In some respects, inexperienced teachers and those who are having major difficulties in the classroom may actually be easier to work with than proficient veterans. Novices are usually eager to please, and teachers whose jobs are in jeopardy tend to be more responsive to directives from superordinates. The real challenge, and the task to which successful district level instructional supervisors tirelessly apply themselves, is that of improving the performance of the majority of experienced and capable teachers who are currently performing at an average or above-average level. This attention to already successful teachers not only ensures that the quality of the overall instructional program is maintained, but supervisors contend that successful and secure teachers possess the greatest potential for further professional growth.

Top–Down or Bottom–Up?

A common view of the change process in education is that change begins with a decision at the top of the administrative hierarchy and filters down to the classroom level. Although the direction of change is certainly influenced from the "top," most supervisors recognize that to be successful the process is inevitably interactive. One central office supervisor distastefully recalled what it was like when he had worked as a teacher in another school system:

> [The district] had plenty of central office help, but they seldom, *seldom* asked us for any input at all because they were the

experts. They were the guys who went out to hear all the experts talk, and they read all the books, and things just filtered down.

Cuban (1984) has challenged the top–down model of district-wide change and suggested instead that truly effective school systems simultaneously provide opportunities for both top–down and bottom–up influence. A curriculum coordinator made this same point in describing how her role relates to the change process:

> The whole role is in changing instruction. It's from the top going down, but it also works the other way when teachers say, "This isn't right. We want to change something." So it goes both ways. . . . When we were introducing computers, I had some definite ideas about what we needed, and those definite ideas are now in place. At the same time, . . . I will listen to teachers because I think that they have an expertise that I don't have, because they're working with it every day.

The introduction of computers into classrooms is probably the most recent major instructional innovation to sweep across public education in the United States. It is not surprising that when talking about change in schools, instructional supervisors often refer to the introduction of computers to illustrate how the change process works. In districts where the impact of computer technology on instruction has been greatest, this change seems to follow the combined top–down/bottom–up pattern.

An assistant superintendent, for example, described how the use of computers in classrooms began in his system with a spontaneous interest among a few teachers. He said that some building administrators were initially uncertain and even a little wary about the propriety of teachers bringing their own computers from home into their classrooms for instructional purposes. At about the same time, school board members began to raise questions at meetings with the central office staff regarding what the district was doing with regard to teaching students about computers. The supervisor explained that in this instance district-wide change eventually came "from two pressures: teachers and central administration."

This example is not meant to suggest that building administrators are typically resistant to change. In another school system, in fact, a young female assistant principal was described by the district supervisor as having rallied early interest in computers at the classroom and building levels, which finally spurred an overly cautious central office staff into action. The point is that instructional innovations are not always initiated and planned from the top and then enforced at lower levels of the hierarchy, as some popular models of change imply. The evidence suggests, in fact, that school districts can be most adaptive by encouraging and openly advocating experimentation among creative teachers and administrators who are on the cutting edge of innovation.

Rather than merely relying on occasional spontaneous bursts of mutual interest and enthusiasm, however, successful central office supervisors intentionally create mechanisms within the organization that facilitate simultaneous top–down and bottom–up instructional-change efforts within their school districts. Involving teachers in curriculum development committees and curriculum councils and encouraging their participation in planning and conducting their own in-service training are the techniques most commonly employed to accomplish this end.

Changing Instructional Practice

One of the most important and most difficult tasks that central office supervisors have is that of convincing teachers and principals to consider honestly and objectively whether instructional programs and practices that may have been in place for years are still appropriate and worthwhile. This can be an especially challenging task if the people at the building level were heavily involved in the original development of the earlier innovations that now represent the status quo.

Strong commitment to an innovation is generally considered to be good from an organizational perspective because it improves the chances of full implementation. An interesting unexamined question, however, is whether a high degree of commitment to a particular innovation limits an organization's ability to adapt to novel situations. Full implementation, that Holy Grail of change agents, actually might be counterproductive if ever achieved because the organization could have problems adjusting to changing circumstances in the future. The greater a group's investment and commitment to a particular innovation, the more difficult subsequent changes may be to introduce.

For instance, a supervisor in one district talked about the difficulty of convincing the high school principals with whom he worked of the academic advantages of eliminating electives for eleventh-grade students in favor of courses that more heavily emphasized the skills of reading and writing. He suggested that a particular principal's reluctance to go along with this change was partly "because [the electives were] his baby back in the 1970s, when we believed, 'If it feels good, do it.'"

A director of instructional services described a similar reluctance among a group of mathematics teachers to alter long-established classroom practices. Although high school students in the district scored exceptionally well on state-administered tests measuring achievement in mathematics, according to the supervisor, a difficulty nevertheless became apparent. The supervisor explained:

> The kids who came back from college said, "Hey, I got all A's in high school, but that isn't the way they teach it in college."

The problem facing the supervisor in this instance was not an easy one to solve. It involved convincing a tightly knit group of able and experienced teachers—who were already convinced that they were doing a good job, both individually and collectively—to consider seriously doing things differently in their classrooms. When the issue was first raised, the supervisor reported:

> We had horrible resistance from the teachers because we have a seasoned staff with probably an average of twenty years' experience in the high school. They've done the same thing for twenty years, and they've done it well.

This supervisor clearly understood that experienced, competent, and confident teachers cannot be treated the same, nor influenced as easily as beginners or those who know they are having difficulty. He

> It simply won't work if you go in there and say to them, "You've been doing this all wrong!"

This supervisor said that even though he approached the members of the mathematics department respectfully and professionally to explain that the rationale for changes in instructional strategies and textbooks was so students would be better prepared for college, the initial opposition from teachers was intense. The supervisor eventually prevailed, but only through a persistent effort over a long period of time, during which he demonstrated a willingness to listen to and discuss the concerns of the mathematics teachers and provided them with both frequent encouragement and material support. But this change in instructional methods and materials meant nothing less than a change in the norms governing instruction, that is, in the collective definition of the situation within the high school mathematics department. Such change necessarily requires the involvement of teachers in their own professional development.

Instructional change is obviously easier to accomplish and is more likely to last if it can be nurtured upward from the classroom level. There are times, however, when resistance to needed change is encountered and a supervisor may have to go beyond simply cultivating the grassroots. When initiating change involving groups of competent but possibly reluctant practitioners, successful supervisors typically follow the very pragmatic rule of beginning where they are most likely to succeed.

A curriculum director, for example, explained how she spearheaded the introduction of computer instruction for elementary students. The plan, which a district curriculum committee comprised of teachers had developed, was to have every elementary teacher in the district voluntarily using computers in the classroom by the following year. Thereafter, some type of computer application would be expected of everyone. Teachers were provided with intensive instruction, sample lesson plans, computers, and access to support staff. The key to accomplishing an ambitious task such as this, the curriculum director explained is to

> start where you have your strength and not your weakness. . . . The first building we went into was [the one] where we had the greatest number of teachers who already used computers and were on the curriculum committee.

The teachers at this first building not only showed more interest prior to the implementation, they also provided a pool of enthusiastic trainers and support staff for teachers at other locations. When teachers at the other schools heard marvelous reports from their colleagues about how well the new program worked, faculty groups at these other schools actually began making requests to the central office that their schools receive the training next. Eventually, all but four teachers in the entire district went through the training voluntarily, according to the supervisor, "and the four were all in the last building, where we knew from day one we were going to have trouble." Beginning where success is most likely helps to ensure that the social definition of the situation reflects positive thinking, optimistic attitudes, and success.

A Contrary Example

Providing opportunities for staff involvement in in-service activities and curriculum decisions has long been advocated as being essential for improving instruction (Wiles, 1967). Before considering how this is done effectively, it may be worthwhile to look first at a contrary example in a district where, by the supervisor's own admission, staff development is not well received by teachers. The instructional supervisor in this district sadly commented that teachers had not appreciated a recent in-service workshop:

> It really hurts when you spend weeks, sometimes months, putting together a conference, spending a lot of money, bringing in guest speakers, only to have people say as they're leaving the building, "What a waste of time. I'd rather the kids had stayed."

It may be instructive to consider how this district went about developing in-service and what factors may have contributed to such dissatisfaction among the teachers. By calling attention to the errors committed, the purpose is not to ridicule but rather to contrast characteristics of ineffective in-service with more-successful examples so that others can avoid the pitfalls that may lead to frustration for everyone involved. The supervisor in this instance explained how the ill-fated in-service session had come about, while describing the kinds of responsibilities included in his job:

> The state requires that we have what they call an in-service day. I have to do as the law mandates and sit down with teachers to find out the in-service needs of the district. So I work with committees, and for two or three weeks I have to spend time organizing that day. The teachers attend a meeting or two during [the morning of] that day, and we bring in guest speakers. In the afternoon, I have to work with the principals on setting up curriculum projects. It could be an evaluation of the curriculum, it could be selecting new materials. So I do spend a lot of time on what the state calls an in-service day.

A source of difficulty, as the supervisor's own words clearly indicate, is that the stimulus for planning the in-service day was a legal requirement, not a conviction that it might benefit students by improving instruction in the classroom. The situation was defined, in other words, simply as complying with state regulations. Involvement of teachers in the assessment of needs was viewed as a matter of conforming with the letter of the law, rather than as an attempt to draw on teachers' expertise or to meet their instructional needs. Outside consultants were hired for what was evidently a one-shot staff development program for every teacher in the district. Furthermore, there was evidently no attempt to integrate the in-service session with the broader instructional program. In fact, it appears that curriculum was considered an entirely separate issue in this district, one in which teachers had little voice.

Incredibly, and apparently as an incidental afterthought, the superintendent of this district decided to enforce a policy of refusing to grant in-service credit to teachers who attended the session unless written application had been on file in the district office and approved prior to the in-service day. As the supervisor explained, "Teachers said that they didn't know that he wanted them to do this." Although the superintendent had never enforced the policy before, in this case "he would not bend." The definition of the in-service session as a matter of legal compliance was thus reinforced by adding a punitive dimension for not following district rules.

While this illustration of poor practice is admittedly extreme in that it was essentially "programmed to fail" through its legalistic and punitive definition of reality, the in-service session itself probably was not too different from what frequently passes as staff development under more enlightened leadership. Specifically, the meeting was conducted by an outside consultant on a one-time basis, without teacher participation, addressing all the teachers in the district simultaneously regardless of their differing needs and interests. In contrast, recent research suggests that in-service training is generally more effective when it is led by professionals from within the district, is ongoing, and accommodates varying needs and characteristics (Joyce and Showers, 1980, 1983). Effective curriculum and staff development, in other words, simultaneously address the normative, motivational, and technical dimensions of a district's social reality.

Normative Change and Professional Growth

Having teachers internalize a norm of collective responsibility for the general quality of instruction within the district may be the ultimate goal of central office supervisors when they work with teachers. The principal mechanism by which supervisors nurture this norm of collective responsibility for the instructional program is by involving teachers in discussions and decisions relating to curriculum and their own professional growth. It was noted in an earlier chapter that supervisors sometimes ironically observe that the more successful they become at this aspect of their work, the less their positions appear to be needed. Among successful instructional supervisors such considerations are apparently outweighed by the improvement of instruction in the district as a whole, the professional growth experienced by teachers, and the knowledge that it is the students who will ultimately benefit.

Broadly defined, professional development for teachers may encompass activities as diverse as reading, traveling, participating in professional associations, supervising student teachers, enrolling in graduate level courses, and visiting other teachers' classrooms and schools. Although central office supervisors may encourage teachers to become involved in any and all of these activities, instructional supervisors contribute most directly to the professional development of teachers in the same way that they promote a norm of collective responsibility: by providing opportunities for teachers to serve on curriculum committees and by involving them in planning and conducting in-service training.

Participation in these activities helps establish expectations among teachers that involvement in decision making and improving the overall quality of instruction are legitimate professional responsibilities. As teachers become involved and accept responsibility for the quality of instruction outside their classrooms, they begin to function more as professionals and less as individual entrepreneurs. In-service training and curriculum development, therefore, may serve as vehicles for socializing teachers into the profession in a more general sense.

The successful induction of individuals in any organization depends upon technical and motivational factors as well as normative considerations (Brim and Wheeler, 1966). Not only must the district present clear expectations of professional involvement and responsibility to teachers, it also must provide adequate opportunities for them to enact the expectations successfully and then reward them for their success.

The relationship between teacher participation and instructional improvement is clear in the minds of successful central office supervisors. An assistant superintendent for instruction, for example, was asked what she believed had contributed the most to consistent gains in student achievement in her district for several years in a row. She responded as follows:

> Most of all, I think it was the teacher involvement in planning curriculum. I think that was important. They helped to identify the objectives out of the textbooks they had chosen. You notice I said that *they* had chosen—for social studies and science, for example—based on the curriculum that *they* said they wanted to teach.

It is worth emphasizing that the simple existence of written curriculum guides does not necessarily indicate that a district is effective or that an instructional supervisor is successful. Curriculum guides are merely the visible manifestations or products of curriculum development. Their content may have very little to do with what is actually taught in classrooms unless teachers have a sense of ownership of the curriculum. Successful supervisors of instruction recognize that having a comprehensive set of guides on the shelf is therefore considerably less important than the active participation of teachers in the process of developing curriculum. Teacher participation contributes to the development of normative standards that have a greater likelihood of influencing teaching behavior in the classroom.

The potential of curriculum for shaping teaching behavior is clearly evident in the following reflections of the assistant superintendent who was quoted earlier. Upon being asked why she identified "teacher involvement" as the primary factor that had led to consistent improvement in student achievement, she responded with several related questions:

> How do we make sure that what we write in a curriculum guide actually takes place in the classroom? What are we doing now? What can we do that will be least offensive to teachers, so that they won't think that Big Brother is watching them *all* the time? Well the key to that is their involvement, so that they're watching themselves.

The curriculum of a district may thus serve as a norm that influences and shapes teachers' behaviors in the classroom. But teachers have to participate in formulating the norm or they will not internalize it as readily. The benefits to a school system of having teachers who are committed, autonomous, and self-monitoring are obvious.

A curriculum director in another district spoke of encouraging a feeling of "ownership" among teachers toward the curriculum and enumerated additional advantages of directly and actively involving teachers in its development:

> I try to get teachers to head up curriculum committees. If we're doing a revision of health, for example, I don't want to do it. I don't want the middle school principal doing it. If curriculum is what we're zeroing in on, I want a teacher to head it up. One, ownership; two, they're teaching it every day, so they have the expertise; and three, we've got better things to do during the summer, like hiring the best new teachers we can find.

When asked to elaborate on why it was important to encourage a feeling of ownership among teachers and to draw upon their expertise, this curriculum director responded with an illustration of the enthusiasm generated among teachers for a special-education curriculum project in social studies:

> I keep getting phone calls from teachers saying, "I want to put this on the agenda. We need to look at it." Those are things that come from teachers. I could sit here and come up with forty topics myself, but these are areas that come from the teachers saying, "Listen, we want to study this, we want to be able to give our input, we want to have an impact."

The curriculum director spoke for most successful supervisors when he observed that he constantly strives to make teachers "feel good about themselves and their teaching." Involving them in decisions through group participation was a way of accomplishing this. He said that teacher morale was important to him mainly because of the influence that teachers have on children. Turning and pointing to a poster on the wall behind him, the curriculum director said:

> My favorite statement by [John F.] Kennedy is up here, "Children are the world's most valuable resources and its best hope for the future." Since we're not going to get paid a great deal of money . . . and we're not going to get a lot of "atta-boys" and "atta-girls" from the outside and the public (we have a very negative newspaper here, and it is always taking us to task), . . . I think there are many things that we can do internally to let teachers know [not only that they are] valuable, but that we value what they have to say. And so I'm big on using committees, on getting as many opinions as possible, and then working that way. Through subcommittees of subcommittees we've been able to do that, and it's really great.

In other words, teachers unfortunately cannot expect to receive rewards or recognition from society for what they do for children. It is therefore up to the people who work in the schools, especially the teachers themselves, to reinforce the understanding that they and their work are worthwhile.

A supervisor can certainly try to help the situation by telling teachers that they are doing well. However, it is far more important for teachers to gain the esteem of their colleagues if they are to develop a professional identity. Providing opportunities for teachers and encouraging them to work with their peers allow them to demonstrate their knowledge, skills, and commitment to one another and also to accept common responsibility for broader instructional issues outside their individual classrooms. As one supervisor put it:

> You get the best results in terms of impact or making a change in a school when you [involve teachers] who already are leaders within that school. Or you can provide teachers with an opportunity to develop leadership and give them a little support while they're doing it. When you can get teachers involved and leading their peers, everybody grows from that. It's amazing.

Involving teachers in curriculum development may not guarantee success, but *not* involving them certainly minimizes the chances for success. A sense of ownership among teachers and relevance of the finished product to classroom realities contribute to a greater likelihood that a curriculum will be taught after it is produced. Furthermore, involving teachers in curriculum development increases the probability of ongoing improvement and experimentation.

Structuring Involvement

The major drawback of extensive teacher involvement for the supervisor is that it takes time to synthesize various points of view and time is a scarce resource in schools. Curriculum improvement projects require a long-term commitment and considerable patience from supervisors who might prefer decisions to be made more quickly. Some supervisors also say that they have difficulty giving groups of teachers the autonomy they need for developing curriculum, because once autonomy of process is granted, the forthcoming results are unpredictable.

Coordinating the development of curriculum in an entire district is a complex task, but it can be simplified by initially using larger groups of teachers to address general concerns. Smaller grade-level and content-area subgroups can then be profitably employed to follow up and focus on more specific issues. A supervisor said:

> I have a general meeting with teachers on each grade level in the fall, and we discuss the new things in the curriculum and areas that they may want to work on. . . . Recently we've made a change in the fourth-grade social studies curriculum. We have been working very closely with the fourth-grade teachers. We had about twelve meetings last year and did some summer curriculum writing on it too.

The work of these subgroups must eventually be integrated, he explained, so that "at the end of grade six certain things are achieved, and at the end of grade eight, and at the end of grade twelve." Ensuring continuity and sequence means that teachers have to be "brought together for a long period of time." The supervisor elaborated on how this could be done using small groups:

> We do an awful lot of work in subcommittees. There's no reason to talk something to death in a large group, about the need to revise social studies k through 12, when the kindergarten teacher doesn't have the foggiest idea of what's needed with psychology electives in the twelfth grade.

Because teachers are accustomed to addressing large groups of students, one might assume that they could easily adapt the skills used daily in their classrooms to other forums. But some teachers apparently are not comfortable when communicating with groups of adults, especially when addressing their colleagues. While working with a curriculum council, for instance, one supervisor reported that he initially had to assign to teacher representatives the responsibility of finding out how their colleagues felt about instructional issues. He said that he told them, with a touch of humor, to expect to deliver an oral report on what they learned from the teachers in their respective schools at the next curriculum council meeting:

> I said, "OK, I want you to go back to the faculty room, to that den of thieves, and find out exactly what's bugging them about the language arts program. And I want you to come back, and I'm going to ask you to give reports. Now some of you can give it to me in writing, but I'm going to ask some of you to stand up and tell us what you learned in the last month."

The supervisor clearly recognized that this practice made people uncomfortable. He said, "Now *that* really scares the heck out of people at first, and they usually give very short reports." He had learned from experience, however, that unless he began by specifically instructing new representatives to talk to their colleagues about instruction and curriculum between meetings of the council, many would not do so. Perspectives and opinions of teachers in most cases were limited to personal experiences in their own classrooms, he found, and he ended up doing most of the talking just to "keep the meeting going."

According to the supervisor, although this procedure caused some initial discomfort for teachers, they invariably came to enjoy discussing issues with other teachers in their schools and then representing the general sentiment at the district level curriculum committee. The supervisor believed that not only did this help the individual representative develop self-confidence and a broader perspective, but a dialogue among teachers at the local building level was also established, which provided a firm foundation for subsequent district level discussion and decision making.

A curriculum director in a different school system pointed out that allowing teachers to exercise leadership while developing curriculum had the additional benefit of reinforcing their perception of the supervisor as primarily a facilitator of the work of responsible professionals:

> We did not have curriculum guides when I first came here, and now we have them in every content area. Teachers are using them, and they are continually being revised. When I ask teachers to work on curriculum guides, I get very positive responses. I feel that the way we work builds good rapport with the teachers, and I think they see me as a support person.

A supervisor in yet another district similarly remarked that it was absolutely essential for administrators and principals to provide as much support to teachers as possible to ensure their success, but without becoming directly involved:

> We don't need to get enmeshed in curriculum, but we ought to be there to help. We should serve as a resource, make the phone calls, and use our influence to get things done for them. Teachers can't get too far without that support. I like to use other people's expertise as much as possible. And they love it too, they really enjoy that.

Thus, while some structuring and direction by the supervisor may be necessary initially, the ultimate goal remains to have teachers assume responsibility for the curriculum and instruction in the district.

Change and Credibility

Although curriculum development and staff development are often treated separately in the literature, as components of district-wide change they are almost inseparable and at times barely distinguishable. Staff development of some sort typically accompanies the implementation of a new or revised curriculum, for example, while the development of curriculum within a school system contributes to the professional development of the district's faculty.

Instead of superiors dictating to and remediating deficiencies in subordinates, teacher involvement can redefine curriculum development and in-service training more positively as a sharing of ideas and responsibility among professional colleagues. For this reason, effective supervisors often rely upon teachers from within the district or from other districts to provide training for their staffs. A curriculum director pointed out that teachers have more credibility with their peers than anyone else:

> Teachers are much more likely to believe something if it is told to them by another teacher instead of somebody in the central office, or somebody at the university, or somebody who is a consultant and travels around the country.

The benefit of involving teachers in planning and conducting staff development sessions is that the result is likely to be a highly collaborative effort:

> One of the myths that we've eliminated is that you're not an expert in your own building. I rarely bring in any outside consultants because I almost always use our own staff for doing workshops. You already have the expertise right there to do it, and the other teachers will very often go ahead and help them. And I set out to do that deliberately, because I think it's very important. It works!

A supervisor in another district observed that utilizing one's own staff for in-service training also provided a continuous and readily available internal support system:

> You don't have to go five hundred miles and pay one thousand dollars. We've got people right here in the district. We did all the in-service for the curriculum for computers with our own folks. . . . It saved us money, but I think it also worked out well in that people in the trenches [understood] that these presenters didn't just whisk in for two days, then whisk out again, and we'd never see them again. When the in-service was over, if they had a problem, they could just call [another building] and say, "Hey, Robin, I'm having trouble. What's the problem with this computer stuff?" They're right here. They're not in Chicago or some place like that. That helps out.

When a teacher from within the district presents an in-service to colleagues, the supervisor continued, both the presenter and the audience can grow from the experience:

> It's important with teachers to identify and build on their individual strengths. We're beginning to use some of our teachers who are exceptional to conduct staff development for other teachers.

> The head of our English department, for example, taught a staff development course on writing that was a k–12 course. He learned a tremendous amount about middle-school and elementary youngsters. He did just a fabulous job, and he understands the kids coming to him better now than ever before.

A practitioner from a nearby district was a critical element in convincing the skeptical members of the mathematics department described earlier that change was both possible and desirable. In the words of their district supervisor:

> We did the same thing for my math folks, . . . who were still skeptical about changing. One of our neighboring districts has a really good program, so we got some of their folks to come out as a freebie and speak to us about the ramifications and pitfalls and the really good things about their math program. That cost us substitutes for about fifteen people that day. That's cheap. And they saw a guy from the trenches, not me, espousing things—a guy who has been living with it for years talking about how that program works, what the success rate is. . . . And he's got the stories of kids coming back, kids being successful, kids doing this and that, and it's hard to discredit that kind of stuff.

A variation of using practitioners from outside the district is to send insiders to another site or special session to gain knowledge or skills, which they bring back to their school. Teachers who are good at communicating information to colleagues are often selected by supervisors to represent the district at workshops and conferences held outside the district. This can serve as a form of recognition and reward for the individuals chosen, and it also directly benefits the district as a whole when they are later drawn on as a resource.

Teachers also have greater confidence in curriculum that has been developed by their colleagues:

> I think teachers feel better knowing that one of their own is up there making curriculum decisions. It would be very easy for me to simply say, "OK, here's the new curriculum," but they wouldn't necessarily accept that.

Supervisors also report that district-wide curriculum councils led by teachers have credibility with school boards as well. One curriculum director proudly described the situation in his district:

> Right now [the curriculum council's credibility] is very, very strong. The curriculum council has a great deal of impact on the

board of education because you have representatives from every building, from about every persuasion that you can think of: librarians, special-education teachers, reading specialists, and so on. It's a high-powered group.

To illustrate this group's influence, the supervisor described an instance when the curriculum council recommended a district-wide "overhaul" of special-education services and curriculum. The initial reaction of the school board was to turn down this recommendation because state and federal guidelines for educating the handicapped were already being met. The curriculum council responded, in turn, by unanimously endorsing its original recommendations a second time and admonishing the school board that meeting the needs of local children was the major issue. Whether or not the district already conformed to minimum requirements established by external agencies was entirely beside the point. The school board in this case reconsidered its position and agreed to fund the proposed improvements. The supervisor observed that the curriculum council functioned as "a lever for us in the central office." It helped him to get new programs approved if he could earnestly say to school board members, "Listen, the teachers want this, and they think it's very important."

A strategy mentioned by many supervisors that serves this purpose is to ask teachers who have worked on curriculum committees to give reports to the board of education. This provides an opportunity for board members to ask questions and learn about the instructional program directly from the teachers. It also gives teachers some recognition for the contributions they have made, and it is an opportunity for the supervisor to share credit. With respect to a new program designed to improve students' writing, for example, a district coordinator reported:

> I plan to bring in teachers to talk to the school board and tell them what the goals and objectives are, how they're going to evaluate the writing, how they expect writing to improve generally, and anything else the board would like to know. The school board feels that they can make better decisions in the future from what they learn from teachers.

Balancing Conformity with Innovation

Fifty years ago, in describing the relationship between cultural values and the social structures that are established to further them, the sociologist Robert Merton (1938) observed that there are five logically

FIGURE 7.1
OUTCOMES OF ACCEPTING OR REJECTING
CULTURAL GOALS AND INSTITUTIONALIZED MEANS

	Cultural Goals	Institutionalized Means
I. Conformity	acceptance	acceptance
II. Innovation	acceptance	rejection
III. Ritualism	rejection	acceptance
IV. Retreatism	rejection	rejection
V. Rebellion	rejection/ substitution	rejection/ substitution

possible adjustments that are available to individuals in the performance of their roles: conformity, innovation, ritualism, retreatism, and rebellion. Each represents a different adaptation to the means and ends prescribed by the culture-bearing group to which the individual belongs. These are presented in Figure 7.1.

As depicted in Figure 7.1, the category of role adjustment labeled "conformity" represents an acceptance of both the values espoused by a culture and the means prescribed for accomplishing them. Conformity ensures that the stability necessary for a group's continued existence is maintained. In fact, without widespread conformity, a "group" would instead be simply an aggregation of individuals whose actions were minimally related to one another.

The category of adaptation labeled "innovation," in comparison, involves an acceptance of cultural values, but a nonacceptance of the institutionalized means for achieving them. The teachers described earlier in this chapter—who brought their own computers from home to use in their classrooms before a commitment to computer technology became board policy—are examples of "innovators" who would fall into this category. The early application of computers to instruction in their district was achieved because these teachers believed that the new technology would interest and benefit students. Whether or not the introduction of computer technology was a priority of the district was a secondary issue to them. Thus, innovation involves replacing established patterns of behavior with new ways of doing things that are consistent with the core values of the group or organization. Innovation helps a group to survive by providing the adjustments needed to deal successfully with changing circumstances.

The remaining three categories of role adjustment, in contrast, are generally counterproductive to a group's effectiveness. "Ritualism" is a demoralization of behavior that may result from an overemphasis on bureaucratic controls and rewards. The nonacceptance of cultural values, but acceptance of the prescribed institutionalized means for achieving them, is a form of goal displacement; it is exemplified by the teacher who "goes through the motions" but lacks a sincere concern for students. Ritualism in schools, of course, is the demon that Goldhammer (1969) hoped clinical supervision would exorcize.

"Retreatism" represents a psychological withdrawal by an individual who rejects both the cultural goals and the norms of the group. With "retreatism," an individual may be said to be *in* the group or organization but not *of* it. Finally, "rebellion" is less an accommodation to the existing structure than it is an effort to institutionalize changes by rejecting the existing goals and standards and substituting new structural patterns in their place. The category of "rebellion" presumably includes physically leaving the group entirely.

"Conformity" and "innovation" are related to some of the concepts introduced in earlier chapters. To function effectively, an organization must maintain a degree of control over the elements of which it is comprised, but sufficient autonomy must be simultaneously allowed for creative adaptation to occur. The central question, however, is, What type of control will bring about such a delicate balance?

Instructional supervisors at the district level are acutely aware of the limited ability they have to alter a specific teacher's behavior. As one supervisor bluntly said about working with teachers, "You can't make [people] change if they don't want to change." She went on to describe perfectly ritualism in action:

> Unfortunately, there are a few teachers who don't want to change. They're very happy going in, putting in their time, and collecting their paycheck. To me that's the most frustrating thing because I think it's unfair to the kids that they are teaching that particular year. Those kids don't get a fair shot at the educational program. It's frustrating.

When teachers retreat and simply do not care enough to improve their instruction, supervisors have little faith in the usefulness of their "going into a teacher's classroom to make sure they are doing things right." Supervisors know that once they leave a classroom, the teacher can and will do pretty much what he or she likes. District level supervisors generally feel that the principal must be relied upon to take action in such cases of retreatism. Principals, after all, have line authority over teachers and evaluate them for purposes of tenure and retention. The principal's location in the school also makes it easier for him or her to monitor a particular teacher's behavior to ensure conformity with minimum standards. However, classroom observation for purposes of evaluation is by no means a panacea.

While standardization and close monitoring of instruction may ensure that teacher behavior conforms to formally prescribed expectations, these bureaucratic functions may actually undermine commitment to basic values while eliminating innovation entirely. The most creative and resourceful teachers are likely to be among the first to feel constrained by the strict enforcement and monitoring of a uniform district policy regarding instruction. The price of securing compliance from every teacher through bureaucratic mechanisms, in other words, may be the stifling of a district's vitality.

What is needed, and what seems to be present in districts that are effective, is a control process that might be termed "channeled nonconformity." Rather than spending time enforcing policy themselves, successful central office supervisors say that they prefer to encourage voluntary compliance and rely on more subtle but far-reaching types of influence, such as praise, facilitating the implementation of good ideas, and leading by example. Although less intense than close monitoring of teacher behavior, these strategies are more likely to result in a genuine change in norms instead of superficial compliance. By far the most important element in achieving channeled nonconformity, however, is the active participation of teachers in curriculum and staff development.

References

Brim, O. G. & Wheeler, S. 1966. *Socialization after childhood.* New York: John Wiley & Sons.

Cogan, M. L. 1973. *Clinical supervision.* Boston: Houghton Mifflin.

Cuban, L. 1984. Transforming the frog into a prince: Effective schools research, policy, and practice at the district level. *Harvard Educational Review,* 54 (2): 129–151.

Goldhammer, R. 1969. *Clinical supervision.* New York: Holt, Rinehart and Winston.

Joyce, B. & Showers, B. 1980. Improving inservice training. The messages of research. *Educational Leadership,* 37 (5): 379–385.

Joyce, B. & Showers, B. 1983. *Power in staff development through research and training.* Alexandria, Va.: Association for Supervision and Curriculum Development.

Merton, R. K. 1938. Social structure and anomie. *American Sociological Review,* 3 (5): 672–682.

Wiles, K. 1967. *Supervision for better schools,* 3rd ed. Englewood Cliffs, N.J.: Prentice-Hall.

8
Working with Principals

Establishing and maintaining good working relationships with principals is absolutely critical to a central office instructional supervisor's effectiveness. The reason that positive relationships with administrative colleagues at the building level are so important to a supervisor's success is that principals possess considerable autonomy and exert a great deal of influence over what does and does not happen in their schools. On a day-to-day basis, the local school can function quite well administratively without the central office supervisor. Principals are able to handle the routine duties of their role almost entirely independent of any involvement from the central office. In fact, many principals appear to prefer things that way.

In the short run, the central office supervisor needs the principals in the district, in order to do his or her job, more than the principals need the central office supervisor. Consequently, in order to have any degree of success, central office supervisors must rely on the cooperation of principals and their willingness to participate in programs of instructional improvement. It becomes the supervisor's responsibility, therefore, to convince the principals in the district that he or she is indispensable to them in the long run and, in the words of many supervisors, that they are both "playing on the same team."

Literature in the area of educational supervision is increasingly focused almost exclusively on the relationship between supervisor and teacher, generally overlooking the importance of interactions between supervisor and principal. Yet many central office supervisors say that they have more contact with principals than with anyone else, that they rarely work directly with teachers without the principal's cooperation, and that they invariably involve principals in some way during large-scale instructional-improvement efforts.

Similarities and Differences

In certain respects, the position of the central office supervisor is similar to that of the building principal. Both jobs involve curriculum development and staff development, for example, and require working with teachers and the superintendent. Indeed, some supervisors think of themselves as being "a principal's principal." The problems in both jobs are "basically the same," they feel, but at the district level, "the problems just get bigger." An assistant superintendent for instruction described her job in the following words:

> It's like an administrative position of a building principal, except at a different level. You are still responsible for the educational program, but the level is different. Instead of being responsible for the education of children in just one building, I'm responsible for the education of children in all the buildings. It's administrative, it's curricular, it's leadership, it's human relations, it's personnel, it's just a different level.

It may be that this individual and others who view their jobs as closely paralleling their former role as principal were originally promoted to district level supervisory positions precisely because they attended especially well to the instructionally relevant aspects of the principal's duties. A curriculum director in another district revealed that as high school principal he had acquired the nickname "the principal in charge of gamesmanship" because he was constantly "pumping up" the enthusiasm of students and teachers at assemblies and in-service meetings. Despite similarities between the positions of principal and supervisor, however, some subtle but important differences are worth noting.

One major difference between being a principal and being a supervisor is the scope of perspective. The principal tends to view decisions affecting students, teachers, and materials in terms of what is best for a single school, the one for which he or she is responsible. The central office supervisor, in contrast, is inclined to balance the needs and wants of all the schools throughout the district and satisfy various constituencies. As one supervisor suggested:

> As a building principal, sometimes you can be very isolated in your own little world. At this level you're not. You're intricately involved with the entire school system at all levels, from the board of education right on down.

This difference of perspective concerning events, one narrow and the other broad, is a constant potential source of tension between the central office and the local school, a tension that the effective supervisor continuously faces and tries to alleviate. District level supervisors spend considerable energy negotiating with principals over compliance with policies and decisions made by the state department of education, the superintendent, and the school board, as well as convincing them that such policies are in the best interest of the local schools. At the same time, the job of supervisor involves "taking some of the heat" from principals who may feel that they, or more likely their schools, are not being treated reasonably. In such instances the central office supervisor usually acts as a patient listener, but may, if convinced that an injustice truly exists, informally plead the case of a disgruntled administrator at higher levels.

Another important difference between the principal's position and that of the central office instructional supervisor, which many practitioners identify, is that the supervisor's influence is typically much less direct than most people assume. Supervisors see their jobs, above all, as performing a service function, the purpose of which is to facilitate higher levels of achievement among principals and teachers. Rather than exercise a directive form of leadership themselves, supervisors more often provide support in the form of resources and encouragement, while simultaneously attempting to minimize potential obstacles to others' success. Supervisors report that they are usually willing to have principals or teachers assume more visible leadership functions, as long as the job of instructional improvement is accomplished.

Thus, while the responsibilities of central office supervisors and principals overlap in some ways, important differences exist in the scope of their focus and the type of influence each exerts. When functioning properly, the two positions complement one another. The instructional supervisor can supplement the principal's efforts in the easily neglected area of instructional leadership, but cannot entirely compensate for its absence. At the same time, instructional improvements that are introduced jointly by the supervisor and principal have a better chance of surviving because of the principal's constant presence and more direct influence at the building level. In the words of an assistant superintendent for instruction:

> The building principals are on the line every day. They're right there with the children, with the teacher, with the program. If they're unwilling to be the educational leader, then, you know, I can't do anything up here that's going to change that for them. But if I have a good working relationship with them, then the kinds of changes we want to see will happen.

Understanding and Credibility

Attaining an understanding of the responsibilities and concerns of principals and establishing credibility with them are essential to the building of good working relationships at the school level. These requirements of attaining understanding and establishing credibility are closely related to one another and can be satisfied through prior experience or demonstrated competence on the job.

One way for a central office supervisor to attain an understanding of principals and establish credibility among them is to have had successful personal experience as a principal. Experience as a classroom teacher, of course, is important too, but it is typically required for state certification as an instructional supervisor and so is taken for granted by principals to a great extent. Prior experience as a principal, however, is not universal among central office supervisors. A lack of building level administrative experience may place the central office supervisor at a slight disadvantage initially, it seems, when working with principals.

Previous personal experience in education at various levels sensitizes an individual to the very real problems and constraints that exist at those levels. This sensitivity makes the expectations that district level supervisors have for teachers and principals more likely to be fulfilled. A curriculum coordinator described the advantage of prior administrative experience as follows:

> I think that if you have been a teacher and you have been a principal, you've had an opportunity to see things through those eyes. You know what kinds of things they're held responsible for, you know the kinds of problems they are dealing with, the kinds of agendas that they have. . . . So I just think that it makes for better understanding in working together.

In addition to gaining insight and understanding of the principal's role, however, a supervisor who has had administrative experience may work more effectively with principals by anticipating the constraints they face. Also, a sense of fellowship may be more easily attainable. The same individual noted:

> I think that it's important to be able to say, with conviction, that you really do understand what the problems are, . . . why certain things can't be done, and why they have to be done another way. And I think it gives you credibility with them. You

can say, "I've been through the principalship for four years, and I know the kinds of things you're dealing with. I really do."

Supervisors who have had building level administrative experience, understandably, feel most strongly that credibility earned in this way is absolutely essential. They often point to their immediate predecessor or a supervisor they know in another district as an example of ineffectiveness that resulted when experience as a principal was lacking. In one case, a supervisor confided:

I'll be very candid about this. The man [whom] I replaced had never been a building administrator. He'd always been a teacher or a department head, . . . and he'd been in the district for about thirty years. He was—in the eyes of the principals, at least, having not had building experience—not on their level. And so he was very subservient to them in many ways. Very capable man, worked very hard, and the people worked well with him. The point was, when push came to shove, he never felt—or was never allowed to have—the authority to really do things. It was always pulse taking and that kind of stuff.

Two central office supervisors in unionized districts suggested that their credibility with principals was enhanced still further in another way. Earlier, during their administrative careers, they had held leadership positions in local associations representing principals in contract negotiations with school boards. Other supervisors, in contrast, believe that being too closely identified with principals, by being a part of their collective bargaining unit, for example, can create a barrier of mistrust between a supervisor and the school board.

Those supervisors who have never been principals, understandably, tend to downplay line administrative experience as a prerequisite, instead emphasizing ways of earning credibility through other means. Actually, there is no evidence that former principals make better supervisors than their counterparts who lack experience at the building level. In fact, one supervisor admitted that he had a great deal of difficulty securing the cooperation of the principals in his district, despite having several years' administrative experience at both the elementary and secondary levels. Thus, it seems that having been a principal does not guarantee success in working with building administrators. Administrative experience, however, does seem to gain the new supervisor an initial advantage in that principals are more likely to grant the benefit of the doubt to someone whom they perceive is much like themselves in understanding and assumptions about how schools operate.

Earning Credibility

All supervisors, whether they move into the central office from the classroom or from a line administrative position, face the challenge of earning credibility with principals while on the job. Essentially, this means demonstrating a willingness to understand and take into consideration the constraints under which principals work, while at the same time proving their competence to principals and refusing to be pushed around or intimidated.

In talking about the support she received from the principals with whom she worked, one supervisor said that it was not something that came "naturally" or "automatically" to her. What she had achieved was an "earned support." When asked how that support was earned, she responded:

> OK, through a period of time and misunderstandings, . . . pulling together, working through things, and being very consistent in your behavior. If I ask that something be done, I make sure that it needs to be done, and then I continue to stress that particular thing, rather than change my mind.

Another supervisor, when asked how one goes about creating a good working relationship with principals, observed:

> You spend some time talking with them. You try to find out what their goals are, where they are. You share materials, you share articles, you share philosophies. You examine curriculum together, examine problems together, and you plan together.

Basically, the best relationship between a central office supervisor and a principal is one of trust and reciprocity that is grounded in mutual understanding and predictability of expectations. Demonstrating an interest in the issues being dealt with in a particular school and one's willingness to provide assistance can be accomplished by letting principals know that one is available to them. A district coordinator explained:

> Although I haven't been successful in all the buildings, I've encouraged the principals to invite me into the meetings at their schools, even though I might not officially have anything to do with the particular topic. It's mainly to enlighten me, so that I can become more knowledgeable and understand their concerns better and then assist people. If I know that there are some things

that I can put my hands on to help them solve their problems, I'm there to help.

Occasional conflicts occur—and may even be necessary—but respect and consideration for one another are essential. As a curriculum director observed about maintaining a good relationship with principals:

> I guess, probably trying to be as fair as possible with each one [is important]. We've had our differences on different occasions, but we're still friends. I think the biggest thing is to listen to them with respect and not pooh-pooh their ideas—allow them input into decisions.

The desired outcome is to establish a recognition on the part of principals that the central office supervisor can be of service to them, but will not tolerate being treated merely as their servant. A solid working relationship with principals is also established by convincing them that the central office supervisor is not in competition with building administrators, but rather that everyone is "on the same team" and working toward common goals.

Predictability and Reciprocity

Supervisors, both with and without administrative experience, are in close agreement about what it takes to maintain a good working relationship with principals once it is established. They are very aware, first of all, that principals want to know what is going on in their schools and that they are likely to consider intrusions from outside the building as being unnecessary disruptions:

> When I go into a building, I always go through the principal's office and say that I'm there. If the principal is available, I say, "I'm here for this reason, and this reason, and this reason. Is there anything else that you want me to do while I'm in the building?"

Rather than representing a subordination of oneself to the principal, such courtesies are obligatory because the principal, after all, is legally responsible for what happens in his or her building. This accountability results in an understandable concern about unusual events, and it is consequently a good idea to keep principals informed about one's presence, if only to ease their minds. The same supervisor continues:

I just think it's important that they know I'm in the building or that I've left the building and where I'm going from there. I don't think anybody from their office should have to run around looking for me if there's a telephone call or something. And I very often will sit with a principal for a few minutes and say, "I've done this, and this is what happened." It's touching base. Those things, I think, build good working relationships. It's a team effort if you want to get anything done.

Another issue for supervisors to consider when working with principals is the importance of avoiding being perceived as a "spy" from the central office. Keeping the principal aware of one's presence, whereabouts, and activities serves to alleviate this suspicion. The supervisor's location at the central office and mobility mean greater accessibility to the superintendent. What the supervisor says about a particular school, even in casual conversation with the superintendent, is a common matter of speculation and worry to principals. It is far better to encourage principals to think of the supervisor as their advocate. As a supervisor in one district explained:

At budget time I'm able to help and support principals with some of their projects by talking to the superintendent or the business manager and saying, "Hey, this is a very worthwhile project. I'd like to give it whatever support we can."

Another supervisor similarly commented:

You can help them by getting them things that they need for their schools. . . . [You] become kind of a helper to them, and then they reciprocate.

On the other hand, the supervisor has to keep in mind that his or her loyalty rests primarily with the district as a whole. One supervisor found that—although the superintendent recognized the importance of her representing the interests of principals and their schools—he thought that at times she carried this advocacy too far, and he reflected this in his annual evaluation of her performance:

He rated me high in the support that I give the elementary principals, and he rated me low for the same thing, because he felt I should not be so supportive at times. That I should "get after them in some cases" was the way he put it. But I felt it was a compliment to be rated high, that I am supportive of them, and I told him that I didn't intend to change. "Because," I said, "I'm the only voice here in the central office for elementary people, and they need the support."

This supervisor made her position clear and refused to become simply a pawn of the superintendent. She maintained her professional autonomy by making known her definition of the supervisory role and how she intended to enact it. Of course, her frankness suggests the preexistence of a very good working relationship with the superintendent. It is important to recognize that although some advocacy of principals is essential, the supervisor also has the sometimes contradictory responsibility of seeing that district-wide policies are properly implemented.

The Central Office and the Local School

On a chart depicting the organizational structure of a school district, the chain of command (or line of authority) looks fairly straightforward. The school board and superintendent determine policy at the top, which is implemented at the building level by the principals through the teachers. The central office supervisor is sometimes positioned as a line officer, with direct authority over principals, and in other instances as a staff assistant to the superintendent. As was discussed in Chapter Three, hierarchical conceptions of how schools function have been challenged in recent years by organizational theorists as being overly simplistic. The experiences of supervisors seem to lend credence to the idea that the bureaucratic paradigm may not be entirely appropriate for understanding the relationships among the various professional positions within a school district. District level supervisors tend to use other metaphors for making sense of how they work with others.

In describing the relationship between the central office and the local schools, supervisors often use language that suggests an analogy with feudalism, in the sense that principals typically maintain operational autonomy within their schools and often seek to protect this independence of operation against intrusions from external sources, including the central office. Supervisors frequently speak of the local school, for example, as being the principal's "realm" or "domain." Even "fiefdom" and "kingdom" are used to describe how principals perceive their positions with respect to the larger organization:

> Principals . . . have their little fiefdoms, and they want to keep them that way, and they don't want anyone interfering.

Such language is not used sarcastically; rather, the feudal analogy simply seems to be appropriate to supervisors for understanding certain organizational dynamics in school districts. Use of the feudal analogy, however, does at times imply a degree of frustration, as is clear in the following example:

> Well, they're all-powerful in their own buildings, and they really don't like central office coming in there to make suggestions and take up their time. They tend to think that their responsibilities are most important. And yet, there has to be some coordination with the central office.

The degree of autonomy enjoyed by principals, of course, varies considerably from one school system to another. In some districts even the superintendent appears to have little control over what goes on at the local school level. But by and large, the evidence suggests that principal autonomy may be waning considerably. Centralization of districts and changes in societal attitudes have eroded much of the principal's traditional independence and influence. In certain cases resistance to central office policy may reflect desperation more than obstinacy. One supervisor observed that principals sometimes openly express anger and frustration to the supervisor, while they recognize the inevitability of compliance:

> I think the role of principal has changed drastically over the last fifteen years. And whereas they once had their own little domain, where they were this father image over all these sweet little female teachers, that isn't true any longer, and I think they've found that hard. They used to be able to do everything on their own, and now it's much more district oriented. And that's been frustrating for them. So you have to listen to, and sometimes ignore, some of the things that they say to get them moving again in the direction that you want.

While it is certainly possible for supervisors with line authority and a mandate from the superintendent to dictate policy to principals, an autocratic approach is usually avoided because it inevitably erodes some of the goodwill that the supervisor has accumulated over time. In the following illustration a supervisor in his first year in the position describes how he inappropriately took a highly directive approach with principals in establishing a computer task force that the superintendent and school board had decided was needed:

> So I went to the elementary principals and said, "Listen, this is going to be our priority. That question's over. Now, here's how we're going to go about it. We need your help." That caused some resentment from some people. Luckily, I had been in the district

for some time, eight years, so people knew me. Had I been new here, I think I would have been looked at like a hatchet man. You know, "Where in the hell did this guy come from? He's like Attila the Hun."

The resentment of principals to an overly directive approach by a supervisor seems to be universal. A supervisor whose title had recently been changed from curriculum director to assistant superintendent for instruction reported that her newly acquired line authority was tacitly understood by principals, but it did not greatly affect the way in which she worked with them. Working relationships quickly became strained if she told principals what to do without at least giving them an opportunity to discuss and modify a new policy prior to its implementation. When asked why it is so important to maintain good working relationships with principals, this supervisor responded simply, "You don't get anything done otherwise."

The active involvement of principals in decisions affecting instruction is critical. This involvement is desirable because it helps secure cooperation and compliance with whatever decisions are made and it serves the purpose of district-wide coordination. Just as the isolation of classrooms can be detrimental to a school building's effectiveness, too much autonomy among local schools can be detrimental to a district. A fairly high degree of consistency among elementary instructional programs, many supervisors agree, is important for ensuring equity for students. An organized sequencing of the curriculum and instructional experiences from the elementary grades through high school is viewed as essential so that students have worthwhile educational experiences at every grade level. A district coordinator put it this way:

> If the high school has a problem with instruction, chances are it doesn't begin at the high school. So there ought to be a sharing on the part of the principals with each other as to what the problem is and what they can all do to solve it.

Once principals recognize that they really can influence policy and contribute to the quality of the instructional program on the district level, the isolation of local schools from the central office and from each other begins to disappear. As one supervisor explained:

> At first the principals seemed to feel that it was their school; you know, they pretty much wanted to do their own thing within the school and not necessarily something that's system-wide and coordinated with every school in the system. It was sort of their

school. But now I find them not only willing to allow teachers to leave school to work on curriculum, but [sharing] things that are going on within their own schools with other principals at the principals' meetings. Very, very often I'll get something in the school mail along with a note that will tell me to freely share this with other principals. That helps me in my job, in what I'm trying to do.

Some districts, though not all, succeed in securing the cooperation and involvement of principals to the extent that principals formally assume responsibility for certain aspects of the district's instructional program and curriculum. In one system studied, for example, principals and assistant principals are assigned to chair various curriculum committees, a responsibility that they accept willingly because it allows them the opportunity to demonstrate their effectiveness as instructional leaders and extend their influence. This also eases the supervisor's work load considerably and allows him or her to spend time more productively by coordinating the various committees instead of providing the leadership alone.

In another instance, a district has begun experimenting with the idea of having principals represent and coordinate various instructional-content areas, such as art, physical education, and social studies for the district. The instructional supervisor in this system believes that principals have become more responsive to the needs of the district's instructional program as a result of this involvement and voluntarily take a more active role in other matters related to supervision. In only a year's time the principals have come to perceive the district's instructional program as a legitimate reason for doing things differently, according to the supervisor who initiated this effort. It should be noted that principals in this same district strongly resisted assuming responsibility for instructional areas that involve extensive state and federal funding, such as special education, Chapter 1, and gifted programs, because of the extra paperwork that accompanies them. Involvement of principals in the district's instructional program, therefore, should not be initiated simply to unload undesirable or time-consuming tasks.

Power and Teamwork

Power is guarded jealously in schools and treated as a limited resource. Central office supervisors, in trying to empower teachers for the benefit of students, may run the risk of being perceived as competing with or trying to diminish the power of principals. It is important, therefore, that the supervisor consistently demonstrate a willingness and capacity to assist both teachers and principals in their efforts to help students. In describing the ideal relationship with principals, most supervisors say that it is best to emphasize a team approach to instructional improvement. As a curriculum director pointed out:

> It is extremely important that central office people work very closely and very well with individual building administrators. You have to build a good working relationship. You have to have the principal working with you or nothing goes. And that's just a fact. . . . If you approach everything as a team, with the principal . . . and you fully informed, and you go at it together, lots of things can happen. But if you're trying to circumvent or confront, it won't work. It will backfire, and you'll lose all that you're trying to do in that school. So cultivating a good working relationship with each individual building administrator is important if you're going to succeed.

The issue of power is a concern when working with principals, both individually and collectively. The best way for supervisors to ensure that empowerment of teachers does not become a threat to principals is to maintain open communications with them at all times. A curriculum director, for example, emphasized that a competitive relationship with principals was counterproductive for everyone:

> I think it's important that a principal be the instructional leader in the school. I don't think you ever need to get into power plays over who's in charge of what, because everybody loses all the way around when that happens. . . . I think a team approach is tremendously important. I think patience is important, sharing philosophies is important, and goal setting together is important. . . . You have to be together.

A curriculum coordinator in another district explained that organizing teachers for the purpose of making decisions could easily be perceived by principals as a threat:

> The curriculum council is made up strictly of teachers, and a few principals feel that the teachers are trying to take over their realm of administration. So when new ideas and new plans come up in the curriculum council, it's very important that I run them through the administrative cabinet so that there isn't that constant

"Who's taking power away from them?" It's important to make sure that principals do not feel threatened by you.

Popular models of classroom supervision presume that the supervisor and teacher comprise the fundamental social unit that underlies instructional improvement. While a simple dyadic model might be appropriate for describing the relationship between a supervisor and a teacher during a clinical supervision cycle, the social dynamics of improvement are usually more complex. Central office supervisors suggest that their work is often more like that of a third-party consultant to principals and teachers. A triadic model of instructional supervision in which influence is shared among supervisors, principals, and teachers, therefore, may be more appropriate for understanding how improvement efforts actually occur, because factors relating to the larger organizational context are considered.

Under ideal circumstances, the roles of supervisor and principal complement one another by providing different types of assistance to teachers. Central office supervisors typically report that they rarely observe teachers in the classroom for purposes of either formative or summative evaluation unless invited by a principal to work with a teacher who is experiencing problems. The advantage of occupying a staff position for the supervisor is described below by a curriculum coordinator:

> My particular position is staff as opposed to line. I do not have responsibility for direct supervision, and I like it that way. I can become a helping person because I'm not evaluating. I'm not judging individuals; I'm judging programs as opposed to people. . . . Principals do the evaluation [of teachers]. And that's very important. I do not become involved in direct supervision because then it would have an effect on my relationship with teachers. . . . Most of the principals, when they're having a problem, particularly with a classroom teacher, will come to me. We'll sit down and we'll talk, first of all trying to improve the instruction in the classroom. Sometimes we'll bring in a [subject area] consultant to work with the teacher, or we may suggest that the teacher take some additional coursework. But the actual implementation of what we decide has to involve the principal, because they're the ones who have the most influence [with the teacher].

Consistent with the idea of the principal as the instructional leader of the school, district level supervisors prefer to see principals assume responsibility for establishing direction within the district's parameters. The distinction between what supervisors do and what principals do is clear to most. A former principal noted in this regard:

> I'm not much involved with working directly with teachers in the classroom anymore. That's something that principals deal with. They should know where they're going and what they're doing. We talk about writing goals and following them, but I think goals become dust collectors. I think that principals should sit down periodically with their staffs and talk about where they are, and what they're doing, and where they want to go.

The supervisor focuses energies of principals and teachers on the essential reason they are all there: to help students learn.

> I'm the only person dealing with curriculum and instruction. It's my office, and I work directly through the principals to the teachers. We have to work with the principals to get their support because they're the ones who really do most of the [classroom] supervision in the buildings.

One might expect that a natural coalition exists between principals and central office supervisors, against which teachers are comparatively helpless, with no alternative available but to comply with the directives of these superordinates. In reality, the relationship among the three positions can take various forms of "two against one." In some cases a principal and teacher will pair off, for example, and resist attempts by a supervisor to influence classroom instruction. Occasionally, however, a supervisor may find himself or herself approached by a teacher who is seeking to form an alliance against the building principal. Needless to say, each of these combinations is likely to be counterproductive to instructional improvement.

Nevertheless, central office supervisors sometimes do have to establish informal coalitions with groups of teachers in order to improve instruction. An associate superintendent for instruction who had met resistance from principals about introducing computers into classrooms described the positive outcome as follows:

> I guess one of the satisfying things about it is the reaction that I now see among the building administrators who had the greatest inertia and whom I couldn't move. I couldn't move them at all. And they were moved from two directions, teachers and central administration. We have a program going that will be exemplary. It will probably be the best elementary program involving computers in the area.

The associate superintendent went on to describe a particular school where the principal had been especially reluctant to get involved with computer technology. But by emphasizing the benefits to students, another member of the supervisory staff was finally able to make an inroad. He continued:

> Now they want to be a real center [of computer technology]. It happens to be due to the work of the supervisor of our elementary program. She's got that principal on board, and she has the staff up and running. They've found so many innovative ways that they can use computers to help them do their jobs better. I'd just like to have my kids in that school.

Principals can pose a major obstacle to improvement in their schools if they choose to do so. A fairly common frustration for district level supervisors, for example, is that sometimes principals will confuse supporting teachers with protecting them from the central office. An assistant superintendent stated:

> I do not subscribe to the philosophy that so many principals hold, that "right or wrong, I'll support my teachers," because I think that's part of what's wrong now with public education.

Occasionally a principal may even try to "protect" an incompetent but loyal teacher from exposure to any form of external intervention. Without the principal's cooperation it is difficult to bring about change. When a principal openly resists, it is virtually impossible. A curriculum coordinator described the problem and implied a possible solution:

> When I first came into this position, principals were very, very protective of their staffs. Any time when I wanted to have meetings with teachers during the school day, they were really opposed to it. Now they have gradually gotten used to that idea, and they do allow people to be released so that we can work on things. But in return, it's because they always know that they will be informed and be a part of it. They have to feel that they're a part of the instructional programs in their schools.

The remoteness of the district office tends to place the supervisor on the outside looking in, when it comes to working with teachers and principals. It is therefore essential that instructional-improvement efforts initiated by the supervisor emphasize a team approach in order to avoid a "we-versus-they" mentality, with teachers and principals pitted against the central office.

A curriculum director described the process of working to improve the performance of an ineffective teacher as

> working with the principal and teacher and getting to the point where you're not evaluating them, but getting them to realize that something's got to be done in the classroom that's not being done. Then you say, "How can I help you to do it?" And trying to get the teacher to tell you how they're going to improve instead of going in and saying, "This is what you have to do."

The ideal relationship among supervisors, principals, and teachers is one in which each accepts a share of the responsibility for improving instruction. Often supervisors will say that the first step involves "sitting down and talking" with a principal and teacher to let them know that the supervisor is there to help them do their jobs better.

Principals who subscribe to the feudal perspective of schools as organizations may have difficulty accepting the idea of allowing teachers to have a voice in decisions. Overcoming this view is a necessary prelude to working as a team. A director of educational services, who recently had been a high school principal, made the following observation:

> Sometimes, some of the principals who have had their own fiefdoms for years, and years, and years have a hard time realizing that they can come down to earth and work with teachers and maybe even, on occasion, lose a battle. I guess I've lost enough battles that I realize you've got to work together.

There are instances, however, when the relationship between a principal and a teacher is less positive, and the supervisor may be drawn into the conflict. A curriculum director described a principal she knew who behaved "rudely," "immaturely," and "unprofessionally" toward the teachers on his staff. While she found this personally very upsetting, there was little that she could actually do because she lacked line authority over principals and could not openly side with teachers without jeopardizing her access to them in the future. An assistant superintendent in another system noted that even with line authority and under generally favorable conditions he preferred that teachers talk directly to their principals concerning complaints about the way the school is run, and he tried to avoid getting drawn into conflicts himself:

> It gets to be a problem sometimes when teachers unload to you about things that they should be talking about with their principals. [The problems] will be things that you're really not

responsible for, but they need to talk. All you can do is say, "You need to talk to your principal about that." You can't really go to the principal and say, "So-and-so would like to have this done" or "The teachers are unhappy about this." It really has to go directly from the teacher to the principal.

Another assistant superintendent, though also pointing out the necessity of not undermining the principal's authority, said that she sometimes intervened with a principal on behalf of teachers in matters relating to instruction. In a case where a principal might arbitrarily tell a teacher to stop using an instructionally appropriate strategy, for example, this individual felt she absolutely had to take action:

As far as possible, I feel it is my job to support the building principal, to listen to the teacher, and then to go back to the building principal and say, "Look, why did you do this? You know she's got some good points here. You've really got to go back and make your peace with her." Because that's where peacemaking takes place, not up here. The building principal is with them every day.

Simply listening to a teacher's dissatisfaction may serve a cathartic function, and at times that is all that is needed. On the other hand, teachers are not always "innocent victims" of overbearing or autocratic administrators. A teacher may, for example, intentionally try to circumvent a principal's decision. A curriculum director in another district observed:

You can get yourself into hot water by going around a principal. An example of that would be where I've had teachers ask for materials to be dittoed or run on the Xerox machine here [at the central office] that their principal didn't want them to use in their classrooms. [The teachers] were intentionally playing both ends against the middle at that point.

Regardless of whether the teachers were right or the principal was right (from an instructional point of view) in this dispute, the supervisor was placed in an untenable position by unwittingly contradicting a specific directive of a principal because several teachers were purposely manipulating the system.

Central office supervisors generally agree that in most situations teachers should be encouraged to "follow the chain of command" and address complaints to their principals instead of to members of the central office staff. Strong norms exist in schools against "going over the head" of a principal, and the willingness of a teacher or group of teachers to do so is usually an indication of significant difficulties (Hanson, 1976). Suggesting that a teacher go directly to the principal with a complaint may be a first step for dealing with conflicts, but serious problems may not be quickly or easily resolved. Supervisors who possess line authority say that when teachers and principals are unable to resolve disagreements between themselves, they will sometimes offer to schedule a meeting between the principal and teacher at the central office. The supervisor then serves as a facilitator of problem solving, while trying to avoid having to impose a solution unilaterally.

Central office supervisors of instruction, whether or not they possess formal line authority over principals, are obligated to rely upon indirect sources of influence because of the considerable autonomy that exists at the local school level. The principal is considered the instructional leader of the school, and successful central office supervisors scrupulously avoid undermining this designation. Essentially, the supervisor's responsibility is to encourage, support, and promote principals' efforts to improve the quality of instruction in their local schools and to get them to contribute as well to the process of instructional improvement on the district level.

References

Hanson, E. M. 1976. Professional/bureaucratic interface. *Urban Education*, 11 (3): 313–332.

9

Transactional and Transforming Leadership

The basis of a central office supervisor's influence within a school district is not immediately apparent. Many supervisors of curriculum and instruction occupy staff positions and lack formal authority over principals and teachers. However, even those supervisors who do have line authority, such as associate superintendents, usually say that they rely on formal authority infrequently, if at all, because they feel it is "counterproductive" and "unrealistic" to give principals and teachers orders and expect them to comply. The influence that supervisors exercise, therefore, does not appear to be derived, to any great extent, from the formal organization.

The expertise of a supervisor is certainly an important factor to consider in this regard. Supervisors and curriculum directors obviously need to possess certain types of technical knowledge, along with managerial and human relations skills (Alfonso, Firth, and Neville, 1981). But locating the source of influence entirely in the person of the supervisor is misleading, given the scope of most supervisory positions. A single individual, no matter how talented, simply cannot attend personally to the multiple and complex responsibilities involved in overseeing an instructional program at the district level without help from others.

Frustrations experienced by district level curriculum and instructional supervisors, in fact, seem to relate in large part to the reality of having a limited capacity to improve instruction. If supervisors had their way, it seems, they would have limitless reserves of money and time to invest in the improvement of instruction and they would be omnipresent, omniscient, and omnipotent. An assistant superintendent, for instance, suggested that frustration was an inevitable part of her job because: "There's just so much to be done in education. We can see so many needs all around." Successful supervisors necessarily come to terms with this reality by viewing their jobs as "facilitating" or "coordinating the expertise of others," rather than as directly exercising personal expertise.

The basis of a supervisor's influence is not easy to locate because there really is no single source. Influence is "earned" slowly over a long period of time, according to supervisors, through innumerable interactions with many people at all levels of the organization. These interactions result in the development of "mutual respect," "trust," and "understanding" between central office leaders and those who work at the building level. Influence is something that teachers and principals voluntarily give to those whom they perceive as furthering their individual and collective goals. The supervisor must gain a reputation for being dependable and consistent, honest and fair, and for not asking others to do things that are unimportant. The supervisor also cannot appear to be interested in seeking personal recognition. The supervisor has to demonstrate a ready responsiveness to others' expressed needs, but at the same time be willing to stand up for his or her own principles, beliefs, and priorities.

Reciprocal Influence of Supervisors

Effective supervisors speak often of credibility when talking about their influence upon others in the school district, especially teachers and principals. Credibility is something that supervisors say they earn gradually over a period of time by working closely with teachers and principals and by demonstrating personal commitment, competence, and usefulness to them in their work with students.

A certain amount of credibility can be brought into the job if a supervisor has previously established a reputation as being an outstanding teacher or an effective principal. It seems that people are willing to give the supervisor the benefit of the doubt when they know that the supervisor has "walked in their shoes." But influence is not something that is obtained once and for all. The influence that supervisors exert is a dynamic, ever changing thing that exists for the most part in the shared perceptions of the people who work in schools. Regardless of how credibility has been earned, it is tested each day. A supervisor's influence therefore must be continually renewed.

Although instructional supervisors admittedly rely on the superintendent's support for actions they may want to initiate, most of the day-to-day influence a supervisor exercises is developed through demonstrations of professional competence and commitment. Teachers and administrators begin to respond positively and cooperate with the supervisor, it seems, only after they develop perceptions of the supervisor as someone who is skilled, who willingly shares credit for success with others, and who is an effective helper, facilitator, and provider of resources and information. When teachers and administrators are convinced that a supervisor is interested in them and can help them solve the instructional problems they face, they begin to respond with cooperation and support for the broader issues of district-wide instructional and curricular improvement.

The influence that supervisors exert often is described by them as "mutual" or "reciprocal" influence. A director of educational services explained it this way:

> I think it's important that I can be a leader but also be led, [that] I can mold but be molded. . . . I think that's very important, that it's a sharing venture. There are no real bosses; there are no winners or losers. We are all working together, and I think that's very important.

Supervisors say that the ideal relationship with other professionals in the school is characterized by mutual respect. The most important dimensions of mutual respect seem to be a sincere attempt to understand one another and the development of trust. A director of instruction, for example, said that the influence she had with principals and teachers was "earned . . . by looking at them as individuals, as humans, and understanding them." A curriculum director similarly noted that "mutual respect with the people you work with [develops from] a genuine attempt to understand their problems." Thus, the ability to empathize seems to be at least as important to supervisors as the ability to analyze situations objectively.

Trust seems to develop from an openness and honesty in communication. An assistant superintendent said that trust depended on everyone's knowing what is happening and what is expected. Another supervisor explained that "mutual respect" was built upon "fairness" and "consistency" of expectations and behaviors. The mutuality of trust is important to appreciate; in order to endure, it must also be demonstrated through action. As a third supervisor phrased it:

> Having mutual respect and trust for one another—I think that's very important. I don't try to "low-ball" them, and I don't expect them to do that [to me].

It probably cannot be emphasized enough, however, that the reciprocal influence that occurs between effective instructional supervisors and those with whom they work is not a strategically contrived case of, "If you do this for me, then I will do this for you." The services that supervisors provide for teachers and administrators are viewed as based upon real needs of the recipients and not as bribes or rewards for cooperation. Such services are seen as deserved because teachers and administrators not only share but literally enact the supervisor's overriding value of providing quality instruction to children.

Although supervisors readily acknowledge that reciprocal influence occurs, they are adamant in emphasizing that reciprocity does not mean doing special favors for some individuals. Assistance provided by a supervisor in response to requests from teachers or principals for resources or training is considered legitimate because it relates directly to maintaining or improving instructional quality. As an associate superintendent for instruction commented:

> "Granting favors"—I don't like the term. I think that requests from teachers . . . or principals [whom] I meet out there . . . stand on their own merit and are of worth. They are earned and not really a favor that I do for them.

Supervisors admit that at times they will assist an individual teacher or principal to maneuver a request or a proposal through the district's organizational hierarchy. If an idea has sufficient merit, a supervisor may even be willing to serve as an advocate of the idea to the superintendent. But such requests or proposals must relate directly to improving the instructional program, it seems, for the supervisor to become involved. Supervisors are careful to avoid granting favors that give an individual or a group an advantage over others, unless such special treatment is perceived as deserved because of exceptionally hard work or original thinking.

Another characteristic of the exchange that occurs between supervisors and the teachers and administrators whom they serve is that it is not often explicitly acknowledged; it is simply understood. Supervisors accumulate influence gradually as people begin to perceive them as competent facilitators of the instructional process. Such perceptions are abstract, but they are based upon very tangible events. Supervisors symbolically demonstrate both their competence and their concern for instruction, for example, through the very practical activity of locating and providing materials that are requested. One supervisor explained as follows when asked if exchange or reciprocity were important to the role:

> It's something that just happens. You don't really think about it in the sense of an exchange. I think it's like mutual respect. When teachers ask me to do something, I always write it down, and I look into it. If I'm not able to do anything, I'll let them know

why. . . . I respond to things that teachers ask for because I feel that they wouldn't ask me if there wasn't a real need. And I feel that they know, in turn, that I will not ask them to do something for me unless it's important as well.

A curriculum director in another district cautioned that materials or services are never offered as bribes. She maintained that instructional materials are always distributed where they are needed and not out of any concern for political expediency. This individual did admit, however, that if a principal were to ask for assistance of some sort, and if she were to provide help, "an unconscious kind of exchange" would occur. She would thereby gain some influence that might be drawn upon at a later time, improving the possibility "that he's going to respond more positively . . . when I need to call him to do something." She insisted, however, that she never planned such an exchange strategically.

Although supervisors assert that reciprocity is never intentionally sought, that they "do things because they're a part of the job" and not because "something is expected in return," they consistently identify mutual exchange as an essential component of their influence. On a purely pragmatic level, the major reciprocal benefit supervisors gain from principals seems to be access to teachers. A major practical benefit supervisors obtain from teachers is their willing cooperation and participation in district level tasks, including membership on curriculum committees and involvement in in-service planning. As one supervisor explained:

I think they see me as one of them, someone they can depend on, that I'm consistent in my behavior and really do things to try to help them. If they request something, I write it down. I've had people ask me, "How do you remember to do all those things we ask you to do?" I think that's important. I think it's little things that really can stick, and later on when you need a payoff in terms of a task to be done in curriculum, the teachers come back ten times more positive than they would otherwise.

Influence and credibility are thus acquired gradually. "You don't get success all in a great bundle," an associate superintendent explained. "It comes in little pieces." Supervisors emphasize the importance of "making sure that the little things get taken care of." These "little things" are details that may appear minor, but are important because of their symbolic value. As they accumulate in the perceptions of others, like the patient accretion of a river delta, their long-range impact can be enormous.

"Little things" are important because they have symbolic meaning for people. Anticipating and responding to others' practical needs, as well as being accessible, convey the message to teachers and principals that they and their work are taken seriously and are appreciated at the district office level. The "little things" represent, in another sense, a token compensation for participation. Supervisors speak of arranging for pay supplements for teachers during the summer months or for occasional released time from teaching during the school day in terms of their symbolic value, emphasizing that such incentives in no way compensate for the time and effort usually invested by teachers in curriculum projects. Like the "coffee and cookies" that supervisors say should precede a teachers' meeting after school, released time and pay supplements are often more important as demonstrations of courtesy than as adequate compensation for teachers' work.

Delegation

Supervisors commonly say that they delegate responsibility in order to build leadership among teachers in matters relating to instruction. Interestingly, it seems that supervisors often first turn to delegation out of practical necessity, but they soon recognize its broader long-term benefits for the entire professional staff. A director of educational services frankly explained:

> There's no way I can do it all. There's no way I can run a k–12 curriculum for five thousand kids with three hundred teachers. I guess they see me work hard, so I'm able to delegate a lot of it, and that's good.

Supervisors generally recognize that there are practical limits to their personal knowledge and skills, that more effective outcomes can be achieved by including the efforts of others. Recognizing that teachers are competent professionals and treating each of them accordingly may run counter to some notions of leadership, but the benefits to instruction are worth it. The same individual observed further:

> This is probably the most capable staff I've ever worked with, . . . and I've been in four different districts. I try to play on their expertise as much as possible. And I'm sure some people would say that's selling the farm, that as the boss you're supposed to be the leader. . . . I believe that you can sometimes lead by consensus. I have no problem with that at all, because I know I don't have the expertise on everything.

Delegation of responsibility, however, under no circumstances means abdication of responsibility. One supervisor commented that delegation is more than simply appointing a teacher to be the leader of a committee; it involves actually "letting them take the leadership role." Nevertheless, the supervisor has to remain available to provide assistance:

> Sink or swim, if they need help, I'll be there to help them. But I let them make the decisions about how to do the curriculum.

The extent to which delegation is possible hinges upon the experience and skill of a faculty and the importance of the particular task. If the capabilities of a staff are as yet underdeveloped, a supervisor may be wisely reluctant to assign responsibility to them entirely. As one individual put it:

> I'll delegate to a certain degree. But there are certain things I'd rather do myself, because if [they fail], I can't say, "Well, he did it!" Other people will say, "Hell, you delegated it to him!" So I'm careful. I'm selective to whom I delegate things and responsibilities. I like to get everybody involved, if possible. But some people end up doing "gofer" work, [while] other people do some high-level things.

While it is important to consider carefully the capabilities of the people to whom a task is delegated, as well as the relative importance of the task itself, supervisors suggest that once a decision is made to delegate, it is essential to delegate completely. This is not easy for many individuals. It requires a high degree of confidence in others and a recognition that there are usually multiple avenues by which any given goal may be accomplished. An associate superintendent said that delegating was the most difficult thing for him to learn to do in his current position. He explained:

> The thing that I've learned, that I had the most trouble with, is that when you delegate, you delegate completely. If I delegate to the Director of Elementary Education, and I'm over there the next day asking, "How is it coming along? What are you doing with it?" then I never should have delegated it to that person. And that has been difficult for me because I'm the world's pickiest individual. The ability to delegate is something I have struggled with. And that was hard for me because I wanted it done the way I would do it to start with, and I've learned there are other ways of doing it that are just as good.

"Letting go" by allowing other people to assume leadership roles is viewed by successful supervisors as essential to effectiveness. It involves the skill of managing by outcomes rather than by "keeping one's finger in the pie all of the time." An instructional supervisor has to be willing to say to an individual or a group:

> This is your project. You take it and go with it. Then come back and tell me everything I need to know.

Many districts have institutionalized formal programs through which promising individuals are identified and provided with opportunities to exercise their leadership abilities. In some districts groups of teachers in each building are assigned to "leadership teams" that plan ways of improving instruction in their local school. In other districts a similar outcome is achieved on a larger scale through system-wide curriculum committees. Supervisors believe it is crucial to distribute leadership in such ways because one person simply cannot influence the quality of instruction unilaterally. Other reasons supervisors give for delegating instructional leadership to both teachers and administrators include the intrinsic satisfaction of seeing another person grow and the belief that the organization has an obligation to the people who are committed to doing good work.

Developing Others

At a functional level supervisors exchange resources, information, and credit for involvement and commitment from teachers and principals. Yet there is a more abstract dimension of exchange that relates to values and to the development of people within the organization. In fact, the exchange of resources, information, and recognition may be subsumed and understood more clearly within this more general context.

An associate superintendent, for example, made the following comment regarding reciprocal exchange:

> My job is at a higher level. Rewards are intrinsic and not expected as a one-for-one payoff, or it demeans the position.

Supervisors derive some intrinsic satisfaction from such things as the diversity of their work and the opportunities for creativity it provides. However, according to supervisors, the most significant personal reward comes from seeing improvement in the quality of learning experiences for children. The indicator of success that central office supervisors consider most closely in this regard is the degree to which other professionals within the district have internalized this value and accepted responsibility for enacting it.

Working with people is what central office instructional supervisors spend most of their time doing. While this can also be said of many other occupations and professions, the uniqueness of the supervisor's role is that practitioners generally see themselves as "helping other people become more effective." They view themselves as providing a service, the primary function of which is "facilitating people's moves to higher degrees of achievement." The ultimate beneficiaries of this service are the students, however, rather than teachers, who benefit indirectly. An assistant superintendent firmly stated that in order for him to be successful,

> the principal and the teachers have to be successful in working with students. Otherwise there is no reason to have the position, a central office curriculum person.

Effective supervisors see themselves as helping to develop teachers and administrators both personally and professionally in a number of areas, including technical skills, autonomy, self-confidence, and leadership. One supervisor in a smaller rural district observed, for example, that "sometimes you have to sort of bring them up before you can get the types of things that you want from them." She said that she had to begin in her school system by first convincing teachers that the things they did and the decisions they made really could make a difference for students.

Empowerment, competence, and responsibility are all dimensions along which professional development is possible. An associate superintendent in a large suburban district pointed out that the people with whom he works vary widely in their skills, training, and experience, and that he had to take those facts into consideration whenever he planned in-service training. Instructional improvement begins with and depends upon the teacher in the classroom, another supervisor remarked, then adding, "The best evaluation, the most effective evaluation, is self-evaluation, but not everybody comes equipped to do that."

Often, developing others requires an "empathic sensitivity" and a time-consuming "laying of groundwork for what one wants to achieve," as well as a capacity to "listen when things go wrong" and the patience to "start over again." At other times, according to supervisors, developing others requires a more assertive "letting people know where you're coming from" and being able to "push, even though they may not think they're ready."

Empowering teachers and principals and developing in them a willingness and capacity to accept responsibility for the quality of instruction in their own classrooms and schools have the effect of making supervisors' leadership somewhat paradoxical in that the closer they come to achieving this end, the less it appears their positions are needed. One supervisor poignantly observed:

> If you do your job effectively, you almost do away with your job. People really don't realize that you're doing anything. Through the leadership training process, I think, you try to identify people in each school who are very capable of doing things at the building level. All these things get done, and I'm not sure that people always realize that I'm really doing anything to help.

The immediate purpose of this distribution and development of leadership among teachers and principals is to improve instruction. But the long-range purpose is to institutionalize the improvement process. The supervisor cited above responded emphatically to the question, "Then what you're doing is giving power away?":

> Yes. If you're really effective, you need to do that. I wouldn't feel right any other way.

This individual continued by saying that if teachers and principals develop the capacity for instructional leadership, "the program is there forever." Otherwise, if the supervisor leaves, the program of improvement is likely to lose its momentum rapidly and eventually disappear entirely.

The Inadequacy of Popular Models of Leadership

Most popular models of leadership are based on the faulty assumption that followers are fairly passive and naive recipients of a leader's influence. Followers are portrayed as objects that are either moved or unmoved by a leader's actions. Leadership might be thought of as a game of billiards, according to this view, where the action of the cue ball represents the leader's actions and the numbered balls are followers who passively react to these actions. The leader's mental processes are represented in this analogy by the player of the game who strategically determines the actions (shots) that are taken. In a few situations a straight, direct shot is appropriate, but in most cases a degree of obliqueness is required. Various angles and obstacles are considered, and often a certain spin is selected and applied to achieve a particular effect. Sometimes an indirect approach is necessary, and the cue ball is made to first rebound off a cushion. While this softens the cue ball's impact somewhat, and is a difficult maneuver to accomplish successfully, the deviousness of a bank shot is also its major advantage.

Most models of leadership, of course, do take into account the fact that followers are alive, at least to the extent of recognizing that they have physical and psychological needs that they seek to satisfy. The key to successful leadership, according to such a view, is for the leader to analyze the situation correctly and then behave in an appropriate manner to achieve the desired outcome. Leaders are instructed by such models to consider followers' needs as a part of the situational context and to manipulate the reward system so that followers' personal satisfaction is contingent upon their accomplishing organizational goals and complying with the leader's directives.

The difficulty of applying such advice when working with living beings is evident in the fanciful game of croquet in *Alice's Adventures in Wonderland*, where flamingos and hedgehogs were used in place of mallets and wooden balls. Anyone who has depended upon others to get a task accomplished can easily appreciate the difficulty and frustration of trying to entice, encourage, and reinforce the flamingos with rewards in order to keep the hedgehogs moving through the wickets in the desired sequence. In the words of Lewis Carroll:

> The chief difficulty Alice found at first was in managing her flamingo: she succeeded in getting its body tucked away, comfortably enough, under her arm, with its legs hanging down, but generally, just as she had got its neck nicely straightened out, and was going to give the hedgehog a blow with its head, it *would* twist itself round and look up in her face, with such a puzzled expression that she could not help bursting out laughing; and when she had got its head down, and was going to begin again, it was very provoking to find that the hedgehog had unrolled itself, and was in the act of crawling away: besides all this, there was generally a ridge or a furrow in the way wherever she wanted to send the hedgehog to, and, as the doubled-up soldiers [the wickets] were always getting up and walking off to other parts of the ground, Alice soon came to the conclusion that it was a very difficult game indeed. (Carroll, 1944, pp. 121–122)

The basic problem with popular models of leadership, especially as they apply to instructional supervision, is that they are far too leader centered. By overemphasizing the leader as the originator of all action, they effectively blind us to the very important fact that followers actively participate in defining social reality.

In truth, followers never simply react to a leader's directives or respond to offered incentives without forming some sort of opinion about the leader and the leader's motives and actions. Followers constantly observe and critically judge everything that a leader says and does. Whether leaders like it or not, followers collectively decide if their leader is wise or unwise, considerate or insensitive, honest or untrustworthy, worthy of respect or not to be taken seriously. Similarly, particular actions the leader may take are judged as brilliant or dull, ethical or unethical, perceptive or obtuse, altruistic or selfish. An argument could be developed fairly easily on the basis of this observation that leadership style is less a personal attribute of the leader than it is a generalized consensual perception among his or her followers.

Perhaps the appropriate game analogy for understanding leadership is the chess match, also from Lewis Carroll (*Through the Looking Glass*), where the pawns, rooks, and knights are alive, form opinions, have discussions, make decisions, and take action independently of the people ostensibly playing the game. Imagine trying to play a chess match in which the pieces on the board considered and discussed among themselves the appropriateness of each move you made, as well as your overall strategy, and eventually began to form and express opinions about your skill as a chess player. Further, imagine that knights argued with you over tactics, pawns voiced resentment about inequities, and bishops confided that some of the other pieces were beginning to have serious doubts about your competence. Or worse, imagine that you knew that the pieces were talking to each other, but you had no idea what they were saying!

While certainly disconcerting, the analogy of animated chess pieces that communicate with one another better captures the reality of what occurs among members of any group or organization in response to leaders' actions than a game of pool or even hedgehog croquet. The view that followers are passive objects and recipients of leaders' actions and largess is simply incorrect. Even under highly controlled circumstances, followers constantly monitor their leaders, form judgments about them, communicate with one another, establish coalitions, and take independent action. Because followers are active participants in creating and maintaining the social reality of a group or organization, their perceptions and opinions concerning a leader and the leader's behavior are critical factors in determining a leader's success. A truly useful model of leadership must take into account the reality that leadership is inevitably a two-way influence process between leader and follower.

Transactional Leadership

A number of authors have described leadership in terms of a transaction that is conducted between a leader and those who follow (Jacobs, 1970; Burns, 1978; Hollander, 1978). According to their view, leaders provide specific services to their followers and receive such benefits in return as loyalty and support. Among the services provided by a leader, beyond tangible and psychic rewards, is the facilitation of the attainment of mutually desired goals. This view recognizes that followers have drives and values in addition to needs upon which they act. The key point of the transactional perspective is that a leader's legitimacy is largely contingent upon followers' perceptions of the leader's effectiveness in facilitating the accomplishment of outcomes that are valued by both.

Two authors who have developed theories of leadership around the concept of reciprocal transaction are Burns (1978) and Hollander (1978). Although their perspectives differ in some ways, the ideas expressed by these authors are by and large consistent and complementary. Of the two, Burns presents a more abstract and comprehensive treatment of leadership, focused mainly on the political realm. He addresses philosophical issues and draws upon actions taken by prominent world leaders for illustrative examples. Hollander, on the other hand, deals with leadership more in terms of an organizational phenomenon and incorporates into his thinking much of the behavioral science research that is familiar to students of educational supervision and administration. Both theorists can offer some useful insights into the role of central office supervisor.

Burns' elucidation of the relationship between leaders and followers is potentially more inspiring for educational leaders, while Hollander's version may offer more practical insights for understanding details of the relationship between central office supervisors and those with whom they work. Writing from an organizational perspective, Hollander presents a model of leadership that he calls "transactional." Like Burns, he sees the essence of the relationship between leaders and followers as a mutual exchange of benefits. Hollander introduces the provocative notion, however, that an effective leader functions primarily as a "group resource" (p. 38). According to this view, the leader serves the group through such routine activities as maintaining the operation, providing direction, clarifying member expectations, locating resources, and minimizing impediments to performance. To the extent that the leader lives up to these expectations, followers will reciprocate by conferring on the leader a variety of benefits, the foremost of which is influence.

Hollander emphasizes that leadership is dynamic in the sense that it must be continuously legitimized. Followers, he notes, closely observe and constantly evaluate leaders' performance with respect to how well the leader is fulfilling the expectations the group has for the leadership role. Essentially, the leader is responsible for reducing uncertainty and defining the situation, which are accomplished in part through routine tasks: establishing goals, setting standards, clarifying expectations, and enforcing rules. But group members also evaluate their leader's motivation and competence, according to Hollander, in terms of two additional general criteria: perceived progress toward goals given available resources, and fair and equitable treatment of group members.

Another concept introduced by Hollander that helps to explain how leaders gain and maintain influence is that of "idiosyncrasy credit." This notion is based on the apparently contradictory findings of studies that suggest that leaders conform most highly to group norms and yet are also most likely to introduce innovations. "Idiosyncrasy credits" are defined by Hollander as shared perceptions of the leader that are developed among followers over time. Initially, a newcomer to a group accumulates credits in two ways: by contributing to the group's main task and by conforming to the group's existing norms. Only after accumulating a sufficient amount of credit through demonstrations of competence and loyalty over time is a leader permitted to introduce an innovation that affects the group's functioning. If the change successfully contributes to the group's effectiveness, the leader amasses additional credits. But if the innovation fails, the leader must return to accumulating credits through routine competence and conformity. Thus, every time the leader proposes an innovation, it is not unlike placing a bet. Success or failure in terms of furthering the purposes of the organization or improving equity determines whether the leader subsequently wins or loses influence.

If the reputation of a new leader, based upon achievements in some other setting, is very positive, a certain amount of "derivative credit" may be brought into the group from the outside and change may be introduced much earlier. Again, however, the innovation has to be perceived as contributing to the accomplishment of group goals, or this advantage will be quickly lost. Another way of losing credits, according to Hollander (1978), is by simply doing nothing. Hoarding one's accumulated credits without wagering them on innovations from time to time is likely to be perceived by followers as failing to fulfill the obligations of the leader role. If action is not taken, in other words, credits simply wither away.

Burns (1978, p. 19) defines leadership generally "as leaders inducing followers to act for certain goals that represent the values and the motivations—the wants and needs, the aspirations and expectations—*of both leaders and followers.*" He distinguishes, however, between two basic types of leadership: the transactional and the transforming. In the transactional relationship, an exchange takes place at a very utilitarian level—that is, one favor is simply traded for another. Examples of such transactions include exchanges of goods for money or jobs for votes, and they typify the lower-level dimensions of Maslow's well-known hierarchy of needs. Such attempts at manipulation through bribery and favoritism, as noted earlier, are avoided by effective supervisors.

In the case of transforming leadership, the relationship between leader and followers is more complex. The purposes of both leaders and followers become more closely joined as they pursue mutual goals related to higher levels of need and value. A transforming leader transcends the tit-for-tat level of exchange by developing followers' awareness and needs away from narrow self-interest and toward a more inclusive scope and higher values. Both parties are "elevated" by this relationship as they seek "moral" ends, such as "justice and empathy" (Burns, p. 42). The function of the transforming or moral leader is essentially to inspire followers to higher levels of consciousness and achievement. This is accomplished through the leader's sense of drama and a bilateral construction of reality by leaders and followers that carries them above the mundane and routine to higher levels of meaning and purpose.

Particularly interesting, for the purpose of understanding the dynamics of instructional supervision, is the fact that Burns (1978) suggests that the process of education most closely parallels the type of leadership that he describes as transforming. Specifically, it is in the relationship between teachers and students that the type of "reciprocal raising of levels of motivation" is most readily evident (p. 448). Teachers and transforming leaders set goals and tasks for their students or followers to pursue "as joint seekers of truth and mutual actualization," rather than out of self-serving motives (p. 449). Teachers and transforming leaders, thus, prepare their students or followers to be leaders themselves. The role of the central office instructional supervisor can be interpreted according to Burns' thinking as the cultivation of this transforming capacity among teachers. Successful central office supervisors, of course, may be viewed as being transforming leaders in their own right.

Toward a Reciprocal Model of Central Office Supervision

By combining elements of the transactional theories of Hollander (1978) and Burns (1978), an understanding of central office instructional leadership can be developed that adequately accounts for both practical and abstract dimensions of the supervisory role. On the practical level, Hollander's conception of the leader as a "group resource" nicely captures the description of what effective central office supervisors say they do. Essentially, supervisors see themselves as facilitating the accomplishment of instruction-related task responsibilities and coordinating the expertise of teachers and principals. The influence that supervisors possess is acquired gradually through innumerable interactions with teachers and principals that generate "trust," "mutual respect," and "understanding."

As was demonstrated in earlier chapters, central office instructional supervisors provide services that help to reduce uncertainty and alleviate structural strain within the district at the levels of values, norms, roles, and tasks. These services (detailed in Chapters Four, Five, and Six) include: promoting and maintaining norms of cooperation, fairness, and equity; clarifying expectations, establishing direction, and coordinating effort; and reducing technical ambiguity and psychological uncertainty surrounding tasks. Such facilitative processes help to define the social reality of the school as being cohesive, purposeful, dependable, responsive, rational, and stable.

By reducing uncertainty, the supervisor is primarily a maintainer of stability and order within the system (Sullivan, 1980). Yet it is also the case that the central office supervisor is an agent of change, growth, and improvement. While these responsibilities at first seem contradictory and paradoxical, Hollander's (1978) notion of "idiosyncrasy credit" makes clear that such functions can be mutually complementary. That is to say, the supervisor is able to gain credibility and practical influence with teachers and principals in two ways: by reducing uncertainty through routine competence and by sponsoring and facilitating changes that improve organizational effectiveness or promote equity.

Changes in organizational processes or structures necessarily require the introduction of some degree of uncertainty into the existing definition of the situation. This uncertainty can be introduced either on the supervisor's initiative or on behalf of teachers and principals. Confidence in the supervisor's ability to restore order and balance to instruction seems to be required, however, before uncertainty can be advantageously reduced and positive change successfully implemented.

The practical influence of the central office supervisor, thus, contributes to a definition of the district's social reality as being stable yet capable of change, growth, and development. This very desirable situation may still be essentially devoid of meaning, however, until it is interpreted in terms of the core value of concern for the well-being of children and commitment to quality instruction for their benefit. As was suggested in Chapter One, the emphasis on this value and the construction of meaning around it seem to be what distinguish effective supervisors from those who are merely competent.

By embodying the core value and exemplifying it in the behaviors they enact, central office instructional supervisors constantly call attention to the fundamental purpose of education, which helps provide focus and meaning to the activities of others. Successful central office supervisors, therefore, function as transforming leaders (Burns, 1978) by helping teachers and principals transcend the mundane and strive toward the common moral purpose or higher ideal of serving children.

According to a transforming view of central office instructional leadership, people in schools do not work toward predetermined organizational goals. Instead, a sense of meaning and purpose emerges from a dialogue that is carried on among educators as they interpret organizational and instructional reality. This dialogue is initiated, encouraged, and facilitated at all levels of the school hierarchy by effective central office supervisors. The result is a consensus of meaning among people who work in schools concerning what they are about, why they are there, and what they need to do, a consensus that is centered on the common core professional value of providing high-quality instructional experiences for students. When supervisors personally embody this core value and act as its advocate, they are able to exert moral influence through the constant collaborative interpretation and reinterpretation of instructional and organizational events and processes.

References

Alfonso, R. J., Firth, G. R. & Neville, R. F. 1981. *Instructional supervision: A behavior system*, 2nd ed., Boston: Allyn and Bacon.

Burns, J. M. 1978. *Leadership*. New York: Harper & Row.

Carroll, L. 1944. *Alice's adventures in wonderland.* New York: The Macmillan Company.

Carroll, L. 1944. *Through the looking glass.* New York: The Macmillan Company.

Hollander, E. P. 1978. *Leadership dynamics*. New York: The Free Press.
Jacobs, T. O. 1970. *Leadership and exchange in formal organizations*. Alexandria, Va.: Human Resources Research Organization.
Sullivan, C. G. 1980. The work of the instructional supervisor: A functional analysis (Doctoral dissertation, Emory University, 1980).

10
Working with the Superintendent

At times the positions of central office instructional supervisor and superintendent seem almost interchangeable. There are often occasions when the supervisor of instruction temporarily assumes the superintendent's role. One district coordinator mentioned that because his superintendent had recently had surgery, he had "filled the bill" and "acted as his replacement." More commonly, the central office instructional supervisor serves as the acting superintendent of schools when the superintendent travels out of town. Under ordinary circumstances, supervisors report, they are called upon to "ghostwrite speeches," "make presentations," and "attend meetings" when the superintendent is unable to do so.

The positions of district level instructional supervisor and superintendent, however, obviously differ in many ways. Of the two, the superintendency is both more visible to the public and more closely prescribed. Established by law, the superintendent's position confers legal authority along with specific duties. The superintendent is ultimately responsible for what happens in the district and is frequently at the center of conflict and controversy (Blumberg, 1985).

Because the central office instructional supervisor's position is less clearly defined, less visible to the public, and less well understood, a danger exists that the supervisor may be perceived as having nothing better to do than "mind the store while the chief is away." While a close working relationship with the superintendent makes it possible for the supervisor to "pinch-hit" in an emergency or temporarily when the superintendent is out of the office, this should never become the supervisor's primary duty. It is important that the individuals in these positions work in close conjunction with each other, but it is crucial to a school district's success that the instructional supervisor clearly establish a professional identity based upon a separate area of responsibilities.

Integration and Adaptation

The major functional difference between the positions of district level instructional supervisor and superintendent is that the attention of the former tends to be directed mainly "inward" on matters affecting operations within the organization. The attention of the superintendent, on the other hand, is directed primarily "outward" toward elements in the school system's environment. The focus of the supervisor is on the primary business of schools—namely, the instruction of students—while the focus of the superintendent is on political and financial matters that support instructional efforts. This specialization of function has certain definite advantages for the school as an organization.

Successful instructional supervisors concern themselves with the perceptions and beliefs of other educators within the school while attending to very practical tasks, such as supplying materials, developing skills, and mobilizing people for collective action. In contrast, superintendents attend more closely to the perceptions and beliefs of those outside the school's immediate boundaries while trying to rally and maintain political and financial support in the community. These specialized functions relate well to Schein's (1984) proposition that there are two major categories of problems that groups and organizations must resolve: problems of "external adaptation" and problems of "internal integration."

Problems of external adaptation involve those elements in the environment "that ultimately determine the group's survival" (Schein, 1984, p. 9), such as acquiring resources and establishing perceptions of legitimacy. Problems of internal integration also affect a group's ability to survive, but they involve matters like rewards, intimacy, and power. Schein points out that external adaptation and internal integration may be thought of as "two sides of the same coin," in that they are highly interdependent. Interaction between the two processes influences the specific form that the culture of a group or organization will take. According to Schein, a culture in a group or organization is continuously redefined as learning occurs "about how to relate to the environment and to manage internal affairs" (1984, p. 10).

A related way of thinking about the problems of adaptation and integration as they pertain to the positions of instructional supervisor and superintendent is in terms of the concepts of "image" and "vision." Although these terms are sometimes used synonymously, an important distinction can be made. The superintendent can be thought of as projecting and promoting a positive external image of the district as he or she goes about the practical problem of securing and maintaining support for the school system within the community. During the process of solving practical problems of integration within the school district, on the other hand, the instructional supervisor is engaged in interpreting and maintaining a positive internal collective definition of the situation. This definition serves as a guiding vision that is collaboratively developed and shared by teachers, principals, and the superintendent.

An organization's image, in other words, is dependent upon the perceptions of people in the environment; it may be thought of as being somewhat akin to an individual's "social self." For both individuals and organizations, of course, how one perceives oneself and how one is perceived by others are interrelated and influence effectiveness. The long-term effectiveness of a school district, for example, depends on how actors within the organization perceive themselves and the work they do, as well as upon the perceptions of parents, taxpayers, and various external agencies (Carol and Cunningham, 1984).

A vision, on the other hand, provides an organization like a school district with an internal sense of purpose and cohesiveness. Although it has been most often associated with the building principal's sense of purpose and direction (Blumberg and Greenfield, 1980; Achilles, 1987), vision also may be considered as a common understanding about the desired state of affairs that holds a group or organization together (Greenfield, 1987). In this sense, it is roughly equivalent to an individual's internal sense of identity, in that the vision defines what the organization means or represents to the people who participate in it.

The Effective Working Relationship

Above all, the superintendent and the central office supervisor have to maintain close contact with one another to ensure consistency and functional interdependence between the internal vision and the external image of the district. In this way, the district can nurture a culture that is both internally viable and externally adaptable. Successful supervisors identify a number of characteristics that make possible a sound working relationship with the superintendent. One important characteristic of an effective relationship between a supervisor and superintendent might be best described as "informality," with the high degree of trust and openness that word implies.

A successful assistant superintendent for instruction explained that frequent visits from his superintendent kept them both informed about events of mutual interest and provided an opportunity for them to discuss more-serious matters whenever necessary. The enthusiasm the supervisor had for this informality is obvious in the quotation below:

> I guess I have actually gone to his office to see [the superintendent] on a matter I wanted to discuss only one time this year. And do you know why? It's because he stops by here most every day. He comes through, he sits down, he drinks a cup of coffee. Anything I have on my mind, I can fill him in on at that point. That kind of relationship is important. Very important! I've worked under a different type of administration in the past, and having this kind of trust and interaction is very, very important. . . . I don't think you can overemphasize that. The relationship that a person in my position has with his superintendent will determine a great deal about the quality of the job he'll be able to do.

"Keep the superintendent informed"—all successful instructional supervisors agree—about ideas that one may have, about new programs underway, and especially about potential problems. Supervisors recognize that a superintendent may be asked at almost any time by anyone about things that are happening in the district, and that superintendents understandably prefer to be able to give a reasonably informed response. It is also important for a supervisor to know which goals the superintendent is interested in achieving in instruction and what his or her expectations are for the supervisor. A curriculum coordinator said that his relationship with the superintendent was such that "we appreciate one another and we anticipate what the other one needs."

Supervisors of instruction feel that they can be most effective when the superintendent "delegates responsibility totally" and gives them "almost complete latitude" in determining the details about how to perform their jobs. Supervisors quickly caution, however, that this does not mean that their superintendents are uninvolved. On the contrary, superintendents who delegate extensively are also described as being mainly "interested in supporting instruction."

Ideally, from the supervisor's standpoint, the superintendent delegates responsibility for the instructional program to the supervisor without subsequent undue direct involvement. Obviously, this requires a high level of trust from both parties. The assistant superintendent for instruction quoted above explained:

The superintendent gives me a great deal of license in terms of operation. He delegates this position to me totally. That doesn't mean that he doesn't want to be involved, but he is not always looking over my shoulder. That's important. That's very important. If you don't have a superintendent who trusts you, you can't do the job. If you're going to be "job-scared," you can't do the job.

In a very real sense, the supervisor of instruction can only do as much as the superintendent will allow. The superintendent can use the supervisor merely as a clerk, assigning only the "menial tasks that must be done." Or, a superintendent can enhance the supervisor's influence by delegating authority and eliminating impediments that require the supervisor to seek permission before initiating action. But it is crucial for the empowered supervisor, in turn, to keep the superintendent informed at all times about what he or she is doing and plans to do. One district level supervisor poignantly observed:

> Being a curriculum director is an amorphous enough job as it is, and enough people look at you wondering what in the world you're doing. You don't need to have the problem of your superintendent saying, "Well, I really don't know what he's doing, either."

It usually works to the supervisor's advantage, and probably to the advantage of the school system as well, if the superintendent was formerly a supervisor of instruction. Supervisors who become superintendents possess a better understanding of what those in charge of instruction are supposed to be doing; consequently, they tend to shield supervisors from unnecessary paperwork. As a curriculum director explained:

> About six months ago [the superintendent] sat in this chair. He knows the many hats I wear and the things I have to do. So he's very sympathetic about trying to get help or trying to divert the Mickey Mouse things that take time away from me, that the clerical folks or somebody else in the central office can do.

A possible pitfall, on the other hand, is that a superintendent who was formerly a supervisor may be less willing to delegate authority and more intrusive in matters relating to instruction.

The key to a sound working relationship between superintendents and central office supervisors is a continuously ongoing, open dialogue between the two concerning how to provide the best educational opportunities for the largest number of students. Obviously, they both must be dedicated above all to developing an instructional program of the highest quality possible. But even when such fundamental agreement exists, occasional minor disagreements inevitably occur regarding details of implementation. Another supervisor reported:

> I have been very fortunate to have a very supportive superintendent. But I've had to oftentimes back off from something that I thought was a very good idea because he just wasn't going to consider it. You just have to sometimes back off, and regroup, and start again.

The give-and-take nature and mutual openness of a sound relationship between a supervisor and a superintendent is evident in the elaboration that followed:

> So you drop it and maybe come back to it later. But I don't ever hesitate to share anything with the superintendent. I think that's important [for] having a good working relationship. And I don't hesitate to say no if he says, "I think you ought to do this in this way, right now." If I don't think it would be appropriate, I certainly feel free to express my position. I think "reciprocity" is as good a word as any.

Although there certainly are times when the supervisor must acquiesce despite his or her own convictions, by no means should the supervisor always yield to the superintendent's wishes. An informal relationship characterized by trust and open communication between the supervisor and superintendent makes it possible for them to work together as a "team [in which] both members complement each other fully." This type of relationship makes it not only possible, but very likely, that the supervisor will privately challenge the superintendent from time to time. A curriculum director explained that although necessary, it is not always easy to disagree with the superintendent:

> Even though it may cause conflict with the superintendent, you have to stand up. Even though it may be frightening and intimidating at times, you have to stand up [for] certain things you believe in.

An associate superintendent, who had competed with the current superintendent for the top position and lost, reported that they nevertheless had gotten along very well for several years. He explained that the basis of this harmony was that they kept their differences of opinion private:

> I know not to challenge publicly, not to circumvent. But in no way does that indicate that I am a rubber stamp.

He went on to explain that in his view the central office supervisor necessarily represents something of a loyal opposition at times, telling the superintendent frankly about problems that others may be reluctant to reveal. However, this supervisor quickly added:

> If you're constantly at odds with the superintendent or at odds with the board, then you ought to do something to change it. Probably the easiest thing to do would be to change jobs.

The superintendent serves the important function of being a reality check against whom the supervisor can test new ideas before action is taken and funds are appropriated. The superintendent's delegation to the supervisor of authority for the instructional program is therefore not an abdication. It is in the interest of the instructional program, as well as both parties involved, for the supervisor and the superintendent to keep each other informed before, during, and after trying out a new idea. The superintendent's active involvement in instructional decisions helps to ensure support of the instructional program because the superintendent continues to feel a part of it:

> When you come up with left-field ideas like I'm prone to do from time to time, and you want to try them, he'll support those things if they have merit. [He has a] willingness to say, "I will go along with that, but have you thought of this?" He plays the devil's advocate, sort of as a sounding board. That's good, because I can get out in left field sometimes. [He shows] support in terms of being available, support in terms of giving me an opportunity to keep the board of education informed of what we're doing and why. [He gives both] professional and personal support. And I'm fortunate to have it. I don't dread seeing the superintendent come by.

Frequent open and honest communication between the supervisor and superintendent thus benefits both. On the one hand, the superintendent is highly dependent on the supervisor to help maintain a positive image of the district. The instructional supervisor could conceivably withhold key information or strategically delay it while the superintendent blindly pursues a course that the supervisor knows would be likely to fail. On the other hand, the supervisor is highly dependent on the superintendent's continued support. Without it, the supervisor is likely to accomplish very little.

Support

Superintendents are able to support endeavors in instructional improvement by providing financial resources and encouragement. Instructional supervisors place a high value on both. The provision of funds that allow time for teachers to work on curriculum development during the summer, attend in-service training sessions, or participate in activities of their professional organizations are examples of financial support for instruction. Some supervisors feel that they have in a sense earned this support for themselves and for teachers through their own hard work because the superintendent "has seen the benefits of investing in professional development." In the best situations, supervisors have internal control over certain expenditures authorized for instruction, rather than being compelled to take each request to the superintendent for approval.

Influence, of course, works both ways. When asked what is most important about working with the superintendent, an assistant superintendent responded by describing the sense of responsibility it entailed:

> Well, you feel a great responsibility, having input into policy making and the decisions that are made for the entire district. And I think that responsibility is a pretty scary one because you know that you're making a decision which is going to affect over ten thousand youngsters. That's got to be pretty serious.

When asked if it was important to have influence over the superintendent, she continued to say that her major contribution in their relationship was one of supplying specialized expertise:

> Not influence over him, but he looks to us as an advisory group when making decisions. And of course, he has not had experience at the elementary level, so he has to look to someone with an elementary background to give him the kinds of input that are important for decisions that affect elementary students. And I feel that that is one of the major responsibilities of my role.

Supervisors say that it is personally important for them to receive occasional verbal praise and encouragement from the superintendent. Support of this sort is psychological and is viewed by some supervisors as necessary if they are to be continuously supportive of others. A curriculum director, for example, pointed out that her position involved providing "service to other people," that one had to be "a giving person" in order to be successful. She said that without occasional encouragement and reinforcement from someone, "we may just reach the point [where we] have nothing left to give." Another supervisor described how his superintendent recently provided important psychological support for him by tracking him down at a vocational school that was geographically isolated from the central office, to tell him personally that an instructional-improvement grant for which he had applied to the state had been funded. The superintendent reportedly told him:

> I called you out of your meeting—and I apologize for doing it—but I just received word that your grant was approved for $72,000, and I knew you would be excited about it, and I wanted to be sure to congratulate you and your staff for doing it.

Then the supervisor added:

> That's the kind of thing that's so important. Because you're in a service position, you don't get as much of that as you perhaps feel you should.

While such occasional "pats on the back" are important for the supervisor, the crucial aspect of support from the superintendent is that it should be ongoing. Supervisors of instruction refer to this quality of support as "consistency." Once a decision has been made to pursue a particular course of action, a supportive superintendent "doesn't change his mind in mid-stream" if some resistance is encountered, but instead "stays right in there" until the goal is achieved. A curriculum director explained it this way:

> If he says, "Do it," I can count on the funds to get it done. I can count on consultants being brought in if I need them. He really gives me the authority to make the decisions in curriculum development and carry [them] through to the end.

Consistency on the part of the superintendent also makes it easier to anticipate how the supervisor can best facilitate their work together. Again, open communication serves the purposes of both persons. An associate superintendent commented:

> He's a consistent person. I pretty much know what he's going to say or how he's going to react to something before I even see him. Really, I guess what I go in there for is to get affirmation of what I'm doing and to keep him informed so that if he gets calls, he'll know where we are and be able to deal with it.

Thus, consistency of material support and encouragement from the superintendent ensure that the internal "vision" and the external "image" of the school district are consistent with one another.

Principals

Because supervisory positions are not often vested with legal authority, instructional supervisors are dependent upon the superintendent initially to establish the central office as an influential component of the district. An organizational chart would suggest that there is no question that the superintendent is in charge of everything that happens in the district. But in reality, it is necessary for principals and teachers to exercise a considerable degree of autonomy and discretion in dealing with the unique characteristics of their particular situations, as well as unanticipated events that arise almost daily. This complicates the exercise of formal authority considerably.

When leadership from the superintendent's office is not forthcoming, particularly over an extended period of time, it becomes very likely that principals will establish a pattern of operations that can be highly resistant to later attempts to exert influence. An assistant superintendent explained it this way:

> Well, we've had a situation here for a long time where we've had three very strong principals who were here when the superintendent came in, and it was very difficult to make changes. . . . We deferred often to principals and their decisions simply because they were strong personalities and they had always done things their way. We made some changes the last year or two, and we'll have a new superintendent coming in next year. . . . If he's a very strong superintendent, there will be more direction from the county office.

It is important, from the perspective of central office supervisors, that the superintendent clearly establish influence among the principals in the district. One supervisor called this "setting the tone for dealing with the schools." Effective principals, as research has shown, tend to be independent and protective of their autonomy. Autonomy alone, however, is no guarantee of effectiveness.

The support of principals for the superintendent and central office initiatives is essential for district-wide improvement to occur. Most supervisors can recount instances when principals successfully resisted a direct order from the superintendent. Resistance is especially effective if principals band together and protect their collective autonomy with passive resistance. It can be extremely difficult in such cases to secure their cooperation, even with respect to simple requests for information from the central office. A supervisor related this incident, which followed a minor accident involving a school bus:

> . . . the superintendent said, "Well, I would like a listing of every student who rides on every bus," and he asked the principals to try to organize it. It was not successful. So this year he just turned it over to them and said, "You must return a bus list of all students." Now that sounds like a simple thing, but the principals don't see the need for it, so they resist.

It is worth emphasizing again that such an organized lack of cooperation from principals seems to result when leadership has not been forthcoming from the superintendent for an extended period of time. Principals react defensively to protect their individual schools, not from some irrational impulse to subvert district policy. Having once experienced autonomy, however, principals may be understandably reluctant to relinquish it unless they can be convinced that the interests of their schools will be served by doing so.

Considerable discretionary autonomy is absolutely necessary for principals to operate effectively; but when it is carried to an extreme, results are unpredictable. If the principal is an energetic entrepreneur, for example, the teachers and students in that school may benefit from the resourcefulness of their leader, though sometimes at the expense of other schools in the system. When a laissez-faire attitude prevails at the central office, the best teachers, the newest materials, and the latest innovative programs can easily end up at a few schools that happen to have the most dedicated and persistent or politically astute principals. On the other hand, if a principal possesses autonomy but does nothing constructive for the benefit of the school, that school suffers. Some coordination from the central office is therefore necessary to ensure that all children in the district have equal access to resources and experience an educational program of equivalent quality.

District-wide instructional improvement is another major reason that leadership from the central office is needed. Even principals who are effective at independently attracting resources to their schools may lack the time and expertise to fully develop these resources once acquired. Staff and curriculum development and direct assistance to teachers are unlikely to occur unless someone takes the initiative to ensure that quality is preserved, extended, and amplified.

A certain degree of tension between the principals' need for autonomy and the district level need for coordination is inevitable. Differences of opinion are likewise unavoidable. There are times when the supervisor must take a stand relative to some issue and defend it against opposition from the local school level. Disagreements can actually be a constructive force when dealt with openly and without vindictiveness. A curriculum director who lacked building level administrative experience described her stormy relationship with principals when first attempting to implement new instructional policies:

> We had some head-on disagreements, and usually I'm a very quiet, reserved person. But if I feel that I've been assigned a task to do by the superintendent, then it's my job to get it done. If we have to have conflict, you know, I create the conflict. But we work through it, and we get the job done. And then it's forgotten. It's not a thing that builds resentment, where people do not speak to each other. The people are very professional, and we work through the conflict, and we're stronger for it.

Ideally, the superintendent is open to principals' ideas and requests. Occasionally, however, a principal may feel for some reason that a proposal he or she wants to present is a bit out of line with the superintendent's thinking, or that it might stretch the bounds of the superintendent's good will. In such cases the district level supervisor may be asked to offer a preliminary opinion about a proposal or even raise the issue informally with the superintendent. This procedure allows some innovative, even risky, proposals to be considered off the record within the organization. An unusual or creative idea can be safely tested through an intermediary without the principal having to make an official request. Furthermore, because a direct request has not been made, the superintendent's position also is eased if it is necessary to reject the idea. Neither party gets embarrassed, and the relationship between them can proceed unimpeded by any residual awkwardness or ill feelings.

It is only when leadership from the central office is perceived by principals as chronically weak and incompetent, or when the relationship between the schools and the central office is defined as adversarial and competitive, that a breakdown in district effectiveness is likely to occur. Again, it is the superintendent who has the most influence in setting the tone for working with the schools.

It should be emphasized that although legally sanctioned line authority is a prerequisite for a public school to operate efficiently, it is not sufficient in itself to overcome the effects of years of poor management, neglect, or bad feelings. Because of the considerable potential principals have for exercising autonomy, they have to be convinced that directives they receive are actually in the interests of their students and local schools and are not merely an attempt by the central office to consolidate power as an end in itself. The supervisor has to work closely with the superintendent to ensure that principals develop an understanding and belief that all levels of the administration comprise a single team that works for the benefit of all the students in the district.

School Board

A central office supervisor's job is considerably easier if the superintendent is respected by the school board. School board members sometimes forget that they actually have no legitimate authority except as constituent members of a convened board at a formal meeting. In cases where the superintendent has not established sufficient influence with the board, lines of authority become blurred and the supervisor is left uncertain about whom to approach for approval of new ideas. An associate superintendent noted that early in her career she was caught in exactly that situation. She described the dilemma it created:

> Whom do you speak to first when you want to get something through? You know, do you go right to the boss, or do you go to somebody else?

Similar problems can arise when newly elected board members do not understand that their function is primarily one of deciding on policy. Newcomers to the board may telephone an instructional supervisor to ask for favors or even to make "suggestions" about how the instructional program should be run. Successful supervisors unanimously prefer that requests and directives from the school board go through the superintendent, and they report that they diplomatically insist that board members do so. Similarly, supervisors say that they rarely if ever call board members directly or seek them out individually for special consideration of some pet project.

It is not that school board members intentionally try to subvert the superintendent; they may simply be caught up in enthusiasm for a new project. For example, a supervisor in one district said that he had mentioned briefly in an oral report at a board meeting held the night before that a committee of teachers had just completed a five-month curriculum project intended to introduce foreign languages into the district's elementary classrooms. A board member became so excited at hearing the news that he called the supervisor at eight o'clock the next morning, asking for copies of the document. The instructional supervisor graciously thanked the board member for his interest in the report, but he also cautioned that it was "up to the superintendent [to decide when] we're going to unveil it to the whole world." The important thing to remember as far as the superintendent was concerned, this supervisor added, was that there should be "no surprises."

Perceptions of the Superintendency

Most central office instructional supervisors claim that they have little or no interest in becoming superintendents themselves, despite the fact that their position might be a logical stepping stone to the superintendency. For some supervisors such statements may reflect what they consider a professionally appropriate attitude, regardless of their real career aspirations. For others a denial of interest in the superintendency may be a rationalization after the fact. In truth, however, the central office supervisor is probably in a better situation than anyone in the district to observe closely and assess accurately the realities of the superintendent's role. On the whole, supervisors do not seem particularly envious of what they see.

An associate superintendent observed that "there's just a lot of punishment" in the superintendent's job. His own decision not to seek a superintendency resulted, he said, "from sitting beside [a superintendent] for seven years in Ohio" and noticing how greatly his superordinate's emotional state hinged upon the actions and reactions of other people. The superintendent became either exuberantly "high" or "angry and depressed" after each school board meeting, depending on how well or poorly things had gone. The supervisor said that he "felt that you really don't have as much control of your life," as superintendent, "because you're right up there in that glass house all of the time, on the firing line, and you get mixed signals from everybody who's out there."

A superintendent acts as something of a "lightning rod," according to the perception of another supervisor, absorbing the shocks of conflict and controversy that originate in the external environment. The superintendent, in this individual's view, protected the school organization from political and economic disturbances, allowing the instructional program to proceed relatively uninterrupted.

The political and financial decisions that superintendents make expose them to greater public scrutiny and criticism than supervisors typically face. The fact that in many states superintendents are the only nontenured educational professionals makes their position still more vulnerable.

Central office supervisors in many districts do seem to hold their positions longer than superintendents. When asked if this observation was accurate, one assistant superintendent responded with a straight face, "I really wouldn't know. This is only the third superintendent I've worked under." The stability of the supervisor's position may be partly due to the superintendent's greater visibility and vulnerability, and partly to the fact that a new superintendent has a high need for a dependable source of information concerning the district's existing policies, practices, and current situation. Accurate information concerning the instructional program is especially elusive.

It frequently turns out that the most convenient and reliable source of information for a new superintendent, on everything ranging from how instructional materials are selected to which school board members are most supportive of the educational program, is the current supervisor of instruction (Floyd, 1986). Once the supervisor has been accepted as a valuable source of reliable information, he or she soon becomes practically indispensable. Furthermore, most superintendents would be reluctant to replace someone who had consistently proven his or her loyalty by supplying essential information at a crucial time.

Commitment to the Superintendent

When working with teachers and administrators on practical problems and building an internal collective definition of the situation and shared vision of what is possible, successful supervisors of instruction contribute to an internal sense of community. Within the district, and especially with respect to the instruction of students, feelings of trust, caring, and support are generated and sustained. At the same time, the superintendent must cope with the factual world of society and develop an image of the district that places greater emphasis on facts and efficiency. Although these perspectives on reality obviously differ, supervisors and superintendents must find a way of giving expression to both if they are to work together well.

The supervisor's concern with vision and the superintendent's concern with image result in each of these leadership positions being highly visible with one audience and less visible with the other. Successful instructional supervisors tend to be highly visible to teachers and principals, for example, but their visibility to the general public in comparison is quite limited. An associate superintendent observed:

> The supervisor is in the eye of the teachers and principals. The superintendent is not as visible to them. We're more visible to

people involved with the instructional program than the superintendent typically is. The teachers and principals are right there on the firing line, and we're the backup for them. The superintendent is kind of like twice removed [from instruction].

As has been emphasized repeatedly, successful district level supervisors possess a strong personal commitment to providing children with the best instruction possible. Supervisors also say, however, that besides this commitment to the well-being of students, it is also important "to have a certain commitment to the superintendent as a person and as a leader." Although the word "loyalty" is currently out of vogue, it describes well the kind of public commitment to the superintendent that successful district level supervisors say they value.

Supervisors generally emphasize that the superintendent should always "take the credit" and be in the "limelight" in dealings with the public and public agencies. Not only does the superintendent make the decisions and take the risks that allow things to proceed, the superintendent symbolizes what the district "stands for" to the outside world. A curriculum director, for instance, said:

In accreditation, I think it would be very inappropriate for the director of instruction to get up and start talking about how it was her work that helped get or keep the school accredited. The superintendent should have the major role there, even though the instructional director actually does a lot of the work.

The wise supervisor of instruction recognizes that the superintendent is vulnerable to criticism because of constant scrutiny. A large measure of the superintendent's success depends on the public's perception that he or she is competently performing the duties of office. One implication of this circumstance is that the success or failure of the instructional program is usually credited publicly to the superintendent.

A supervisor may find an absence of public visibility difficult to accept when accolades are given, but he or she should recognize that the superintendent has taken the greater risk and therefore deserves the praise when things go well. The wise superintendent, on the other hand, allows the instructional supervisor to bask in some glory among professional colleagues. This arrangement provides for a more equitable balance of recognition between the two leadership positions.

It is conceivable that a central office supervisor might successfully maintain a sound instructional program, while the superintendent failed in dealings with the public. As assistant superintendent for instruction observed, for example, that a superintendent could lose his or her job by making unpopular personnel decisions or for proposing a budget that sets the tax rate too high. "The public gets much more upset over their money," she observed ironically, "than they do over the quality of education." However, a curriculum director noted that although a supervisor might be successful in improving instruction, if the "superintendent fails, then that [supervisor] would fail at the same time—if not in the eyes of the public, then within themselves." The internal vision and external image, although quite different in terms of specific details, after all, are reflections of one another.

References

Achilles, C. M. 1987. A vision of better schools. In W. Greenfield (ed.), *Instructional leadership*. Boston: Allyn and Bacon.

Blumberg, A. 1985. *The school superintendent: Living with conflict*. New York: Teachers College Press.

Blumberg, A. & Greenfield, W. D. 1980. *The effective principal*. Boston: Allyn and Bacon.

Carol, L. N. & Cunningham, L. L. 1984. Views of public confidence in education. *Issues in Education*, 2 (2): 110–126.

Floyd, M. K. 1986. *Meanings that outstanding central office instructional supervisors associate with their role* (Unpublished doctoral dissertation, University of Georgia).

Greenfield, W. 1987. Moral imagination and interpersonal competence: Antecedents to instructional leadership. In W. Greenfield (ed.), *Instructional Leadership*. Boston: Allyn and Bacon.

Schein, E. H. 1984. Coming to a new awareness of organizational culture. *Sloan Management Review*, 25 (2): 3–16.

11
The Dilemma of Invisibility

Most central office supervisors of instruction or curriculum are acutely aware of a peculiar characteristic of their role, namely, that it tends to be an invisible one. That is to say, many of the tasks in which supervisors engage, such as helping a teacher solve an instructional problem, either have intangible outcomes or take place outside the direct view of others and so go unnoticed. In addition, much of a district level supervisor's effort is aimed at improving the image of the school district by making those in more visible positions—such as the superintendent, principals, and teachers—"look good."

A dilemma therefore arises for the supervisor because one must be somewhat self-effacing when highlighting others' successes. Yet the more successful the supervisor is in making others appear successful, the more likely the impression may be inadvertently fostered among the general public, and even some professional colleagues, that the role of supervisor is superfluous.

In the office of a curriculum director (who participated in the interviews on which this book is based) hangs a cartoon depicting a swimming duck. As its feet thrash frantically beneath the surface of the water, the duck manages to maintain a tranquil smile. Beneath the cartoon a caption reads, "The secret to success is to stay cool and calm on top, and paddle like HELL underneath." The cartoon seems to capture an essential truth about instructional supervision: The hard work that is necessary for schools and school districts to operate smoothly is invisible to most people.

The experience of invisibility seems to be common to large numbers of practitioners, and yet it has been overlooked almost entirely by theorists, researchers, and authors in the field of supervision (Costa and Guditis, 1984). Central office supervisors frequently use the term "invisible" when asked to describe what their jobs are like. One supervisor, for example, put it this way:

> I see the director of instruction's job as being sort of an invisible, underlying type of support that is given to classroom teachers and principals; and if things go really, really well, if it's done in a way that's effective, the schools feel extremely successful. . . . It's almost like an invisible role, but it's getting the job done, and it's getting the job done in a way that people feel good about.

A curriculum director similarly observed:

> Your leadership is not the visible leadership; it's the behind-the-scenes leadership. Does that make sense? Do you know what I'm saying?

When asked to elaborate, she continued:

> Well, I would say that the first requirement for a curriculum director is not to have an ego problem. If you want the credit for what's going on and want to take the credit for programs, or things that you begin and supervise, you'll really have problems.

Although supervisors tend to view the invisibility of their role as inevitable and actually necessary to their effectiveness, they are also aware that the consequences of being invisible are not always favorable for them personally. At the local district level some supervisors feel that they are infrequently recognized for their accomplishments. They rarely receive praise and sometimes are denied more tangible rewards as well. Monetary incentives and salary increases seem to go first to others whose jobs produce outcomes that are more easily measured. Also, recent state and federal reports on the status and quality of education focus almost exclusively upon the more visible roles of teacher, principal, and superintendent. It is particularly ironic that legislators, acting upon the recommendations of such reports, plan extensive programs of instructional improvement while ignoring the supervisory positions and services that already exist in most local districts.

It is worth emphasizing, however, that "invisibility" for central office supervisors of instruction is not necessarily something to be eliminated. Rather, it is a part of the reality of being a central office supervisor that must be recognized and reckoned with.

Ambiguity and Remoteness

As was noted in Chapter One, the position of public school central office supervisor is poorly defined in both theory and practice. This absence of a clear definition of the supervisor's role is probably an advantage for the local school system in most cases because a degree of ambiguity leaves room for individual interpretation and improvisation, allowing the supervisor to adapt the role to suit local conditions and changing circumstances within the district. Some supervisors, however, believe that ambiguity is potentially a disadvantage for them personally in the long run. Because people in the community, for example, lack a clear understanding of the role in the school district, supervisors sometimes feel vulnerable at budget time, when cuts are being proposed.

The central office supervisor is also physically and psychologically remote from others. Much of what a person in that position does to improve instruction occurs outside the direct view of the public and involves little direct contact with them. Although it is probably true that members of the public fail to comprehend fully the roles of teacher, principal, and superintendent, the average citizen has at least a general understanding of and some familiarity with what these people do. If one knows from experience as a student that teachers teach and principals and superintendents run the schools, then one can imagine what a typical day for a teacher or administrator must be like. But a member of the general public is less likely to have had direct contact with a supervisor or curriculum director. Without some understanding of the subtleties of how schools function, instructional-support roles remain comparatively mysterious. As a curriculum director explained:

> You do a lot of things that people don't see you do, the community doesn't see you do. They see things happening, and they think that's great. But they don't think about who's responsible for it happening. They see the principal, they talk with the teachers, they come to the district office to see the superintendent. There are an awful lot of things that we do that are really kind of invisible as far as the community is concerned.

Physical remoteness of the central office from the local school buildings contributes to the supervisor's also being invisible to teachers. This seems to be true not only of supervisors of instruction and curriculum, however, but of all central office personnel. For example, one supervisor said that his superintendent was seen so infrequently in the schools that the teachers had nicknamed him Dr. Who? Although supervisors unanimously say that they would like to be out in the schools more often themselves, most also agree that they too often get "closeted" in their offices.

Visiting local schools regularly and often is viewed by successful supervisors as valuable, not only to improve instruction, but also for maintaining credibility among teachers and building administrators. As was noted in an earlier chapter, it is a responsibility that supervisors often find difficult to fulfill. September and June seem to be times when district level supervisors can most easily fit school visitations into their schedules. They point to paperwork, especially that required by state and federal governmental agencies, as keeping them from making the rounds at other times during the year. Paperwork is a serious problem for supervisors in smaller districts, where secretarial help is often inadequate and where a single individual may be responsible for the entire instructional program. The small school system, after all, must file the same number and types of reports as larger districts.

Partly because of externally imposed constraints on their time, most central office supervisors structure their efforts expeditiously—for example, directing change efforts toward groups instead of working with teachers individually. The constant competition between efforts aimed at improving instruction and other responsibilities is evident in the following quote from a curriculum director in a smaller district:

> At the central office level we get caught up in a lot of paperwork and other types of things, and you're not able to be visible as much in the schools. So you find yourself looking for large targets, audiences, in terms of staff development, for instance, so that you can hit all the schools. Or you look for leadership teams to help you implement. It works sort of like a Catch-22. I mean, people are assigned certain responsibilities, and they can't carry them out because of other kinds of duties that conflict.

In many districts teachers seem to have a rather vague understanding of the organizational structure and processes at the central office level. In very large districts uncertainty about such simple things as who answers to whom may extend, surprisingly, even to principals. One associate superintendent noted:

> I find at times that there are people out in the schools who aren't aware, for example, that in my division there are eight departments, and they may not be aware that special education is under my direction and that [the special education coordinator] answers to me.

A curriculum director thought back to when he was a building principal in a large urban district. He remembered that one day he confronted an apparent stranger wandering in the halls of his school, only to discover that the individual was in charge of testing for the district. After five years in the district he did not recognize the man on sight.

The problem of central office remoteness is compounded in larger school districts by the number of bureaucratic levels that further separate and insulate the central office from the classroom. In a large suburban district the associate superintendent meets regularly with his supervisory staff, which is composed of eight subject area specialists. As a group they plan and conduct in-service training for building level instructional supervisors who, in turn, conduct staff development workshops for teachers. Curriculum development, textbook recommendations, and instructional-materials selection are handled similarly, though in a bottom-up fashion. Teachers initially contribute opinions and ideas at building level meetings, which are conveyed through representatives to district level meetings. Those are chaired by individual members of the central office supervisory staff. Final decisions on recommendations are made at the central office by the associate superintendent in consultation with his staff.

The associate superintendent in this case was very aware that "a lot of people don't know who I am." He attributed this fact directly to the hierarchical manner in which supervisory services were delivered in his district:

> When you deliver services that way, after a while teachers will say, "Well, we never see you" or "What's that person doing up there?"

A related difficulty in larger districts is simply the sheer number of teachers who fall under the scope of a supervisor's responsibility. As an associate superintendent in another district succinctly put it:

> You can only be in one school at a time. A large school system means less contact with the teachers.

A curriculum director similarly noted the problem created by being able to be in only one place at a time and having to work with several schools simultaneously:

> When you're not in [a particular] school and doing something for that school and with that staff, then they really don't know what

you're doing. But they suspect it's a lot better than what they're doing.

Intangibility of Instructional and Supervisory Tasks

Another cause of invisibility for central office supervisors of curriculum or instruction is the intangibility of the instructional program and what supervisors do to support it. Most specialists in the central office are associated with easily identified areas that provide essential services for the schools. These areas include transportation, finance, and buildings and grounds. Although the instructional supervisor deals with that aspect of the school which is absolutely central to its mission, contributions in this vital area are comparatively difficult to demonstrate clearly—if at all—with respect to the quality of services rendered.

Members of the public, upon whom the school and the instructional program depend for financial support, really have no accurate way of knowing what, if anything, is going on in a particular school or district. Even if they happen to have children who attend school, the information they receive as parents will be understandably subjective and narrowly focused. Each child's perception of the school is likely to be limited to experiences in a single classroom and to interactions with one or two staff members.

A part of the job for many supervisors, therefore, is to make the instructional program more visible to the public. One way this can be accomplished is by speaking before various community groups about the instructional program and explaining what it is that teachers are doing. Another way is to invite representatives of the news media into the schools to report on what is happening that is new and exciting. As a curriculum director in a district with financial problems explained, he frequently had to interpret the instructional program to the public through the media and personal appearances before community groups:

> I have to make sure that the public understands; otherwise people won't know what we're doing. How would they know? I mean, I don't know what's going on at [a local college] right now, unless I read about it in the paper, unless I see it on TV or something. Otherwise, it's just another college to me. Well, we're just another school system, and I want to be sure we put our best foot forward, and so I'm not afraid to talk with groups, go places, do things, get the media involved, because I think it's important.

Among the outcomes of extensively publicizing his district's reading program locally was a full-page spread in a large metropolitan newspaper, followed by a spot on the regional *PM Magazine* television show. "None of that would have happened," the curriculum director observed, "if we had not made some contacts." His assumption was that good publicity was necessary in order to acquire and retain public support.

This particular school system had an especially difficult time getting budgets passed each year. The curriculum director, therefore, spoke frequently at meetings of civic organizations, like the Lion's Club, and at state level education conferences in order to increase his instructional program's visibility and credibility:

> I've got a traveling road show with slides and all that kind of stuff, about a hundred slides which show what the program's all about, how easy it is to develop, how to replicate our program.

Beyond increasing the credibility and reputation of his own district's instructional program by having it recognized publicly, the director felt that he was performing a professional service to other districts. He seemed to believe sincerely that the locally developed program he represented and touted publicly would benefit other schools and their students if replicated, and that other districts could profit by avoiding the mistakes he and his own district had made during the original development.

An associate superintendent in a well-funded suburban district said, in contrast, that he simply pointed to test scores to justify to board members and the public the number and types of instructional programs in the district, "especially nationally normed tests" and state criterion-referenced tests. Not surprisingly, in this district students typically scored well above average on tests and the tax base was growing. In cases where students perform less well, however, or where the public is reluctant or unable to support education fully, it seems that attention is called more often to alternative-outcome measures and to technological facets of the instructional program, such as the use of computers.

Supervisors report that they heighten the visibility of the instructional program in other ways, including such activities as preparing and distributing monthly newsletters that describe to parents the programs in which children are enrolled and organizing annual fairs that display student work as tangible products of instruction. One supervisor said:

> We have a curriculum fair each spring. It's to highlight student work and what's going on in the buildings, and it's to highlight the instructional programs.

Curriculum work organized by supervisors and completed by teachers becomes visible in the guides they write for their own classroom use. Some supervisors make certain that, in addition to the teachers who will be using them, all administrators and central office staff receive copies of the guides as well. Frequently, curriculum guides are also presented to school board members at meetings where teachers have the opportunity to explain in detail the work they have accomplished and how it will continue to benefit the district and its students. Such measures are a way of demonstrating the existence and quality of the instructional program, as well as the work that teachers have performed, beyond regular classroom teaching, in service to the district.

Another way to communicate a commitment to quality in the instructional program and to rally community support is to focus attention on concrete objects, such as technologically sophisticated equipment, especially computers. For example, one director of curriculum was able to boast:

> Mine was one of the few budgets that wasn't cut. Curriculum and instruction and in-service were not cut at all. Everybody else took a shot and lost parts of their money. Mine didn't because we're doing things with computers and things that are very visible.

Most successful instructional supervisors never view themselves as being intentionally self-serving when engaged in making the instructional program visible. They focus attention on teachers and the job they are doing instead of on themselves. This commitment was demonstrated by one of the supervisors interviewed, who had arranged a visit by a local newspaper photographer and reporter to the classroom of an innovative teacher. Following that event he observed:

> My name will be mentioned, but I'm not the guy that's standing there smiling in front of everybody, because that's not important to me. I want the kids involved, and I want people to see them. I want to see teachers.

A director of instruction similarly said he thought that people in the central office, like himself, needed "to have strong enough egos to allow other people to take the credit for what they do." A degree of voluntary self-effacement seems to be commonly perceived by supervisors as a necessary part of their job. As another director of instruction explained:

> I just did a PTO presentation last week, and the focus was teachers and what they are doing. I never said "I"; I always say "we." People are unaware of what teachers are doing. In everything I write, everything I do, I focus on what teachers are doing and how they have helped bring things about.

District level instructional supervisors generally believe that their emphasis always should be on encouraging teamwork, cooperation, and accomplishments of the group. This effacement of self is done consciously and voluntarily, not out of shyness or some personality defect. Actually, many opportunities arise when the supervisor could easily "steal the show." More-flamboyant supervisors, in fact, say that they sometimes have difficulty restraining themselves from upstaging others and basking in the limelight a bit. A strong ego is essential, one director of instruction said, "from the standpoint that you've got to be convinced that what you're doing is important." At the same time, he added, it is critical not to let "your ego get in the way," and to let someone else take credit, even for something that may have been initiated by the supervisor.

Calling attention to the instructional program and what teachers are doing in the local schools, however necessary it may be, does contribute to the supervisor's invisibility. An idea from Gestalt psychology may help illustrate how this process seems to work. By constantly calling attention to the instructional program and away from oneself, the supervisor, in effect, becomes part of the background against which the figure of the instructional program stands out. When an observer's attention is focused on the figure in the foreground, the background necessarily becomes less conspicuous, less a part of the viewer's consciousness. Thus, the supervisor intentionally tries to draw public attention toward instruction. The more successful supervisors are at accomplishing this, the less visible they inevitably become.

Having to attend to public relations, however, takes time away from working directly with teachers in schools on the improvement of instruction. The possibility exists that the quality of the instructional program will suffer as a result. The supervisor may also become further removed from instruction in people's minds. When the supervisor is not actively engaged in such tasks as staff development, curriculum development, and direct assistance to teachers, people inside and outside the school are likely to begin questioning the supervisor's real usefulness. Ironically, as noted earlier, inordinately energetic attempts to make visible the instructional program are likely to occur precisely when public confidence and support for education on the local level are already low. By working too extensively on public relations, therefore, supervisors may work themselves right out of their jobs.

Part of the cause of the supervisor's invisibility to the public and to professional colleagues is the intangible nature of the services they provide. Supervisors report that it is difficult to explain instructional support services to noneducators, even when they have genuine interest and a sincere desire to understand. If one says to the average citizen that "supervisors help teachers," the impression is given that supervisors must be something akin to teachers' aides. On the other hand, if one explains that supervisors are involved in directing and coordinating instruction, the assumption usually is made that supervisors differ little from line administrators or that they are similar to foremen in a factory. Further attempts to clarify may result only in the unwarranted conclusion that supervisors are really an extravagance, not at all essential to the functioning of schools and classrooms.

An interesting aspect of the central office instructional supervisor's position is that many of the things they do for the improvement of instruction are initiated independently and at their own discretion. In a sense, the supervisor's job involves a constant fine tuning of the educational delivery system by identifying and tinkering with various aspects of the instructional program. They seem to be continuously on the lookout for needs to be satisfied, gaps to be filled, and processes to improve. While this fine tuning may be one of the most important facets of the supervisor's job, it is also the least visible. An example of this fine tuning was offered by a curriculum director who explained that he had recently worked many hours getting a new summer reading program in place. He was very much aware that if he had not attended to this need of the students in the district,

> probably a lot of people wouldn't even know it. If I said, "Well, let's just not worry about a summer reading program," I wouldn't get fired. And the job would still go on, and people would either like me or dislike me regardless. But I just . . . want to help those kids out, and so I bust my buns to make sure that that program works and take my vacation some other time.

Supervision, according to the perspectives of central office practitioners, is in large part a matter of initiating and facilitating changes for improvement while encouraging others to take responsibility and credit for the outcomes. One person described her job metaphorically:

In some ways you could compare it to the yeast in bread dough: not always visible. Sometimes you get a little whiff of it as the bread is baking and you think, "Mmm, that's nice." But it certainly makes a difference in the bread.

Functional Outcomes of Invisibility

An occasional source of unwanted visibility for central office supervisors arises from involvement in controversial issues. One supervisor explained it this way:

There are times when I get more visibility than I want. We've had this big thing about drugs and drug abuse, a lot of publicity. . . . So, you know, I wind up having to make a presentation on the drug and alcohol abuse prevention curriculum to the board of education with a very vocal little body of people there to pick apart every word that you have in the curriculum and every activity that is there. And the press is sitting there taking notes like mad, and I would just as soon not be on that kind of hot seat. That's a little more visibility than I want.

Usually, involvement in controversy is scrupulously avoided by central office supervisors because they view it as making them less effective. Taking a position in the foreground is likely to lead to closer scrutiny by the public, which makes behind-the-scenes work more difficult. For the most part, supervisors view involvement in controversy as something that superintendents do; they want no part of it.

On the basis of their experience, in fact, supervisors generally accept the proposition that invisibility of the central office supervisor's role may serve the very practical function of insulating and protecting the instructional program from the turbulence of politics and capricious interference. The superintendent, who is usually at the center of controversy (Blumberg, 1985), is much more likely to lose his or her job—for instance, if the public becomes dissatisfied with the system's performance—than is the supervisor of instruction. Because the central office supervisor is not constantly in the public eye, he or she is likely to have a better chance of surviving during times of turmoil.

An associate superintendent for instruction explained why he had made a decision early in his career not to seek a superintendency:

I felt that you really don't have as much control of your life [as superintendent] because you were right up there in that glass house all of the time, on the firing line. . . . But as the number-

> two person, and I see my position as a career position, . . . I do have that invisibility, or a certain amount of it. [Instead of] being on the firing line all the time, I can, I think, perform my job more effectively and get things done that need to be done. Because the superintendent is really the one out there who's taking the brunt of a lot of things, and is sort of insulating me from a lot of things that are happening, . . . I can get my job done.

A result of this situation may be that the role of central office supervisor lends a certain degree of stability to the school system and its instructional program in what may be a politically volatile environment. Even during a time of high turnover among superintendents, the invisibility of the instructional supervisor insulates him or her to some degree from the turmoil and allows for continuity of the instructional program. As noted in Chapter Ten, a new superintendent will be dependent on the supervisor to answer questions relating to instruction, ranging from how and when to select and order textbooks to what is currently being done to improve the quality of instruction. Of course, the new superintendent may replace the instructional supervisor or curriculum director with someone else, but this is probably unlikely to occur at least until after the period of transition is completed. Most importantly, the educational experiences of students can proceed uninterrupted despite the turmoil at higher levels.

A second possible functional outcome of the relative invisibility of the supervisor's position is that the symbolic importance of his or her physical presence may be enhanced. A supervisor's appearance at a school-related event attended by either teachers or members of the general public conveys a special value to the event, which suggests that attendance or absence by the supervisor can be used strategically. An associate superintendent observed:

> It's important that we attend in-service meetings. It's important to show that the meeting is important enough for me to be there and to stay there. It conveys to all of us, you know, "This is a pretty important meeting, this is worthwhile."

Similarly, a curriculum director in a small district attended plays, concerts, and athletic events regularly, believing that this conveyed to parents the idea that these were an important part of the instructional program of the school and that she took them seriously. In a larger district, however, an associate superintendent said that she found it impossible to attend many school functions, because if she attended an event at one school, she would have to attend similar events at the other schools so as not to slight them by her absence.

Interestingly, as long as this associate superintendent's children had attended school in the district, her role as parent had afforded her the opportunity to attend any school events in which they participated. But once her children went on to college, her presence at local school functions took on a different meaning, related solely to her professional role. Consequently, she thereafter confined her attendance to district-wide events only.

A third possible function of invisibility among supervisors, which may be most important in terms of day-to-day activity, is that it allows them to be an unobtrusive source of reassurance and reinforcement to others involved in or interested in the educational enterprise. Faced with an organization characterized by multiple and shifting goals, uncertain technologies, rapid turnover and weak affiliation among participants, and an unstable environment, the necessity of avoiding crises of confidence becomes paramount. These characteristics of loosely coupled systems are issues that central office supervisors of instruction constantly confront.

Meyer and Scott (1983) have suggested that schools as organizations enact public rituals of rationality in order to maintain their legitimacy with other institutions and agencies that are sources of the schools' funding and accreditation. A school maintains the confidence of its external environment, and thus its existence, by satisfying the demands of rationality that are imposed upon it by legislative bodies, the courts, state and federal bureaucracies, accrediting agencies, and business interests. Schools not only have to comply with these rational procedures, they also must maintain the appearance that the rational structures work (Meyer and Rowan, 1978).

Related to this notion of having to maintain the confidence of various external publics and agencies is the idea that internal confidence among members of the professional staff must be maintained as well (Carol and Cunningham, 1984). By helping teachers and administrators to establish direction and decide on procedures to follow, and by dramatizing the effectiveness and efficiency of the instructional program, supervisors may be a primary source of confidence for those who enact the program as well as those who view it and judge its success (the public and other institutions). Both internally and externally directed performances require extensive backstage preparation, which invisibility almost certainly facilitates.

Becoming More Visible

As noted earlier in this chapter, the consequences of remaining invisible and working behind the scenes are not always favorable for the instructional supervisor. Supervisors feel that they are sometimes overlooked at the local level when salary increases are awarded and at the state and national levels when proposals are made for instructional improvement. Ironically, the better a supervisor is at successfully promoting the work done by others, the less visible he or she becomes. "If you do a really good job," a curriculum director lamented, "it's like you do not exist."

Supervisors say that they are accustomed to not getting recognition for their efforts; they know that it comes with their job. But as an associate superintendent said, "Although it's not important to me to be the number-one man—I don't want to be—it's important to me for others to recognize my contributions and to tell me about them." A curriculum director, speaking about the supervision profession as a whole, observed: "We do things in a vacuum. . . . I just wish there was a way that we'd get more prominence for the things that we do behind the scenes." Implications of invisibility, thus, exist for both the individual practitioner and the profession as a whole.

Supervisors generally feel that it is inappropriate and, in fact, counterproductive to promote themselves publicly as the primary causal agents of success. Teachers, principals, and the superintendent are typically given credit instead. Even in situations where someone might actually attempt to present an award or other form of recognition to supervisors, they feel compelled to deflect attention away from themselves. This almost reflexive humility may contribute to the public's confidence in the schools and even inspire the mutual confidence of other professionals, that what teachers and administrators are doing has great value. The supervisor at times serves almost like a chorus in a Greek play, calling attention to the heroes of the drama and singing their praises.

One opportunity for central office supervisors to achieve a degree of internal visibility is before the school board. Perhaps this is because the board, too, occupies a position that is typically in the background. As one supervisor said:

> I don't think there's any invisibility for me with the board. You know, they know you're there. They may not understand the full magnitude of what you do, but at least you're more visible with them because you are at the board meetings with them. Every board meeting, you're there.

As with speaking before community groups, attendance at meetings of the school board provides a chance to impress the public with the quality of the instructional program and with one's own capabilities. One supervisor put it this way:

I try not to get my name in there too much, but the point is, in the process, they know I'm in charge of these programs. They see me present often enough at board meetings or at local functions. They know, if my name's not on there, at least I'm running the show. So that's good.

Another acceptable way to make oneself more visible, some supervisors believe, is to take steps to ensure that people associate the supervisor with success. This can be done "by leaving tracks" in subtle ways, while allowing others to continue in their visible roles as causal agents. Any communication or document originating in the supervisor's office, for example, should have the supervisor's name on it, some supervisors believe. The source of various memos, minutes of meetings, committee reports, and curriculum guides should be clear to everyone. Although other supervisors are uncomfortable with even this modest degree of self-promotion, it may be the only practical way of reminding people that although one may not be personally visible to them at every moment, the supervisor is in fact busily at work on improving or promoting some aspect of the instructional program. A curriculum coordinator explained how she accomplishes this:

I have made sure that [my job] is very visible. I have regular reports that I give to the board of education every week. I make sure that I get written reports to the superintendent constantly. I make sure that as many people as possible know what I'm doing, because otherwise I can just be excessed.

By this same token, establishing a physical presence in the schools is considered so high a priority by many supervisors that the interminable paperwork is set aside periodically so that visits to the schools can be made. The stated and intended purpose of these visits may be to improve instruction in the local buildings, but supervisors believe that the visits also demonstrate their continuing interest in the instructional program and a commitment to the people who implement it at the school and classroom levels. More often than not, such occasions provide an opportunity for the supervisor to deal with problems that teachers face or to react to new ideas that teachers may have. A curriculum director observed in this regard: "It's not just to go and drink coffee with them, but to get in and watch some of the programs we've set up."

The purpose of getting into the schools and classrooms obviously should never be to spy on teachers, but to demonstrate a helpful interest in what they are doing and the problems they face. This need was expressed by one supervisor in this way:

> The teachers really appreciated it when I first started visiting the schools and said, "Is there anything I can do to help? Are there things I can do to facilitate things for you? Can I watch you? I'm not going to write it up . . . , but can I just sit in here? Because I'd like to watch the way you operate with kids, with a computer, with doing stories, doing this and that." And they really appreciated it, because I think they too long felt neglected.

At the same time, this supervisor observed, there is no question that increased visibility in the schools also served to legitimize his role before his professional colleagues in the district:

> Everybody's a martyr in education. They think they're working the hardest and getting screwed the worst. They believe that. I think that you've got to let them know that you're there and that you're putting in an eight-to-five day like the rest of them.

Making certain that others are aware of one's presence and the services that one provides can ensure that the supervisor is recognized as an indispensable part of the team. An additional advantage is that it may actually make the supervisor's job easier by distributing responsibility for improvement onto a broader network. A curriculum director explained the importance of communicating with as many people in the school district as possible in terms of the assistance they can provide:

> I think that when you're visible, people will say, "Hey, you know, I could probably help you with this in computers because I know this person to contact," or, "I know some people who have expertise in this foreign-language thing," or "this thing we're doing in health," or, "I have this book you might be interested in," or something like that. I think that if they know what you're doing, it makes it easier for you.

In summary, because supervisors so often deflect recognition away from themselves and suggest publicly that success is actually due to "the hard work of our teachers," or "the unflagging support provided by our principals," or "the strong leadership of our superintendent," a difficulty may arise if people begin to take such statements at face value. As one supervisor observed, other professionals may ask each other, "If we're so good, then what do we need this guy for?" Augmenting one's visibility as a supervisor is therefore sometimes necessary to avoid becoming a victim of one's own success.

References

Blumberg, A. with Blumberg, P. 1985. *The school superintendent: Living with conflict.* New York: Teachers College Press.

Carol, L. N. & Cunningham, L. L. 1984. Views of public confidence in education. *Issues in Education,* 2 (2): 110–126.

Costa, A. & Guditis, C. 1984. Do district-wide supervisors make a difference? *Educational Leadership,* 41 (5): 84–85.

Meyer, J. W. & Rowan, B. 1978. Institutionalized organizations: Formal structure as myth and ceremony. *American Journal of Sociology,* 83 (2): 340–363.

Meyer, J. W. & Scott, W. R. 1983. *Organizational environments: Ritual and rationality.* Beverly Hills: Sage Publications.

12

The Backstage World of Classroom Supervision

The idea of looking at the classroom as a dramatic performance has been proposed many times (Grumet, 1976; Lessinger and Gillis, 1976; Horning, 1979; Milburn, 1985). One version of this notion explores the concept of teaching as dramatic expression and develops such themes as the classroom as theater, the teacher as actor, and the lesson as staging (Rubin, 1984). Evidence exists that some teachers in fact use a theatrical metaphor while making sense of classroom events (Jackson, 1968, p. 121; Ben-Peretz and Sheinman, 1987).

The theatrical metaphor has been applied less often as a way of understanding instructional supervision. The most fully developed conceptualization of instructional supervision from a theatrical perspective may be that of Lewis and Miel (1972), who proposed that the supervisor might be thought of as a kind of "critic" of teaching and the instructional environment. More recently, Zimmerman (1985) suggested that the theater also may provide some useful insights for understanding the functions of the position of central office instructional supervisor.

Supervisors frequently use language suggesting a theatrical metaphor when talking about their job responsibilities, often referring to themselves as working "behind the scenes" or "backstage," for example, and talking about the importance of not "upstaging the teacher" or "stealing the superintendent's limelight." For the most part, central office instructional supervisors believe that it is their work "backstage" that makes the instructional program succeed. They derive satisfaction from seeing the success of others, especially teachers and principals, who may be said to be more frequently "onstage" (Goffman, 1959). For example, one director of educational services explained:

> Now no one knows that or understands it, but the point is, that's what makes [instructional] programs run. [Supervision] is behind

the scenes—most of it is. . . . I guess I'm a bit of an egoist, and I like to be front and center with a high profile. Sometimes that works and sometimes it doesn't. But when I see a program working well, then I guess that's the reward you get from it.

Another supervisor similarly said: "For a person in this position to be successful, that person has to see others be successful and not steal their limelight."

The fully developed theme of "working backstage"—including work with principals, the superintendent, the school board, and teachers—is described more completely in the next chapter. This chapter presents six categories of behaviors that supervisors suggest represent the ways in which they work "backstage" with teachers: upgrading instructional materials and techniques, communicating informally, organizing groups, initiating and facilitating innovation, training staff, and rehearsing presentations to the school board.

Upgrading Instructional Materials and Techniques

In the minds of many educators, the phrase "supervision of instruction" has come to mean classroom observation followed by some form of feedback conference. According to the views of many central office supervisors, this definition is much too narrow. In fact, classroom observation is done rather infrequently by most district level supervisors, except when they are invited into a classroom by a teacher or principal who is particularly proud of what students are doing, when a tenure decision is to be made, or when a teacher is having a difficulty that the principal cannot resolve alone (Zimmerman, 1985).

Most supervisors say that the task of classroom observation typically falls to principals, mainly because the large numbers of teachers in school districts make frequent visits by central office supervisors impractical and ineffective. Some supervisors report that they try to avoid becoming involved in what one called "direct supervision" of teachers because evaluation is viewed as interfering with the informal working relationships they try to establish with the faculty.

Central office supervisors do sometimes serve as consultants, when asked by principals and teachers, the first step of which usually involves "sitting down and talking." Working backstage with individual teachers in this way is described by supervisors as largely a matter of upgrading resources and skills. In the words of a curriculum coordinator, it involves

> going in and working with [teachers] on their instructional materials, improving classroom techniques, you know, what they

need to do the job, . . . [and] helping them to get the kinds of things that they need.

The perspective and concerns of central office supervisors, however, usually lie beyond the solitary classroom. A curriculum director in another district explained that before deciding what to do about a problem that surfaced in a teacher's classroom, she thought about it a bit longer in her present role than she had when she was a principal. As a principal, she said, her inclination was to try to solve the problem as quickly as possible. Now, she believed, "there are no short-term answers and no quick fixes." The role of curriculum director required that she "step back and think, 'Is this an isolated problem or a more generic one?' " If the problem was simply one of a single teacher having difficulty with some aspect of instruction, then she offered to help, after explaining to the teacher why she was concerned about that particular area. But if the problem appeared to be part of a general pattern for a grade level, a school, or the district as a whole, her approach was much different and more typical of what central office supervisors refer to as working backstage with teachers.

Working backstage with teachers in one sense involves simply locating and obtaining appropriate instructional materials for classroom use. It includes "getting samples of good materials, getting activities to teachers, and getting good textbooks . . . and the tools that go along with them." The instructional materials and equipment that a teacher uses during a performance in the classroom might be considered analogous to the props that actors use when staging a play. Because "teachers don't have time to go out searching for materials every day," central office supervisors report that they act as links to state education agencies, textbook publishers, and colleges and universities that have instructional materials available.

Routine purchases and distribution of materials and supplies, according to most supervisors, are usually done by principals at the building level, with varying degrees of coordination from the central office. Supervisors often get directly involved, however, in the initial selection. As one district level supervisor explained:

> I help people by providing resources or providing information. One of my jobs is to be like Sherlock Holmes, in a way, and find materials for teachers . . . because they don't have the time.

Supervisors not only locate instructional materials that have district-wide application, they also stay alert for special types of materials needed by individuals or requested by groups of teachers who have common interests. Generally, successful district-level supervisors have confidence in most teachers' abilities to use these instructional materials appropriately and independently within the constraints of the curriculum. Thus, working backstage with some teachers can be simply a matter of "giving them materials and letting them go ahead in their classes."

Communicating Informally

Another way that central office instructional supervisors say that they work backstage with teachers is by spending time in the local school buildings, making themselves accessible to teachers for the purpose of solving problems. An associate superintendent for instruction said that "going into the buildings and talking" to teachers was very important. "Slipping into the teachers' lounge and talking, just being there," provided opportunities for teachers to relate both problems and successes to him. A district coordinator explained it this way:

> I think you should be in the buildings; you should be walking around, talking to people informally, hearing what they have to say, having lunch with them. I think that if they have something to tell you, it breaks the ice. It gives them a chance to say, "Oh, by the way, now what do you think of this?". . . When you're too busy to do this, you're not doing your job.

Problems that teachers typically face were reported to range from local shortages of supplies to serious concerns about the curriculum. By being physically present in the schools on a regular basis, supervisors learn firsthand about general difficulties teachers are facing and can try to remedy them. By dealing with such issues directly, disruptions to the implementation of the instructional program are apparently minimized. Supervisors sometimes will work especially closely with a principal and faculty in a single school to improve its overall instructional effectiveness, focusing energy, funds, and materials there until improvement is shown.

Organizing Groups

Supervisors explain that they actively try to involve others in the backstage work of the school, rather than trying to do everything themselves. Providing opportunities for teachers to work together on committees seems to be a common way of accomplishing this end. Assigning responsibility to groups of teachers for tasks such as selecting textbooks, developing instructional programs, or planning in-service is viewed by supervisors as desirable because teachers become more self-invested and committed to the final decision or product.

Supervisors also believe that opportunities for cooperating with colleagues in making decisions about professional matters help build teachers' self-esteem and confidence, particularly when teachers receive some type of public acknowledgment for their work. Saying that he wished he could pay teachers more for their contributions to curriculum development during the summer months, a district supervisor commented:

> They get $55 a day. Big deal. That's really not much money when you think about it. And it's a lot of work, because they do a lot of work behind the scenes. They do a lot of work during the year, . . . after they're finished with [the curriculum], to get it all ready for publication and all that. So they don't get rich at it, but . . . their ego is invested and they do get the credit, and they do get the things done that are important.

Another important outcome of working backstage with groups of teachers, according to supervisors, is that it helps develop a sense of teamwork, shared responsibility, and mutual confidence. Developing this sense of team membership may compensate for the fact that the nature of teachers' work onstage—in the classroom—tends to be isolating. A necessary part of developing a capacity for teamwork, as supervisors see it, is a willingness by the supervisor to allow teachers to assume leadership and take credit for accomplishments. A curriculum director explained it as follows:

> There are times when you really need to be the supportive member of the team and let others carry the leadership role. You can provide a lot of help, a lot of support, but let the other [person] take charge . . .

Another curriculum coordinaor said:

> Our role is not one of pushing but leading. And not leading in a way to be directing, but trying to be unassuming and a team, where it's a balance of all, rather than one person.

Initiating and Facilitating Innovation

Supervisors often use the terms "initiating" and "facilitating" to describe the backstage nature of their jobs. These behaviors seem to follow one another sequentially in actual practice. "Initiating" refers to the process of identifying an area for needed improvement and introducing a project or course of action. This is often done in response to a direct request from teachers or principals. "Facilitating" relates to providing encouragement and support for the ideas and processes that emerge within a group composed of teachers who are involved in planning or implementing the project. An associate superintendent, for example, said:

> I've got a couple of pilot things going now, out in the schools, that I personally initiated through a request of a principal, or having sent them a challenge saying, "I'm ready, I'll give you all the resources in my office."

A curriculum coordinator explained:

> A part of my job is starting something, . . . and then providing the support and the behind-the-scenes help, without always being the one in charge, or leading the group. . . . What you do is facilitate the leadership in an individual school so that something can happen within that school that's good.

Many supervisors report that they make suggestions, provide materials, and introduce information and ideas continually, while allowing a group to develop its own identity and ultimately its own direction. Because their responsibilities are so diverse, supervisors frequently are unable to "follow through and complete" projects that they have begun. Processes are initiated and support provided, in other words, but the actual tasks are often completed by others.

Supervisors report that they sometimes formulate a tentative initial plan of action based upon a group's discussion, which is then used as a springboard for further deliberation. Such facilitative activities are seen as necessary because teachers ordinarily lack the time, due to their classroom instructional responsibilities, to attend to such backstage committee functions themselves.

Facilitation of the group sometimes means the supervisor has to support people's efforts even when he or she disagrees personally with the direction the group is taking. Many supervisors seem to believe generally that a "hands-off" approach is best when working with committees of teachers because in the end the collective "wisdom of the group" will prevail. One supervisor suggested that in planning for in-service, it is important to know one's teaching staff and understand their point of view because "my role is [as] a facilitator. . . . My role is to understand where they're coming from and to work at grassroots."

In bigger districts, with large numbers of committees, the supervisor often really has little choice but to allow curriculum and in-service planning committees considerable autonomy once they are established. Because of other duties and commitments, he or she may attend only the first and last meetings of a committee—and perhaps one or two others, if specifically asked by teachers for help or for more information.

Training Staff

In-service training, according to supervisors, most frequently deals with either new classroom techniques or changes in federal, state, or local policies, of which teachers have to be apprised. In one sense, an in-service or staff development session may be thought of as a kind of rehearsal of the instructional program. A curriculum coordinator said:

> Whenever you do any in-service with teachers, you're doing a behind-the-scenes preparation for their performance back with the kids.

At times supervisors conduct training sessions themselves, but at other times they hire outside consultants. Many say that they involve teachers in making presentations whenever possible. In another sense, therefore, a staff development meeting may itself be considered as a kind of performance that the supervisor produces and stages for internal audiences. In either case, preparation for in-service involves "backstage" work in terms of organizational logistics and rallying support:

> You've got to make sure that you've got in-service days, that you've got people who are supporting you, that you start where you have your strength and not your weakness.

Another supervisor explained:

> When you meet with the group to begin a project or make plans for something, you need to be knowledgeable about what you're doing and then just be prepared. Always be prepared to the greatest extent that you can, then be willing to stand back and let others be in the limelight whenever they can.

Careful preparation, again, is followed by active support in the forms of resources and encouragement. The supervisor may track down information needed by a group in order to proceed. A director of educational services related the following example:

> When we did the foreign language study, . . . we sent away to thirty-nine districts across the country that are doing foreign language in the elementary schools. We got twenty-one responses. We then "Xeroxed" copies for each teacher on the committee, and they did their homework by reading the material. If I had said, "Well, find whatever you can," hell, we wouldn't have gotten anything done with it. But I took it upon myself to send off to all these different districts. I feel that's an important resource I can play: to get information, find materials for them, and so on. Then we can get down to the important part of reading, digesting, and tailoring the program to [our district].

Rehearsing Presentations to the School Board

Written guides that are products of curriculum committees or demonstrations of innovative instructional techniques utilized by teachers represent a culmination of committee work. As such, they are frequently staged as special presentations for the board of education. Besides being informational, these programs dramatize to the board and the public the positive aspects of the instructional performances that are staged daily for the student audience. These presentations to the school board tend to be quite formal and can involve considerable preparation on the part of teachers and the instructional supervisor.

An assistant superintendent described how she had recently met with two elementary teachers and coached them about such details as what to wear to a board meeting at which they were presenting a curriculum project. After making suggestions regarding timing and after reviewing the visual aids the teachers had prepared, the supervisor had the teachers actually rehearse their presentation, while she played the part of the board of education. When asked why it was important to spend so much time on preparing for this presentation, the assistant superintendent replied:

> Because you want them to come through in a positive way with the board. You don't want anybody to fall flat on their face when they're in that kind of public situation, with the public . . . and the board there. They are the decision makers for the school system, and the policy makers. And you want your [teachers] to come through in a positive way.

The Role of Teacher

According to role theory, social interaction of any kind requires that an actor communicate an idea to another actor or an audience. While actors in the theater follow a fixed script from the beginning of a performance to its end, in ordinary life people continually adjust and modify their presentations according to the responses of the listeners. The theater, therefore, may be said to be "script driven," while everyday social interaction is "character driven" (Hare, 1985). In other words, outside the theater, people are freer to make up their own scripts as they live their lives. If what one says and does is not getting the reaction desired, for example, one's script can be changed in midsentence (or midlife), if necessary.

Teaching seems to fall somewhere between script-driven theater and character-driven social interaction (see Figure 12.1). Teachers are constrained, in a very real sense, by predetermined behaviors, routines, and vocalizations to a greater extent than individuals engaged in normal social intercourse. A teacher has a set of specific information, ideas, and skills to communicate to students in a certain length of time. Both the lesson plan and the curriculum may thus be thought of as representing types of scripts that the teacher follows when conducting a lesson.

On the other hand, a teacher interacts with the audience (students) to a greater extent than is possible for actors in the theater in order to be certain that the message transmitted is in fact received. The teacher will slow down, or back up and repeat a portion of the performance (more than once if necessary), or even skip ahead a bit if the audience is quickly catching on to the main ideas. Thus, good teaching is necessarily also character driven to a large degree, because

**FIGURE 12.1
DEGREES OF ROLE ENACTMENT**

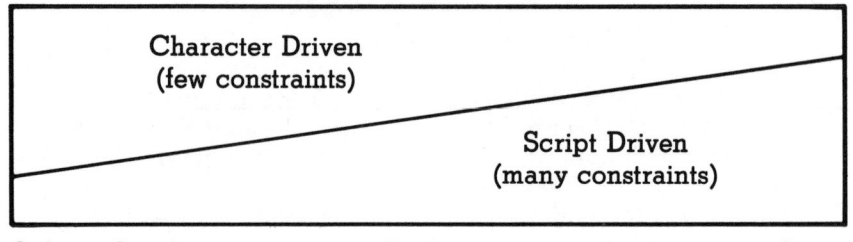

Character Driven
(few constraints)

Script Driven
(many constraints)

Ordinary Social Interaction — Teaching — Acting

the teacher adjusts the performance to the reaction (or lack of reaction) of the students.

This analogy with theater also reminds us that the word "performance" has more than a single meaning. On the one hand, there is the functional, or instrumental, meaning of "executing a behavior," which is often used among educators in phrases such as "student performance," "performance objective," or "performance test." Another common meaning of the word "performance," however, refers to an expressive dimension of behavior, as in the phrase "dramatic performance" or the more general "artistic performance."

All human social behavior, in fact, may be viewed as having a functional dimension as well as an expressive dimension. The blink of an eye serves to soothe irritation, for example, while the wink of an eye expresses a message, e.g., "I'm kidding," or "I'm interested." Similarly, a person's voice, manner of walking, and other behaviors convey impressions to observers that may or may not be intended by the person being observed. Clarity of communication is enhanced when the functional and expressive dimensions complement and reinforce one another. Yet a discrepancy between the two often will attract and hold our interest. Implicit in the theatrical metaphor, as applied to teaching, is the idea that teachers can become more effective by improving the expressive as well as the functional dimension of their classroom performances.

The Supervisor as Theatrical Director

Several authors have based recommendations for the practice of instructional supervision upon a theatrical metaphor of teaching (Lewis and Miel, 1972; Horning, 1979; Milburn, 1985). In each case, the suggestion has been made that the instructional supervisor ought to function as a "critic" of classroom performance. According to this view, the supervisor observes a classroom lesson and focuses attention on specific elements, which tend to vary from author to author.

Lewis and Miel (1972), for example, suggest that the supervisor-as-critic should attend to aspects of the craft and artistry of teaching, to hidden assumptions and values of the teacher, and to the cultural context of teaching. Horning (1979) recommends that "critics" of teaching ought to analyze elements such as setting, structure, theme, and plot, as well as stage presence and style of the teacher.

More recently, Milburn (1985) has illustrated by means of a case study how a supervisor-as-critic can focus on the human presence in the classroom. Among other things, he suggests that the classroom observer make note of the development of character and activity within the act, identifiable segments and connections between them, the influence of prevailing conventions, the utilization of space, the unfolding of thought, and unique features of the act.

Although the conception of the supervisor-as-critic is an illuminating and potentially valuable perspective for certain types of interactions, a major limitation is that it tends to focus attention on the "onstage" performance of the teacher while overlooking those preparatory behaviors "backstage" that make the performance possible and in large measure determine its quality. It is this "backstage" realm where successful district level supervisors suggest they make the greatest contribution to teacher effectiveness.

Thinking of the supervisor as a "director" of performance, rather than as a critic of performance, may better capture the reality of the role of central office supervisor. For example, materials that are located by the supervisor—such as textbooks, audiovisuals, worksheets, and computer software—are, in effect, the "props" utilized by teachers in staging their lessons. The selection and preparation of such props and their incorporation into an "onstage" lesson, of course, takes place "backstage" prior to the actual classroom performance. Occasionally, however, central office supervisors may coach individuals on specific techniques for improving their performance. Supervisors report that the suggestions they make in such cases are offered more in the spirit of a critique than criticism.

By making themselves available to teachers informally during the school day, supervisors learn firsthand about potential obstacles to the "onstage" instructional performance of individuals and groups of teachers. Much as a theatrical director might attend to minor details while the actors are busily involved in enacting a dramatic performance, supervisors identify and solve emerging problems informally "backstage," before they develop into full-scale disruptions to the instructional performance.

Supervisors-as-directors involve others in the backstage work of the school by establishing committees to deal with generic problems at the grade, building, or district level. In some districts networks of standing curriculum committees encourage commitment, confidence, and a sense of unity of direction and purpose among the faculty. A cohesive team with members who trust one another is essential for successfully producing an onstage performance (Goffman, 1959). Getting teachers to work backstage with colleagues is believed by practicing supervisors to promote such cohesiveness and trust.

In-service training may be thought of as a type of rehearsal for what teachers do in their classrooms. It, too, usually involves a performance or presentation of some kind. Often, like a true rehearsal, in-service sessions allow participants opportunities to practice what they have learned. The actual planning and preparation for an in-service meeting, furthermore, may be thought of as being still farther backstage than the session itself. Supervisors may "cast" an outside consultant or another member of the professional staff as the presenter. Or, when supervisors conduct in-service sessions themselves, the backstage preparation supports their own performance onstage, before the faculty. The inherent backstage nature of staff development work is evident in that, even when making a formal presentation to the professional staff, supervisors are still backstage with respect to the school system's major audiences: students, parents, and other taxpayers.

Curriculum development, from a theatrical perspective, is especially interesting because it involves nothing less than writing and rewriting the "script" that is followed by teachers during their classroom performances. The practice of involving teachers in this process disperses the function of "author" to the "actors" themselves and contributes further to the character-driven quality of teaching.

Thus, as "director," the supervisor is allowed access "backstage" and may help teachers individually and collectively plan with "scripting" and "staging" their lessons. The supervisor-as-director is someone who is trusted as being interested in helping individual teachers and groups of teachers present the best possible performance to their primary audience, the students, as well as to secondary audiences of the teacher's performance, which include other teachers, the principal, the school board, and the public. Whether the performance goes well or poorly, as in the theater, the director shares responsibility for its success or failure.

Supervisors who think of their role as one of critic, on the other hand, are likely to run into considerable difficulty getting an accurate assessment of instructional performance. The chances of their being able to contribute to the improvement of instruction are therefore very limited. The tendency of even chronically insubordinate students to protect their teacher from a negative evaluation, by becoming models of decorum whenever the supervisor is in the classroom, is well known.

The use of "stage cues" by teachers to let colleagues know when the central office supervisor is in the building, such as sending an eraser from room to room, likewise presents an obstacle to determining what is actually happening instructionally in a particular school (Blumberg, 1974). Principals may view the critical supervisor as a spy from the district office who is looking for something negative to report to the superintendent. Thus, students, teachers, and principal may consciously or unconsciously conspire in presenting a false image to the habitually critical supervisor whenever he or she visits a local school building.

The supervisor-as-critic is limited to evaluating a lesson only on the basis of the observable performance. With no participation in, and little knowledge of, the backstage preparation that makes a lesson possible, the critic is aware of only the "act" that is performed for his or her benefit. This act may or may not reflect the reality of daily life in the classroom.

Thinking and behaving as a director, in contrast, enables supervisors to contribute in a variety of ways to the backstage preparation of the instructional performance that is enacted by teachers. The director may critique a lesson with an eye for improving the backstage preparation, the onstage enactment, or both. Thus, the supervisor-as-critic sees only an illusion conjured up by the teacher, while the supervisor-as-director participates in the reality of lesson preparation and instructional improvement.

It should be mentioned that it would be incorrect to think of the central office supervisor as merely a "gofer" for individual teachers or committees, although some supervisors say that they voluntarily and consciously fulfill this function from time to time. A director of educational services explained his relationship to the onstage performance in this way:

> People by and large know that if I'm not up there leading the way, . . . I'm there tinkering behind the scenes, running whatever's going on or getting things going. I don't mind being a gofer. I don't mind making phone calls, doing all the things to get somebody the things they need, when they've got the expertise.

Most supervisors, in fact, report that they take a more assertive approach in promoting district-wide considerations. The individual just quoted, for example, also said that a group of teachers occasionally must be "arm-wrestled" away from a self-serving perspective and toward a direction that is beneficial to the entire district. Supervisors generally prefer to avoid strong-arm tactics, however, and are more likely to limit in advance the direction a committee can take, if they think it is necessary, by initially selecting needs that are in line with district priorities.

Although they function primarily backstage, supervisors are constantly generating new ideas and looking for practical ways of improving instruction. One individual pointed out that the central office supervisor's backstage supportiveness, although indirect, is not at all an indication of passivity:

We need to be constantly trying to do something out there to improve the operation for which we are responsible. And in the end, the kids are going to gain from that. So I think that a major role of the [associate] superintendent for instruction ought to be continually looking for new and better ways to do things [in classrooms] and promoting those ideas with the staff.

On Classroom Observation

As noted earlier, in terms of both time allocation and expenditure of effort, formal classroom observations represent a comparatively minor part of a central office instructional supervisor's job-related activities. The fact that district level supervisors do occasionally work with individual teachers, however, and the popularity of classroom observation as a prescription for improving instruction warrants a few words about how the supervisor-as-director might approach this responsibility when called upon to do so.

When originally conceived, "clinical supervision" essentially represented an engagement of teachers and supervisors in a collegial dialogue for the purpose of improving instruction by solving problems directly at the classroom level. It was intended to eliminate meaningless ritual in schools (Goldhammmer, 1969), and it involved peerlike interaction between teachers and supervisors as they jointly planned lessons and shared responsibility for successes and failures (Cogan, 1973). Since the early 1970s, however, as the popularity of the term "clinical supervision" has steadily increased, its meaning seems to have been altered drastically. Though the words "clinical supervision" are now invoked by practically every author in the area of instructional improvement, the phrase frequently describes a technique used by administrative superordinates for monitoring and evaluating teacher behavior.

A lesser known version of the preconference, observation, postconference cycle was once proposed in a model by Hill (1968), which he called "I-B-F supervision." The letters I-B-F stand for "image," "behavior," and "feedback," and they represent the major themes of each phrase of the traditional supervisory cycle. According to this model, the preobservation conference begins with the supervisor helping the teacher to express the ideal "image" that he or she wishes to project in the classroom lesson to be observed. Hill defines "image" as a mental picture held by the teacher of the role he or she wishes to play with respect to such things as the relationship with students, instructional skills, and classroom management. The classroom image is presumably based on a teacher's prior experiences, training, values, and attitudes and is likely to vary from person to person and over a period of time. A similar use of imagery for enhancing the lives of individuals in therapeutic situations has been described more recently by several authors (Kelly, 1974; Forisha, 1978; Gowan, 1978).

Assuming that teachers strive to behave in a manner that they believe is consistent with the ideal image they want to project, Hill suggests that the supervisor should try to help the teacher to state as specifically as possible the behaviors that he or she intends to enact while attempting to achieve the image desired, along with the behaviors that students are expected to enact. During the observation phase the supervisor then records instances when the intended behaviors are seen to occur. The resulting data and other artifacts provided by the teacher are later discussed during the postobservation, or feedback, conference session, which focuses on consistencies and discrepancies between the ideal image and the actual enactment of the lesson.

Among the advantages of I-B-F supervision identified by Hill (1968) is that the elaboration through discussion of the ideal image of the lesson provides intrinsic motivation for the teacher to study objectively and plan his or her teaching behavior. The teacher thus perceives the need to change because of differences between the real and ideal: the need for change is not imposed. The supervisor serves mainly by helping the teacher to identify ways of reducing possible discrepancies between real teaching behaviors and the ideal image. This process is fairly nonthreatening to the teacher because attention is focused on images and behaviors rather than on the worth of the teacher or quality of the lesson.

Social action can be analyzed using five categories of dramatic action: "what was done (act), when or where it was done (scene), who did it (agent), how he did it (agency), and why (purpose)" (Burke, 1969). This same framework has been suggested very recently as a useful guide for decision making in schools (Wales, Nardi, and Sager, 1986). By addressing such questions while planning a lesson or analyzing observation data, a teacher and supervisor may be able to understand better both the functional and the expressive dynamics at work in a classroom. Teachers may be helped to think of their own behavior in the classroom in terms of roles they must play. Be stepping out of their usual role, they may try out different roles to achieve the kinds of classroom results they want.

I-B-F supervision is compatible with the backstage metaphor of supervision because it emphasizes the teacher's construction of an image to be projected and the supervisor's role in helping the teacher to enact that image successfully. In effect, the supervisor helps the teacher to interpret and bring to life the script that the teacher has written for a praticular lesson. The part played by the supervisor in determining the degree to which the image has been achieved and in helping to reduce discrepancies between reality and the ideal enactment are also similar to the functions performed by a theatrical director.

References

Ben-Peretz, M. & Sheinman, S. 1987. *Gestures and context: The classroom as theater.* Paper presented at the Annual Meeting of the American Educational Research Association. Washington, D.C.

Blumberg, A. 1974. *Supervisors and teachers: A private cold war.* Berkeley: McCutchan.

Burke, K. 1969. *A grammar of motives.* Berkeley: University of California Press.

Cogan, M. 1973. *Clinical supervision.* Boston: Houghton Mifflin.

Forisha, B. L. 1978. Mental imagery and creativity. *Journal of Mental Imagery,* 2 (2): 209–238.

Goffman, E. 1959. *The presentation of self in everyday life.* New York: Doubleday Anchor.

Goldhammer, R. 1969. *Clinical supervision: Special methods for the supervision of teachers.* New York: Holt, Rinehart & Winston.

Gowan, J. C. 1978. Incubation, imagery, and creativity. *Journal of Mental Imagery,* 2 (1): 23–32.

Grumet, M. R. 1976. Toward a poor curriculum. In W. F. Pinar & M. R. Grumet (eds.), *Toward a poor curriculum.* Dubuque, Iowa: Kendall/Hunt.

Hare, A. P. 1985. *Social interaction as drama.* Beverly Hills: Sage Publications.

Hill, W. M. 1968. I-B-F supervision: A technique for changing teacher behavior. *The Clearing House,* 43 (3): 180–183.

Horning, A. S. 1979. Teaching as performance. *The Journal of General Education,* 31 (3): 185–194.

Jackson, P. W. 1968. *Life in classrooms.* New York: Holt, Rinehart & Winston.

Kelly, G. F. 1974. Mental imagery in counseling. *Personnel and Guidance Journal,* 53 (2): 111–116.

Lessinger, L. & Gillis, D. 1976. *Teaching as a performing art.* Dallas: Crescendo Publications.

Lewis, A. J. & Miel, A. 1972. *Supervision for improved instruction.* Belmont: Wadsworth.

Milburn, G. 1985. Deciphering a code or unraveling a riddle: A case study in the application of a humanistic metaphor to the reporting of social studies teaching. *Theory and Research in Social Education,* 13 (3): 21–44.

Rubin, L. 1984. *Artistry in teaching*. New York: Random House.
Wales, C. F., Nardi, A. M., & Stager, R. A. 1986. Decision making: New paradigm for education. *Educational Leadership*, 43 (8): 37–41.
Zimmerman, I. K. 1985. Changing roles, differing perspectives. *The Principal's Center Newsletter: Harvard Graduate School of Education*, 4 (2): 7–8.

13
The Backstage World of Central Office Supervision

It is not enough for educators simply to do a good job, several supervisors suggested, they must also be perceived as doing a good job. Administrators and school board members, as well as teachers, are concerned with the images they project through their actions and how they are perceived by others. An important part of the supervisor's responsibilities seems to involve helping others to create and maintain a positive public image of the district's instructional program. Sometimes this concern with image requires rehearsals of performances and careful attention to staging by the teachers and administrators who are more directly and more visibly involved with instruction. Furthermore, it seems that the audiences of the instructional program are multiple and include people both within the outside the formal school district organization.

A theatrical metaphor for understanding human behavior was suggested by Burke (1941) as a supplement to the mechanistic metaphors that dominate the behavioral and social sciences. He proposed the dramatic perspective "as the logical alternative to the treatment of human acts and relations in terms of the mechanistic metaphor," but added, "mechanistic considerations need not be *excluded* from such a perspective, but take their part in it, as a statement about the predisposing structure of the *ground* or *scene* upon which the drama is enacted."

This is to say, with respect to schools, the traditional concerns of administration, such as finance, law, scheduling, plant management, and transportation, may be appropriately thought of in mechanistic terms because they represent the "background" against which the "drama" of education is enacted. But our understanding of such human processes as classroom instruction and instructional supervision are severely limited when they are treated in the same manner.

Goffman (1959) elaborated upon the metaphor of drama for the purpose of analyzing social interaction, especially as it occurs within institutions and organizations. He demonstrated that behavior may be categorized and analyzed as occurring onstage, backstage, or offstage. Thus, much of the work done by supervisors of instruction in the school district may be thought of as occurring "backstage" of the official "onstage" public performance that is enacted by teachers, principals, and superintendents.

When viewed in terms of drama, the central office supervisor's role is seen to involve much more than simply making technical adjustments to the instructional program. Working with teachers, for example, requires from the supervisor a simultaneous awareness and anticipation of the reactions of multiple audiences: students, other teachers, administrators, parents, and taxpayers. Both functional and expressive dimensions of events and procedures must also be considered.

Thinking about schools and educational processes in terms of theatrical imagery certainly does not simplify things for us. In fact, it complicates our understanding of how things work by adding multiple dimensions of meaning. Complicating our understanding a little, however, may be a necessary antecedent to grasping the complexity of the reality of school districts as organizations and the contributions that central office supervisors make to their preformance.

The Backstage Perspective

A few years ago, *The New York Times* published an interview with the director of a highly acclaimed Broadway musical production. The director was asked by the reporter if, in staging the musical, he had achieved the objectives he had set out to accomplish. His response to this question was something along these lines: "As a director, I never work toward objectives. I play with images instead." In a similar sense, it might be said that instructional supervisors "play with images," the images that teachers, principals, superintendents, and school boards project to their various audiences. Of course, the functional dimension of a school district's performance requires that these images relate in some way to definite outcomes, which are often stated as objectives.

Supervisors generally suggest that the audiences of the instructional program are multiple and include people both within and outside the formal organization. A curriculum coordinator in one district included as audiences only people and agencies that view the schools from the outside, occasionally, or from a distance. She identified parents and the local community, the state department of education, state standards committees, and professional accrediting associations. In Goffman's (1959) terms, external audiences such as these may be thought of as being offstage. A curriculum director in another district, however, when asked about his use of an analogy with drama responded to the question "Who is the audience?" as follows:

> Teachers, the board of education, the community, I think they're all the audience. . . . and also kids.

Although the people who occupy various positions within schools may be considered to be audiences of the instructional program, they are by no means passive observers. Students, teachers, and administrators generally cooperate in staging performances for each other, as well as for people and agencies external to the school. Students help to dramatize the success of the instructional program for the "offstage" audiences, for example, through artistic and athletic performances (plays, games, contests, and pageants) or through demonstrations of activities in which they are involved at meetings of the PTA or the school board.

Similarly, superintendents give speeches at meetings of community groups and make public presentations at board meetings extolling the virtues of the local academic program. Central office staff spend a great deal of time ensuring that state department paperwork is completed, that federal reports are filed, and that deadlines for grants are met. In each of these examples, a performance of some type may be said to be staged to project an image to the public or outside agencies that the school is responsibly and competently doing its job (Meyer and Scott, 1983).

What goes on in schools can be interpreted as drama on several levels. The images projected and impressions fostered by individual actors within a school as they go about their daily activities and interact with one another is one possible level of analysis. Looking at the school as an organization in terms of the ways it strives to maintain legitimacy and viability within its environment (Meyer and Scott, 1983) represents another dimension. Between these micro and macro levels of interprettion lies a third possibility, that of examining the relationship between the among various groupings (i.e., students, teachers, and administrators) within the school system.

This third alternative is most useful for understanding the relationship of central office supervisors to those who occupy other positions in the school. When asked what happens "onstage" and who the "audience" is in schools, supervisors frequently indicate that students, teachers, principals, superintendents, school boards, and central office supervisors themselves are both actors and audiences at different times. In other words, these levels function alternately as spectators to each other's performances while they interact with one another within the school context.

While it is important for those who occupy various positions in schools to do an adequate job according to some objective standard, as noted earlier, it is also important for them to be perceived as doing a good job by both internal and external audiences. Students, teachers, administrators, and school board members, thus, may be viewed as independently and collaboratively performing for one another as well as for the public.

Working Backstage with Principals

Principals have a number of audiences to whom they play, most directly to teachers and the superintendent, but also to students, parents, and the school board. One way that supervisors say they work "backstage" with principals is by trying to improve the classroom performance of an individual teacher or a group of teachers at the school level.

Classroom observations of individual teachers by central office supervisors occur most often, it seems, when supervisors are called into the schools as third-party consultants by principals (Zimmerman, 1985). When done collaboratively and in a spirit of professionalism, the supervisor's and principal's skills can complement one another. A high level of instructional leadership may be generated as they work with teachers on simultaneously improving both the "backstage" and "onstage" aspects of instruction. However, situations that are likely to breed mistrust quickly occur if the supervisor works "backstage" with the principal to establish documentation for teacher dismissal. This practice immediately casts the supervisor in the role of critic rather than director, even if it occurs unwittingly, and eliminates the supervisor's access to the "backstage" of teachers. Little more than cosmetic improvements to teachers' classroom performance can then be expected.

Another way that supervisors say that they work backstage with principals is by serving as a mediator or consultant in the principal's dealings with the superintendent. Gaining access to the principal's backstage world is important if supervisors are to be effective in helping them solve problems and difficulties at the school level. Ideally, principals come to recognize the value of working with the supervisor and offer access to their school without the supervisor having constantly to earn it. Because supervisors have more contact with the superintendent, they can informally provide useful advice to principals concerning the superintendent's preferences and priorities. A curriculum coordinator, for example, observed:

> You help principals . . . if they really need something. If they need somebody to get to the superintendent [informally], very often you'll do that, so that you can become kind of a helper to them.

A district coordinator similarly explained:

> I work backstage with [principals] on their budgets, helping them to get their budgets in line so that they will have a better chance of getting what they ask for.

The supervisor's ability to help in this way is dependent in part on the principal's willingness to disclose ordinarily private information about himself and his school. Supervisors can establish trust over time by contributing positively to the principal's image and by taking care not to undermine it. Access to the "backstage" of the school may be gained, in other words, by repeatedly demonstrating that one is interested in enhancing the impression that others have of the principal's performance. A curriculum coordinator explained how he did this while running a summer school program at an elementary school in his district. At every meeting attended by parents concerning the summer program,

> we always introduce him as our host principal and say how cooperative he is. . . . We always mention him in articles in the paper. We always get a picture of him with the kids. . . . Now he's not playing any active role at all in the program—at all! We just borrowed his school.

In exchange for such image building, according to the supervisor, this principal actually began to feel that he was a part of the instructional program and was willing literally to unlock doors, secure cooperation from custodians, and actively seek the housing of the summer program at his school for the next year. The curriculum director continued:

> His role is very tangential, to say the least, but the point is, we don't say, "We're taking over and see you in September." He feels that's important to him. He looks good with his own folks, because a number of his own [students] are in the program. It looks like he's one of the "pooh-bahs" in the organization.

Supervisors can also contribute positively to the image that principals project to their teachers. It is difficult for principals to play the part of instructional leader, if they are unfamiliar with the "script" or "props" that teachers utilize in the classroom. One way the supervisor can assist principals is by providing in-service training for them that relates to the district-wide instructional-improvement thrusts. A curriculum coordinator, for example, described how he convinced a group of reluctant principals to attend a workshop on computer utilization with the argument that they would otherwise "look bad" in front of their teachers, who were receiving more intensive training:

> And I said, "Well, that's nice, to have [computer instruction] the biggest emphasis in the district, and you guys don't know how to turn [a computer] on or what to do [with one].

The curriculum coordinator in this case suggested hypothetically to the principals that a teacher might approach them with a piece of broken equipment some day, and while they certainly would not be expected to fix it, they at least ought to know the name of the equipment piece and have a general idea of what it was supposed to do when it worked. The coordinator said that the principals quickly became "very appreciative" of the two-hour in-service sessions, which met once a week for ten weeks, when the relevance of the content was explained in those terms. The importance of image building or "impression management" (Goffman, 1959) is evident in that the point of the in-service was not to get principals to use computers, it was to give them only a general familiarity with computers. This ensured that principals maintained credibility with their teachers. The curriculum director continued:

> Now they're literate. They may not be able to program; they can't. But that's not important. The thing is, they can fake their way through it now. And I think it makes them look good when they're up there [saying], "Every one of you is going to teach [about computers] this year." And the teachers are saying, "Yeah. You don't even know how to turn the thing on."

Working Backstage with the Superintendent

The superintendent is very much a visible symbol of the school system in the community. Because the superintendent is constantly in the public's view, it is important that he or she, as well as the instructional program, "looks good" in terms of the image that is projected. Mutual trust and loyalty, it seems, are at the core of the relationship between the superintendent and the central office supervisor.

Lewis and Miel (1972) suggest that the superintendent is somewhat akin to a producer of the public performance staged by the school district. The superintendent, however, is also the district's primary author and principal actor. (Both "author" and "actor," according to the *Oxford English Dictionary*, can be traced to the Latin root "auctor," which means "originator"; it is also the root of the word "authority.") The superintendent formulates policy governing the district, and in doing so "authors" the "script" that others will follow. Unlike the typical playwright, however, the superintendent is expected to enact the performance as well. The superintendent must interpret the script through his or her actions before the public, the school board, and professional colleagues (Pajak, 1987). A part of the supervisor's job, according to one participant, is to "make the superintendent look good," while being careful at the same time that one does "not steal his limelight."

Because the superintendent plays an active part in "frontstage" school affairs, he or she cannot easily attend to the "backstage" matters that ensure a smooth and credible overall performance. Attending to the projection of a positive image for the district is a full-time job in itself. The supervisor's responsibility, in part, is to make certain that the district's "script" is enacted by others in a way that is consistent with the intended image of the instructional program. Roles enacted by principals and teachers ideally complement the role being performed by the superintendent.

An associate superintendent explained how, when he first assumed his current position, he met with an official at the state department of education who gave him some advice that he thought had proved accurate and useful:

> He said to me, "You know, you think you're going in there as the planner for your district. But that will not be the case. It doesn't work that way in school districts." He said, "The real planner is the superintendent. He will plan with the board." And he said, "You are going to be the implementer of those plans. You're going to support and carry out." And he was really right on target, I think.

As a "director," however, the supervisor has considerable room to interpret the superintendent's plans, or script. Supervisors in most cases seem to have considerable autonomy to introduce new ideas and allow modifications when working in conjunction with principals at the school level. Supervisors uniformly warn, however, that the superintendent should be kept closely informed of progress and developments as changes in interpretations occur.

Central office supervisors seem to accept as part of their job the responsibility for helping the superintendent deliver as smooth a performance as possible. This may include gathering background information or writing reports and speeches for the superintendent—even appearing in public as his or her proxy. Superintendents and supervisors usually cooperate closely in making backstage preparations for any presentation to the public or school board:

> Everything we do with the board of education we have gone over as a central office staff. We get our act together before we meet with the board of education. That's important, because if you're not prepared, you can get caught in public with a lot of problems.

Sometimes supervisors get directly involved in protecting the integrity of the superintendent's image. Besides providing background information and rehearsing meetings, supervisors also stay alert for possible intrusions or disruptions that might embarrass the superintendent by catching him unprepared. An associate superintendent in a large district related the story of how a high school principal had spent money that was ordinarily allocated for library books to purchase computers and other instructional equipment. This misappropriation was not noticed until the district began preparing for reaccreditation, and it became evident that the library would not meet the standards of the accrediting agency because the number of books in the library was insufficient.

In an attempt to shift responsibility for the problem to the central office and get additional funding for his school so that books would still be purchased, the principal secretly approached a school board member who planned to raise the issue unannounced at the next public board meeting. The supervisor somehow got wind of this plot and decided that it was essential to warn the superintendent:

> I knew that the superintendent was most likely to hear about it that night, that the board member would ask him about that. So I got to him and I said, "Hey, here's the problem up there. The principal has spent [only] 18 percent of his money over the last three years for books. The average is about forty-six percent for the other schools. Therefore, he really hasn't met his maintenance effort. . . ." And I said, "There are some other schools which are kind of in the same situation."

When the board member raised the issue that evening, not only was the superintendent not embarrassed, he came across as being remarkably knowledgeable about the specific details of the problem, its origins, and similar situations in other schools. Furthermore, he came armed with specific suggestions about how to deal with the problem within the context of the entire district and how to avoid similar problems in the future. A potential disruption, in this instance, was anticipated by the supervisor and turned into a superior performance by the superintendent.

Working Backstage with the School Board

The school board is a key audience, of course, for the district's instructional program. Board members' impressions of the program and of those who run it determine how well it will fare financially. School board members, however, are also very concerned about the images that they themselves convey to the public. With the current public emphasis on instruction in mind, a curriculum director observed:

> They want to look good. There are a lot of things that make them look bad. And so, when it's things like curriculum work, they want a piece of that action. They want to have stuff ahead of time so that they can ask questions. Sometimes they'll even ask me for some questions, some intelligent questions, [that] they can ask, so that at the board meeting they don't look like they're just interested in, you know, "How many tires are you gonna buy this year?"

It is in the interest of the central office instructional supervisor to "educate" the board about the instructional program so that they truly understand it. One supervisor referred to spontaneous outpourings of information as "mini-in-services," which he provided to board members every time an opportunity arose. Having access to information about instruction not only makes board members feel involved and "part of the action," it also helps them project a positive image of themselves to the public. A curriculum coordinator observed:

> If they look bad, we look bad. And if they look bad, then we have a harder time getting things done.

The point is that while it is true that the central office staff at times plays to the school board as audience, at other times both groups are simultaneously onstage and are cooperatively playing to the general public. The agenda of board meetings usually has been agreed upon beforehand and perhaps even rehearsed a bit at a closed session. Some superintendents privately poll board members individually in advance of a public meeting to get a sense of how they will vote before allowing an issue to be placed on the agenda. In districts free of major animosity, there seem to be few surprises at board meetings. The school board and the central office staff have an informal understanding that neither will introduce issues publicly without first informing the other group.

In some cases, board members do not get along well with one another. Central office staff wisely tries to avoid getting involved in such disputes and attends instead to the things for which it is directly responsible. A curriculum coordinator said:

> Sometimes [board members] zap each other. That's their problem. I can't do much about that. But if it's talking about curriculum, or in-service, or testing results, or things like that, things that I have control over, they have all the stuff way ahead of time.

A director of educational services noted, for example, that the members of the school board in his district agreed privately as well as publicly about most issues concerning education. But the mere mention of money at public meetings invariably resulted in some heated exchanges among board members. Central office staff helped the board present a united front to the community, in this case, by simply avoiding bringing up financial expenditures that had not already been discussed and agreed upon privately. While this tactfulness was never formally recognized, the supervisor believed that board members reciprocated:

> I think they appreciate the fact that we don't mousetrap them, and so they don't usually do it to us. Sometimes they throw us some ringers that are really tough, you know, or they'll ask some bizarre question that you don't have [the answer to] at your fingertips. And you just have to say, "Well, I can give you an off-the-cuff answer, or I'll have to get back to you at the next meeting and . . . give you a full report on it."

What Is Reality?

Although roles enacted by people in organizations can be understood in terms of theatrical imagery, it does not necessarily follow that the actors are being insincere. It is true that in any social setting individuals may be found who are only "going through the motions" and lack a real sense of commitment (Goffman, 1959), but the majority of people usually are quite serious about what they do and say. Even those who are sincere, nevertheless, are often aware of the impressions they make upon other people and strategically adjust their own behavior accordingly.

Because education is so open to public scrutiny and subject to public sanctions, an awareness of vulnerability to criticism may be heightened beyond what occurs in ordinary types of social exchange. Educators, like other public figures, are forced to take the reactions of others into consideration before they act. But this is not to say that educators are any less sincere than most other people in their intentions and actions. A curriculum coordinator pointed out that the behavior of educators can be compared to what happens in everyday life:

> I'm not sure that the actors are always aware that they are putting on a performance. . . . They are doing what they feel would be appropriate for the moment. I guess we all want to appear in the best light in whatever situation. So we're always performing, I guess, to some degree.

Supervisors use the terms "backstage" or "behind the scenes" when describing what they do, in the sense of supporting an onstage performance of some kind (Goffman, 1959). A teacher's lesson in the classroom, a superintendent's presentation to the board of education, or a school board's report to the public, for example, share the common characteristic of being intentionally staged for an audience and are all illustrative of the types of performances that central office supervisors are called upon to support. Other activities supported by the supervisor, such as work done by a committee of teachers on a curriculum project, may have no audience immediately present but are actually a type of backstage preparation for future classroom performances. The instructional program as a whole also may be viewed as a type of performance in the sense that the general public and various institutions must retain confidence in its integrity and effectiveness if the school is to maintain its legitimacy and continue receiving financial support (Meyer and Rowan, 1978; Meyer, Scott, and Deal, 1981).

A hypothesized relationship among the performances staged by the various groupings within a school district is depicted in Figure 13.1. Essentially, each performance may be viewed as nested within a broader and more inclusive performance. This arrangement is somewhat like that of a play within a play within a play. Students, for example, project a certain image to teachers in the classroom at the

FIGURE 13.1

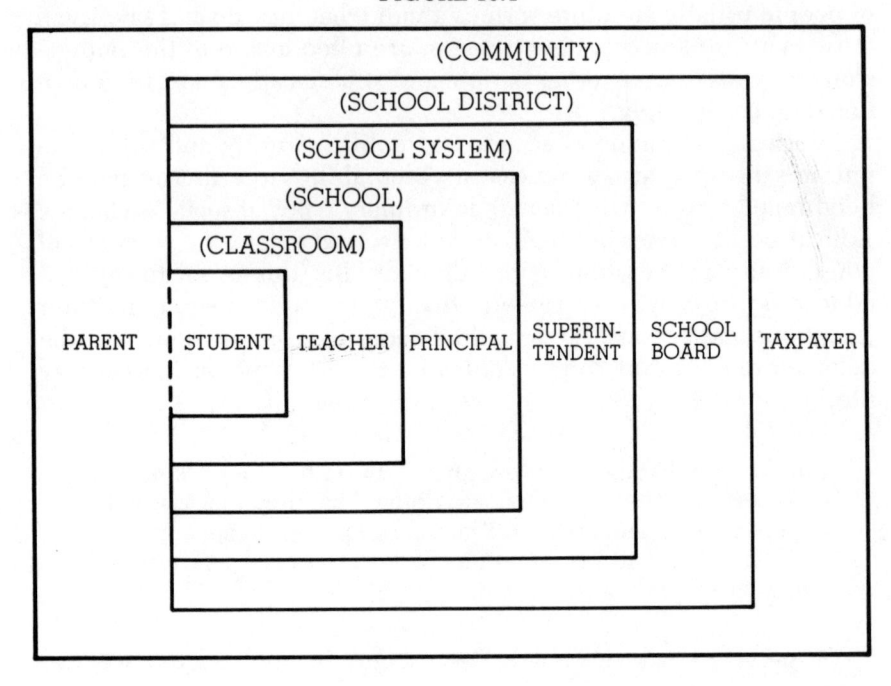

(COMMUNITY)
(SCHOOL DISTRICT)
(SCHOOL SYSTEM)
(SCHOOL)
(CLASSROOM)
PARENT | STUDENT | TEACHER | PRINCIPAL | SUPERINTENDENT | SCHOOL BOARD | TAXPAYER

same time that teachers project an image to students. Each group allows another group to see only what it wants to be seen. Much of what occurs among students, for example, or among teachers or administrators, is not disclosed to other groups. Furthermore, the performance of a member of a group cannot be inconsistent with the broader performance that represents its context without causing a disruption to the more general performance.

The model of interrelated nested performances presented in Figure 13.1 has been anticipated in the work of Barr and Dreeben (1983), and also by Deal (1985). In the former instance, the authors propose that instructional subgroups, classrooms, schools, and school districts can be understood as "a set of nested hierarchical layers, each having a conditional and contributing relation to events and outcomes occurring at adjacent ones" (p. 7). Barr and Dreeben, however, emphasize the concept of "production" in a strictly functional sense. Their metaphor is an industrial one, as they analyze allocations of time, resources, and personnel in each hierarchical layer with many references to "specialized labor," "production workers," and "managerial levels."

Deal (1985), on the other hand, depicts schools as having identifiable cultures that are comprised of several related subcultures. He points out that students, teachers, and administrators possess and enact distinct norms, rituals, and patterns of language that influence behavior within each subculture. These differences can lead to misunderstanding and conflict as individuals interact across groups. Deal suggests that in effective schools, school-wide cultural values, heroes, ceremonies, and rituals "keep various subgroups pulling roughly in the same direction" (p. 611).

As was noted earlier, "mechanical" considerations like those that Barr and Dreeben highlight can be viewed as representing the background, or scene, against which social drama is enacted. Routine administrative decisions, such as scheduling and allocating resources and personnel, which have been shown to affect student outcomes (Barr and Dreeben, 1983), however, need not be excluded in order to recognize the symbolism and pageantry underlying school culture emphasized by Deal (1985). A model of nested performances based on a metaphor of drama represents something of a middle ground between the functional and the expressive extremes. A model of school organization of this sort, therefore, has the potential for representing both dimensions of social behavior (the wink as well as the blink) simultaneously and in conjunction with one another.

Actors and Audiences

Teaching, like acting, requires the presence of spectators. Also like acting, teaching is constrained somewhat by a script, more commonly referred to as the lesson plan or curriculum, which prescribes the transmission of specific information, skills, attitudes, and values within a certain period of time. While students are the primary audience of the performance staged by a teacher, unlike most theatrical audiences, they frequently participate directly: in supporting roles, acting as antagonists, or as spectators to competing performances staged by their peers.

The performance of a teacher is viewed not only by students but by other audiences as well, including parents, other teachers, and the principal. The most important of these external audiences, as far as the teacher is concerned, is likely to be the principal, because the principal has regular and direct access to the teacher's onstage performance through classroom observations. The principal also functions as a critic, who evaluates the quality and worth of the performance in much the same way that a teacher acts as a critic of student performance. However, the principal is also engaged in staging a performance at the school level for an audience comprised of students, teachers, parents, and the superintendent. How well an individual teacher complements this larger performance by playing his or her part well, and by successfully getting students to play their parts appropriately, undoubtedly influences the evaluation he or she will receive.

In a similar fashion, the performance of the local school is something like a play nested within the still larger performance of the school system, which includes the central office and local schools collectively (see Figure 13.1). This system-wide performance is staged by the superintendent for the school board, which in turn stages a performance of its own for taxpayers. Each protagonist (i.e., student, teacher, principal, et al.) has considerable autonomy in determining the nature of the performance he or she will stage, but the operating assumption is that each performance will conform to the more inclusive performance in which it is nested. The expectation is that the prescribed script of each broader performance will constrain the performances nested within it, although much of the action that takes place in schools is improvised by the actors as they go along.

In contributing to the overall performance of the school system and the various performances nested within it, the central office supervisor functions much like a theatrical stage director. Although directors, for the most part, neither write nor act in a play, their backstage function of bringing actors and script together in a credible and even masterful way is essential.

Directors regularly attend to such mundane duties as casting and coaching individual actors; selecting props, costumes, and scenery; and holding rehearsals. But by far the most important responsibilities of a theatrical director involve the creative interpretation of the author's script and the merging of the various elements of the "mise-en-scene" into a cohesive and coherent whole (Schechner, 1985). The earlier chapters of this book described in detail how successful supervisors of instruction manage to accomplish this through a process of interpretation of social reality within the school in terms of what is of benefit to students. The fact that the environment of the school district is comprised of various audiences that have different expectations concerning the specific type of performance that is appropriate for schools complicates the supervisor's work considerably.

On the local community level, parents and taxpayers comprise the external audience for the overall performance staged by the school district. These two groups of spectators rarely play an active part in the onstage drama of education, except for voting on bond referendums or for board members, which nevertheless can have a significant impact. The interests of parents and taxpayers are quite different, although the two groups do in fact overlap, of course, when parents are also taxpayers. The primary interest of parents is to secure the best education for their children, while the major interest of taxpayers is to limit costs. By and large, parents also tend to prefer a nurturing social configuration within the school, while taxpayers prefer an emphasis on efficiency.

A certain amount of image building or impression management is inevitably a part of the central office instructional supervisor's job because public performances are so centrally a part of what schools do. When the supervisor coaches a teacher in the classroom or assists the superintendent in presenting information to the school board or taxpayers, for example, both functional and expressive dimensions come into play. The requirements of impression management imposed by the institutional environment, however, may interfere with a school's attending to instructional improvement (Meyer and Scott, 1983), which is generally understood to be the primary purpose of instructional supervision. The central office supervisor may be caught between the conflicting demands of the ostensible purpose of his or her role (i.e., improving instruction) and the time-consuming legitimizing tasks (e.g., federal program and state education documentation) that must be completed in order to maintain the credibility of the school within its institutional environment. An overemphasis on impression management within the external institutional environment at the expense of attending to the quality of the instructional program, in other words, can undermine the success of a supervisor and a district's effectiveness.

References

Barr, R. & Dreeben, R. 1983. *How schools work*. Chicago: University of Chicago Press.

Burke, K. 1941. Ritual drama as hub. In S. E. Hyman (ed.), *Perspectives by incongruity*. Bloomington: Indiana University Press, 1964.

Deal, T. E. 1985. The symbolism of effective schools. *Elementary School Journal*, 85 (5): 601–620.

Goffman, E. 1959. *The presentation of self in everyday life*. New York: Doubleday Anchor.

Lewis, A. J. & Miel, A. 1972. *Supervision for improved instruction*. Belmont, Calif.: Wadsworth.

Meyer, J. W. & Rowan, B. 1978. Institutionalized organizations: Formal structure as myth and ceremony. *American Journal of Sociology*, 83 (2): 340–363.

Meyer, J. W. & Scott, W. R. 1983. *Organizational environments: Ritual and rationality*. Beverly Hills: Sage Publications.

Meyer, J. W., Scott, W. R. & Deal, T. E. 1981. Institutional and technical sources of organizational structure: Explaining the structure of educational organizations. In H. D. Stein (ed.), *Organization and the human services*. Philadelphia: Temple University Press.

Pajak, E. 1987. *A dramaturgical model of district-wide change: The many faces of instructional supervision.* Paper presented at the Annual Meeting of the American Educational Research Association, Washington, D.C.

Schechner, R. 1985. *Between theater and anthropology.* Philadelphia: University of Pennsylvania Press.

Zimmerman, I. K. 1985. Changing roles, differing perspectives. *The Principals' Center Newsletter: Harvard Graduate School of Education,* 4 (2): 7–8.

14

Making Sense of It All

DUKE S.
Thou seest we are not all alone unhappy;
This wide and universal theater
Presents more woeful pageants than the scene
Wherein we play in.

JAQUES
All the world's a stage,
And all the men and women merely players;
They have their exits and their entrances;
And one man in his time plays many parts,
His acts being seven ages.

>William Shakespeare, As You Like It,
>Act II, Scene 7

BEN JONSON
If but stage-actors all the world displays,
Where shall we find spectators of their plays?

SHAKESPEARE
Little, or much of what we see, we do;
We are both actors and spectators too.

>"The Life of William Shakespeare,"
>p. li, The Complete Works of William Shakespeare,
>Henry Irving (ed.),
>New York: World Syndicate, 1926.

Information theorists have come to recognize that the human brain is not a passive audience but actively chooses what it perceives and retains. It tries to grasp the entire scene and the relation to one another of all the elements it sees. In perceiving and trying to make sense of its environment, the brain examines multiple perspectives, hypotheses, and interpretations. The human brain constantly creates patterns out of unconnected and meaningless inputs, order out of disorder (Campbell, 1982).

Successful central office instructional supervisors may be thought of as functioning in a manner somewhat like the human brain in bringing sense and order to the diversity that exists within their school districts. Supervisors reduce uncertainty surrounding instruction and help provide the stability and predictability that are necessary for the operation of the instructional program without sacrificing variety and the capacity for innovation (Pratt, 1982). They accomplish this by emphasizing the core value of providing high-quality instruction to students; by promoting norms of cooperation, fairness, and reciprocity; by mobilizing effort and coordinating roles; and by clarifying tasks and outcomes for teachers and administrators.

This structure is not imposed upon teachers and administrators as explicit commands. It is achieved through less formal understandings and agreements, which are arrived at during ongoing interactions and discussions of issues relating to curriculum and instruction. Groups are initiated and facilitated by supervisors and serve as forums for these discussions. The informality of the understandings allows teachers and administrators to retain freedom to exercise their professional judgment in applying information that is accessible only to them because of their closeness to a particular classroom or school.

Collectively, the understandings and agreements concerning curriculum and instruction that develop through discussion comprise a cultural definition of the situation. The abstract ideal of benefiting students through instruction is gradually negotiated at increasingly specific levels (i.e., norms, roles, and tasks) until it is concretely enacted by teachers in the classroom. The involvement of teachers and administrators in the process of negotiation enhances commitment from them and permits change to be introduced from either the top or bottom of the organizational hierarchy.

Most importantly, perhaps, an ongoing conversation among professional educators concerning curricular and instructional issues drives out magical thinking that relies upon the quick fix as a solution to structural strain. Magical thinking oversimplifies reality and short-circuits the rational pursuit of solutions to complex problems. Districts afflicted with magical thinking are likely to be highly susceptible to fads and crazes in both curriculum and instruction. Panaceas are quickly embraced and rapidly abandoned in an almost involuntary and repetitive cyclical pattern. Changes are superficial and cosmetic under these circumstances. Rumors and wild speculation are often rampant in such districts, and irrational hero worship and scapegoating are likely to be common.

Successful supervisors of curriculum and instruction, in contrast, tend to be patient realists who tirelessly cultivate a district-wide culture that is capable of continuous internal integration and external adaptation. Such a culture is characterized by stability and continuity, as well as gradual adjustment of its structure and purposeful mobilization of effort and resources to specific situations. Events are interpreted positively and lead to generalized beliefs that contribute to the definition of the situation as one that exists primarily to benefit students. A rich variety of instructional methods is cultivated, but meaningless chaos is avoided. The key to such a culture is hard work on the part of the supervisor to keep communication open and ongoing at all levels of the district. Change then becomes an evolutionary process instead of an anarchic one.

The way in which successful district level supervisors of instruction and curriculum bring order and meaning to the school districts they serve appears to be quite consistent with descriptions of the thought processes engaged in by other professionals as they do their work. Schon (1983) has noted, for example, that complexity, uncertainty, and instability are inherent in the problems and institutional contexts faced by practitioners in professions as diverse as architecture, psychotherapy, engineering, town planning, and managing. Rather than applying a standard body of specialized knowledge and established techniques to recurrent and well-defined tasks, Schon reports, practitioners in these professions must constantly improvise in order to handle successfully the variety, ambiguity, and novelty that they regularly encounter.

Schon (1983, p. 95) describes the process by which a professional faces uncertainty and reduces it to tolerable levels as a "reflective conversation with the situation." He suggests that this process describes the "art" by which practitioners deal successfully with ambiguity, instability, and unpredictability.

Upon encountering a new situation, according to Schon, successful professionals first allow themselves to be surprised and even confused by its novelty and uniqueness. Next, practitioners reflect upon the phenomenon encountered in terms of prior understandings concerning their practice that have been acquired through previous experience. Some tentative or exploratory action is then taken, and the outcomes are considered in terms of the original implicit assumptions, which may subsequently be revised according to the new information.

The practitioner's tentative actions are based upon an initial appraisal of a puzzling situation or problem, and they function as probes that generate information relevant to his or her understanding of the specific case. Scattered pieces of information are gradually pulled together into a coherent whole in a process much like solving a puzzle (Schon, 1983, p. 124). These tacit understandings comprise a theory-in-use and serve to guide further action. An appropriate intervention is eventually derived that fits the particular features of the specific situation. In Schon's words:

> The unique and uncertain situation comes to be understood through the attempt to change it, and changed through the attempt to understand it. (P. 132)

Like the managers Schon describes, district level supervisors of instruction and curriculum may be said to contribute to the "learning system" of the organization (p. 242). Through their efforts both to shape and understand the dynamics of the school district, supervisors add to the store of information available to its members. Supervisors organize and clarify both the ends and means that may be appropriate in a particular situation by interacting with it. By bringing sense to an uncertain situation in this way, they may attempt a tentative application of practical knowledge themselves, or more often prepare the way for other professionals to act (Olson, 1980; Elbaz, 1981).

Although instructional supervisors make sense of ambiguous situations themselves, they by no means do it alone. Successful instructional supervisors undoubtedly possess a sense of mission, a personal vision of what schools should be like, and guiding principles and beliefs. However, the work that they consider most important involves creating opportunities for teachers and administrators to structure specific details in ways that make sense to them, their students, and communities. Their facilitation of sense-making and improvisation among other individuals and groups, in fact, is crucial to the effectiveness of the school district as a whole. Unlike the inert materials with which some professionals work, the situation in schools not only "talks back" to the instructional supervisor, it converses and makes sense within itself as well. The supervisor should keep the conversation focused on what is the best thing for students instructionally.

A negotiated definition of the social situation is developed within effective districts that ensures that order and meaning exist, but not at the expense of novelty, creativity, and the capacity for change. Initiating and facilitating discussions of issues relating to instruction and curriculum among teachers and administrators generates the narratives, images, and myths that enrich an organizations's culture. By personally modeling and reinforcing norms of cooperation, trust, and reciprocity, the supervisor ensures that a positive definition of the situation is eventually enacted in classrooms.

An interesting alternative to viewing culture as a set of rules and norms that govern roles and behavior is suggested by Jerome Bruner (1986). He considers it advantageous to consider culture as if it were an ambiguous text that is constantly undergoing revision as members interpret and reinterpret, negotiate and renegotiate meanings that guide their actions. According to this perspective, instead of merely enacting the roles assigned to them, participants assume a more active posture in shaping and reshaping their culture through their interactions with one another.

An apocryphal tale about William of Normandy illustrates the point well. As William led his invading army onto the shores of England in 1066, he is supposed to have stumbled and fallen to his hands and knees. Being a superstitious lot, his troops immediately halted, aghast at the omen of ill fortune they had just witnessed. According to the story, William suddenly raised himself and turned to face his men. Displaying a fistful of sand, he triumphantly yelled, "See how easily this land comes into my grasp." The rest, of course, is history.

According to Bruner (1986), education should involve not only the transmission but the creation of knowledge and culture. He suggests that the passive acquisition by students of existing facts is insufficient. Students ought to be encouraged to participate actively in speculation and interpretation of meanings. By reflecting upon what they learn, students can go beyond having knowledge and culture control them. They can select, interpret, and use knowledge to create new and better definitions of reality.

Central to Bruner's argument is his observation that human reality is comprised of two distinct yet complementary spheres of experience and ways of thinking. One is structured by the logic of causation that governs the natural world. The other follows the logic of narrative and drama, which more closely fits the human experience of social reality. In order to engage in reflection and the creation of culture, according to Bruner, education cannot rely upon the "uncontaminated language of fact and 'objectivity' " (p. 129). The process of reflection requires a rich multiplicity of meanings and interpretations that are only found in the narrative mode.

The primary problem that society must soon face, according to Bruner (1986, p. 149), is:

> [H]ow to create a new generation that can prevent the world from dissolving into chaos and destroying itself. I think that its central technical concern will be how to create in the young an apprecia-

tion of the fact that many worlds are possible, that meaning and reality are created and not discovered, that negotiation is the art of constructing new meanings by which individuals can regulate their relations with each other.

Historically, our thinking about schools has drawn upon an industrial or factory metaphor (Callahan, 1962). While this mechanistic perspective of schools as organizations may be useful for understanding certain processes—such as facilities maintenance, transportation, or food services—it is unsatisfactory as a model of less predictable processes, such as instruction (Weick, 1982). The indeterminate nature of the goals and processes of schools inevitably makes them open to a variety of meanings that can be interpreted in multiple ways. It may be profitable to think about the culture of a school as a narrative, or script, that is both authored and enacted by the people who inhabit it. Central office instructional supervisors seem to view their positions in this sense as "setting the stage" for action that is taken more directly by others.

This narrative, or dramatic, perspective is useful because it alerts us to the fact that adults in schools collaboratively "set the stage" for students' experiences in schools (Connelly and Clandinin, 1988). The social reality that they create, consciously or unconsciously, is the script that students must live day after day. It is through such scripts that students develop understandings of who they are and what they are capable of becoming.

Teachers may be thought of as performers who specialize in playing to audiences comprised mainly of children, while superintendents and other central office personnel specialize in playing to adult audiences. Principals are in a particularly untenable position because they must constantly mediate between the playful and serious, the child's world and the adult's world. This means that principals have to interpret policies or events appropriately according to the expectations of different audiences. Computerized records of student achievement, for example, might be explained to parents and teachers as beneficial for improving opportunities for children to receive individualized attention. The same program might be touted to board members and taxpayers, on the other hand, as desirable for enhancing efficiency and accountability.

A school is something like a play written with alternative scripts whose actors are faced with the dilemma of trying to present various versions simultaneously in order to please multiple audiences with very different preferences. Students and parents (especially of younger children) prefer a lighter script wih a happy ending, while taxpayers insist on a serious and sometimes sad one. Innovation in education might be viewed cynically as often little more than an occasional shift in emphasis from one type of performance to the other, depending upon which audience clamors loudest at the moment.

The problem seems to come from being forced to choose one type of performance over the other. The result is that a large part of the audience will always remain dissatisfied. Perhaps a solution is to emphasize what comedy and tragedy have in common instead of how they differ. Hare (1985) observes that in both comedies and tragedies the characters control the plot, unlike in melodramas and farces, where the plot controls the characters.

For educators, the implication may be to avoid mistaking either the "playful" image or the "serious" image as truer, more real than the other. It simply will not work to drive one or the other out. Both are necessary for the educational enterprise to function. Recognizing this fact may enable us to be less controlled by the scripts written for us by others and better able to direct the plot ourselves. As spectators, the public will continue from time to time to criticize education. Perhaps what needs to be done is to educate the public so that they become at least knowledgeable spectators of what is going on in schools. Instead of simply enacting comedies or tragedies, educators might author scripts wherein students are prepared to experience their lives as heroic epics in which they determine their own destinies.

References

Bruner, J. 1986. *Actual minds, possible worlds.* Cambridge: Harvard University Press.
Callahan, R. E. 1962. *Education and the cult of efficiency.* Chicago: University of Chicago Press.
Campbell, J. 1982. *Grammatical man: Information, entropy, language, and life.* New York: Simon & Schuster.
Connelly, F. M. & Clandinin, D. J. 1988. *Teachers as curriculum planners: Narratives of experience.* New York: Teachers College Press.
Elbaz, F. 1981. The teacher's "practical knowledge": Report of a case study. *Curriculum Inquiry,* 11 (1): 43–71.
Hare, A. P. 1985. *Social interaction as drama.* Beverly Hills: Sage Publications.
Olson, J. K. 1980. Teacher constructs and curriculum change. *Journal of Curriculum Studies,* 12 (1): 1–11.
Pratt, D. 1982. A cybernetic model for curriculum development. *Instructional Science,* 11 (1): 1–12.
Schon, D. A. 1983. *The reflective practitioner: How professionals think in action.* New York: Basic Books.
Weick, K. E. 1982. Administering education in loosely coupled schools. *Phi Delta Kappan,* 63 (10): 673–676.

Index

Action, 44, 86, 146, 153, 155, 162
Adaptation, 40, 49, 76, 88, 90, 108, 122, 123, 162, 163, 231
Alice's Adventures in Wonderland, 154, 160
Ambiguity, 8, 14, 16, 19–20, 34, 39, 45–49, 88, 96, 102, 159, 231, 233
and remoteness, 181–184
Anxiety, 41–42
Association for Supervision and Curriculum Development, 3, 19, 34
Audiences, 176, 205, 207, 213–216, 221, 223, 225, 234–235
internal and external, 202, 216, 225–226
primary and secondary, 207
Autonomy, 8, 81
principal, 125–143, 171–174

Background, 187, 213–214, 225
Barr, R. and R. Dreeben, 224, 227
Behavior, 9, 39, 122, 124, 146
"Big picture," the, 11–12, 36, 158
Bounded rationality, 85
Brain, human, 229–230
Bruner, J., 233–234, 235
Bureaucracy, 2, 19, 25, 39–41, 122, 124, 133, 183
Burke, K., 213, 227
Burns, J. M., 156, 158–159, 160

Campbell, J., 17, 39, 50, 235
Carroll, L., 154–155, 160
Change and innovation, 28–29, 40, 43, 49, 52, 89, 106–109, 112, 118, 121–124, 157, 160, 230, 232

Change and innovation *(cont.)*
bottom–up and top–down, 106–107, 230
capacity for, 16
gradual, 29, 31, 48, 231
initiating, 28, 52, 110, 188, 200–202, 232
normative, 112
resistance to, 52, 110
Chaos, 40, 231
Classroom(s), 1, 11, 20, 26, 35, 46, 79, 81, 86, 88, 90, 94, 97, 105, 110, 114, 122–123, 183
observation, 22, 105, 123, 197, 206, 209–211, 216
supervision, 188, 196–211
Clinical supervision, 105, 123, 138, 209
Cohesiveness, 74, 164
Collective behavior, 44, 45, 48, 71, 112–113, 162, 176
Colleges and universities, 1, 92, 95–96, 198
Commitment, 45, 49, 90, 102, 105, 108, 115–116, 124, 145, 160, 176–177, 186, 200, 206, 223, 230
Committees, 23, 54, 62, 66, 72, 81–82, 84–86, 93, 100, 102, 108, 110, 113, 117, 121, 136, 148, 150–151, 174, 199–203, 206, 208, 223
ad hoc, 82
standing, 82
task force, 87
Communication, 7, 8, 22, 59, 72–73, 81–82, 137, 146, 155, 167–168, 170, 186, 193, 231
informal, 10, 12, 21, 199
verbal, 7, 10

Community, 5, 54, 164, 176, 184
Complexity, 9, 28, 86, 231
Components of social action, 42–48
Computers, 30, 95–96, 107, 110, 122, 134, 139, 140, 185, 186, 218
Confidence, 101, 150, 159, 188, 191–192, 199, 200, 206, 223
  building, 88, 91, 100
Conflict, 52–53, 58–59, 62, 72, 130, 141, 143, 162, 167, 173, 175, 225
  confrontation, 58
  tension, 127
Conformity, 121–123
  channeled non-conformity, 124
Consensus, 32, 39, 71, 97, 160
Consistency, 36, 55–56, 79–80, 145–146, 164, 170–171
Constraints, 5, 15, 19, 23, 27, 39, 128, 130, 166, 182, 204
Constructing meaning, 1–2, 12, 14, 40, 160
Continuity, 11, 36, 49, 80, 116, 231
  and sequence, 116
Cooperation, 10, 54, 56–57, 59, 63–64, 90, 125, 129, 135, 140, 147–148, 159, 172, 187, 200, 230, 232
Coordination, 40, 70–87, 90, 116, 135, 145, 159, 172, 198
  of procedures, 74
Core value, 1–2, 10, 16, 147, 160, 230
Creativity, 29, 62, 77, 92, 108, 123, 151, 232
Credibility, 27, 90, 118–120, 128–130, 145, 159, 182, 185, 219
Credit, 62
  exchanging, 57, 62–69, 192
  idiosyncrasy, 157, 159
  losing, 157
  sharing, 66, 121, 145
  taking, 63–65, 177, 200
Cuban, L., 107, 124
Culture, 9, 40, 43, 48–49, 100, 122, 164, 224, 230–234
  organizational, 38–42
Curriculum, 4, 8, 24, 27, 35, 54, 72–78, 85, 90–93, 100, 103, 105, 108, 110, 111, 113–116,

Curriculum (cont.)
  118, 120–121, 124, 135–136, 149, 151, 174, 183, 186–187, 193, 199, 207, 225, 232
  councils, 76, 108, 110, 113, 117, 120–121
  development, 118, 126, 169, 172
  guides, 113–114

Deal, T. E., 41, 50, 52, 224–225, 227
Deal, T. E. and A. A. Kennedy, 40, 50
Decision making, 8, 86, 118
Definition of the situation, 45–46, 49, 52–54, 59, 109, 111, 157, 159–160, 164, 230–232
Delegation, 149–150, 165–166, 168
Details ("Little things"), 148–149
Developing others, 151–153
  building on strengths, 99
Dialogue, 10, 16, 34–36, 71, 85, 118, 160, 166, 209
Direction, 36, 38, 71–72, 85, 159
Diversity, 1, 4, 6, 8, 16, 19–20, 28, 31–32, 36, 39, 49, 74, 83–84, 151, 230
Donmoyer, R. and A. R. Neff, 7–8, 12, 17

Empowerment, 87, 136–137, 152–153
Encouragement, 97–98
Enthusiasm and excitement, 29, 94
Environments, 16, 29, 38–39, 45, 78, 163, 175, 190, 215
Equity and fairness, 52, 54, 56–57, 72, 74–77, 90, 103, 135, 145–146, 159, 172, 178, 230
Evaluation, 5, 32, 123, 132, 138, 152, 157, 197, 209
  self-monitoring, 114
Evolution, 39, 49, 231
Exchange, 147–148, 151
Expectations, 33–34, 38, 40, 45, 55–56, 65, 70, 72, 76, 79, 85, 89, 100, 102, 113, 124, 128, 130, 146, 157–159
Expertise, 72, 83, 92, 94, 144–145, 169
Expressive behavior, 205, 214, 227
External agencies, 5, 33, 103, 164, 182, 191, 198, 215

INDEX

Facilitation, 77, 79, 84, 118, 124, 143–147, 156, 188, 200–202, 232
Fads and crazes, 45–46, 230
Favoritism, 52, 147
Feedback, 31, 73, 98
Feudal analogy, 133
Fine tuning, 31, 188
Flexibility, 8, 16, 80
Floyd, M. K., 14, 16, 17
Focus, 8–9, 80, 160
Followers, 153–158
Foreground, 187, 189
Fragmentation, 6–8, 14, 16, 19, 36, 39, 46, 80
Freud, A., 38, 50
Frustrations, 19–20, 23–27, 111, 134, 140, 144
Functional behavior, 205, 227
Funds, 23–24, 33, 89, 95, 103, 144, 169
  budget, 5, 178
  cost of materials, 90
  financial difficulty, 4, 30, 75
  financial incentives, 63
  financial support, 163

Games:
  anagrams, 13–14
  billiards, 153–154
  chess, 155
  croquet, 154
Generalized belief, 46–47, 97
Genetic code, 39
Gestalt psychology, 187
Glickman, C. D., 40, 50
Goals, 20, 31, 35–36, 38, 39, 72, 77–81, 86, 150, 157–158, 165, 170
  displacement, 123
Goffman, E., 213, 215, 227
Goldhammer, R., 105, 123, 124
Gouldner, A. W., 68, 69
Grants, 24, 91
Group resource, 156, 159
Groups, 23, 41, 45, 55, 84–85, 87, 95, 110, 116–117, 123, 139, 155, 163, 182, 187, 201
  hands-off approach, 103
  organizing, 199–200

Hare, A. P., 235
Helping, 152, 160
Helping others, 21, 49, 60, 146
Helping teachers, 172, 179, 187
Heroic epics, 235
Hero worship, 46, 231
Hill, W. M., 209–210, 211
Hills, R. J., 44, 50
Hollander, E. P., 156–157, 159, 161
Honesty, 56, 146
Horning, A. S., 206, 211

I-B-F supervision, 209–211
Ideas, 1, 89, 92, 94, 183
"If-only" mentality, 47
Images, 179, 208, 210–211, 213–214, 217–218, 220–221, 235
  building, 217–218, 227
  making, 10
  and myths, 9, 163–164, 168, 171, 176, 178
  and narratives, 10
Impression management, 218, 227
Improvement, 94, 99
Influence, 5, 7, 10, 21, 23, 26, 62–63, 80, 82, 109, 114, 124–125, 127, 134, 136, 143–145, 147–148, 151, 153, 156–157, 166, 169, 171, 174
Informality, 22, 68, 94, 105, 127, 139, 164, 167, 206, 217
Information, 1, 7–9, 15, 22, 32, 44, 46, 55, 59, 71, 73, 84, 89, 92, 94–96, 102–103, 120, 146, 172, 176, 201, 203, 225, 232
  brokering, 92–94
  processing, 14, 227–230
In-service training, 5, 21–22, 30, 86, 88, 94–96, 102, 108, 110–113, 118–119, 126, 148, 152, 169, 183, 199, 201–203, 207, 218
Instruction and instructional improvement, 1, 4–5, 8, 24, 46–47, 53, 56, 59, 72, 78, 84, 88–90, 105–106, 108, 110–111, 113, 123, 125, 127, 137–138, 141, 143–144, 147, 151–153, 169, 172, 180, 182, 188, 192, 194, 199, 207, 209, 227
Integration, 44–45, 49, 72, 80, 116, 163–164, 231
  cohesiveness, 74, 164
  collaboration, 1, 74

INDEX

Interpretation, 1, 9, 13–14, 16, 40, 44, 54, 86, 160, 164, 181, 215, 220, 226, 231, 233–234
  numerical, 9
Involvement, 53, 77, 85, 110, 113, 115–116, 119
Invisibility, 179–194
  functional outcomes, 189–191
  self-effacement, 186

Job descriptions, 2, 4–5, 70–71
Job titles, 2

Larger districts, 25–26, 78–80, 152, 183, 190, 202
Leadership, 15, 42, 46, 55–56, 65, 87, 94, 118, 124, 127, 136, 143, 149–151, 153–154, 156–158, 172–173, 176, 178, 206
  transactional, 156–158
  transforming, 158–160
Legislation, 47, 49
Lewis, A. J. and A. Miel, 196, 205, 212, 219, 227
Library, 83, 91
Line of authority, 59, 133–135, 141, 143–144, 171, 173–174
Link or liaison, 1, 22, 86, 198
Listening, 59–61, 109, 127, 152
"Little things," (*see* Details)
Long-term perspective, 11, 36
Loose coupling, 15, 39, 45, 68, 191
Loyalty, 132, 156–157, 168, 177, 219

"Magical" thinking, 47–48, 230
Making sense, 9, 11–13, 35, 63, 84, 133, 196, 230, 232
Managing
  conflict, 57–62
  objectives, 32
  outcomes, 151
Manipulation, 41, 142
Materials, 1, 5, 74–75, 77, 83, 89–92, 96, 102–103, 148, 162, 183, 198, 201, 206
Meaning, 9–10, 15–16, 36, 40–41, 44, 46, 73, 75, 158, 160, 205, 231–234
Means and ends, 70, 122, 164, 232
Mechanistic metaphors, 213, 234
Mediator, 60–61, 147, 216
Medium, 14–15

Meetings, 83–84, 117, 185, 192
Merit pay and career ladders, 32, 46
Merton, R. K., 121, 124
Methodology, v-vii
Meyer, J. W. and W. R. Scott, 191, 195
Milburn, G., 206, 212
Mobilization, 32, 46, 72, 162
  of effort, 70–87, 162, 230–231
Monitoring, 7, 22, 105, 124, 155, 209
Mutual adjustment, 86–87
Mutual confidence, 200
Mutual respect, 58, 145–146, 159

Narratives, 9, 11, 233–234
Nation at Risk, A, 48
Needs assessment, 95–96, 111
Negotiation, 8, 35, 72, 127
Nested performances, 224–226
Networks, 72, 77, 81–82, 85, 87, 103, 194, 206
News media, 83, 184
Norms, 20, 33–36, 41, 43–44, 47, 49, 52–69, 72, 80, 109, 112–114, 123–124, 142, 157, 159, 225, 230, 232
Novelty, 29, 32, 42, 231–232

Organization, 7, 36, 39, 59, 72, 85, 122–123, 155
  conscience, 80
  learning system, 163, 232
  structure, 85
Outcomes, 71, 88
  tangible, 33
Ownership, 114, 116

Panaceas, 46, 123, 230
Paperwork, 5–6, 22, 24–25, 33, 84, 136, 166, 182, 193, 215
Parents, 58–59, 61–62, 67, 84, 164, 184–185, 207, 214, 226–227, 234
Parent–Teacher Organizations, 91
Participation, 74, 96, 103, 124, 148–149, 169
Patient realists, 231
Patterns, 43–44, 55, 225
Patterson, J. L., S. C. Purkey, and J. V. Parker, 47, 50
Perceptions, 40, 145, 148, 157, 162, 175
Personal growth, 28, 30, 34

Personal traits, 16
Personal worth, 30
Planning, 5, 72, 77, 79, 86, 90, 103, 108, 113, 151, 201
Power, 136–137, 153, 163, 174
Praise, 29, 66, 97, 98, 102, 124, 169, 177, 180
Predictability, 40, 56, 75, 77, 85, 96, 102, 131, 230
  variable situations, 86
Prestige and status, 30, 33
Principal(s), 1–3, 19–20, 26–27, 32–33, 39, 46, 58–59, 61, 63–65, 71, 75, 77, 79–80, 86, 88–91, 94, 97–98, 100, 102–103, 108, 118, 123, 125–127, 129–131, 133–137, 143–149, 153, 159–160, 164, 171–173, 177, 179–180, 182–183, 192, 197–198, 201, 208, 214, 216–219, 226, 234
  consultant to, 138
Problems, 19, 33, 40, 143, 165, 198, 231
Problem solving, 21, 41, 61
Professional growth, 30, 34, 106, 112–113, 118, 152, 169
Professional standards, 34, 56
Public, the, 178–179, 181, 184–185, 189–190, 207, 218, 220–223, 235
Publicity, 185
Public relations, 187–188
Purpose, 2, 36, 72, 75, 158, 160, 164, 206
Puzzles, 12–14, 232

Rapport, 3, 21, 97
Rationality, 38, 41, 47, 61
  rituals of, 191
Reality check, 168
Rebellion, 122–123
Reciprocity, 56, 68, 101, 130–131, 147–148, 157–158, 230, 233
  reciprocal influence, 145–147
  reciprocal interdependence, 86
Recognition, 19, 29, 63–64, 101, 114, 120, 145, 151, 180, 192
Reflection, 233
Reflective conversation, 231
Regulations, 43, 76, 83, 87, 111
Requisite variety, 15–16

Resources, 1, 4, 7, 72–73, 75, 82, 86, 88–89, 92–93, 96, 120, 151, 163, 172
Responsibilities, 4, 6, 85–86, 100, 112, 152
Retreatism, 122, 123
Rewards, 44, 63, 71, 95–96, 115, 120, 151, 154, 156, 163
  altruistic, 30
  tangible, 156, 180
Ritualism, 122–123
Role conflict, 20, 32–34
  central office spy, 132, 208
Roles, 3–4, 32–33, 55, 71, 81, 83, 122, 230, 233
  character-driven, 204–205
  clarifying, 70–72
  organized, 42, 44, 49, 70
  script-driven, 204
Role models, 55–56
Role set, 33–34
Role theory, 204
Routines, 72, 74, 77
Rules, 86–87
Rules of grammar, 15, 39, 44
Rumors, 45–46, 231

Salaries, 30, 89, 149, 192
Sarason, S. B., 48, 50
Satisfactions, 19–20, 28–32, 62, 92, 151
Scapegoating, 46, 231
Schein, E. H., 40, 49, 50, 163, 178
Schon, D. A., 231–232, 235
School board, 33, 58, 61–62, 64, 66, 77, 79, 81, 84, 107, 121, 127, 129, 133, 175, 185–186, 192, 203, 207, 213, 215–216, 220–222, 226–227, 234
School(s), 38, 66, 81, 85, 88–89, 91, 97, 110, 117, 123, 125, 133, 179, 182, 185, 188, 234
  and central office, 133–135
Secretaries, 25, 58, 95
Securing resources, 88–92
Self-confidence, 88, 99, 102
Self-fulfilling prophecy, 100
Sergiovanni, T. J. and R. J. Starrat, 42, 50
Service, 72, 131, 148, 160, 169
Service to children, 10, 49, 231
Sharing ideas, 118
Sharing responsibility, 200

242 INDEX

Sharing understandings, 40, 73
Skills, 44, 94, 96, 115
Small districts, 5, 24, 79, 91, 152, 182
Smelser, N. J., 43, 45, 47, 50
Social drama, 225
Social movements, 47–49
Social and psychological distance, 20–23
Social reality, 40, 155, 159, 226, 233–234
Social structure, 48–49
Social system, 32–33, 42–45, 68
Solutions, 19, 42, 62, 179, 209, 230
Stability, 16, 39, 49, 68, 122, 159, 176, 190, 230–231
Staff development, 5, 90, 92, 95–96, 105, 111–112, 118–119, 124, 126, 187, 202
Standards and standardization, 40, 72–77, 81, 86, 123–124
Standards of conduct, 43, 55, 114
State department of education, 1, 27, 127, 214
Structural strain, 45–46, 49, 88, 159, 230
Student(s), 1, 6, 24, 29–31, 33, 35, 38–39, 54, 72, 105, 107, 110–112, 121–122, 126, 136, 139–140, 152, 160, 162, 166, 169, 177, 185, 190, 197, 207, 210, 214–216, 225–226, 231–233, 235
  achievement and, 114
Sturges, A. W., 34, 37
Success, 31, 35, 64–65, 87, 89, 92, 99, 101–102, 110, 113, 116, 127, 144, 148, 151–152, 155, 162, 170, 192
Sullivan, C. G., 7–8, 17, 92, 103
Superintendents, 1, 3, 32–33, 59, 62–64, 66, 71, 77, 79–80, 90, 95, 98, 112, 126–127, 132–134, 145, 147, 162, 164–167, 175, 179–181, 183, 189–192, 214–222, 225–227, 234
Supervisor
  defined, 14
  effectiveness, 1–16, 39
  theatrical director, 205–210, 219, 226
Support, 63, 88–89, 94, 96, 102–103, 105, 130, 156, 168–170, 176

Support system, 102
Symbols, 41, 148–149
  abstraction, 9
  importance, 190
System-wide perspective, 10–11, 36, 158

Tanner, D. and L. Tanner, 89, 103
Tasks and activities, 4–6, 8, 12, 32, 36, 42–43, 45–46, 49, 54–55, 71, 88, 150, 159, 166, 179, 187, 230
  intangibility of, 184–189
Taxpayers, 164, 207, 214, 227, 234
Teachers, 1–3, 19–27, 30–33, 35, 38–39, 46, 53–54, 58–59, 61–65, 71, 73, 75–77, 79–84, 86, 88–97, 100, 103, 105–106, 108, 111–119, 121–122, 133, 137–145, 147–150, 152–153, 159–160, 164, 169, 177, 179–186, 190, 192, 197–206, 209–210, 213–216, 218–219, 226–227, 230, 232, 234
  closing the gap with, 20–21, 23, 36
  contact, 21–22
  recognition, 101
  role, 204–205
  veteran, 26
Teamwork, 10, 56–57, 66, 72, 136–137, 141, 167, 187, 200, 206
Tenure, 26, 123, 176, 197
Test scores, 31, 185
Textbooks, 5, 32, 53, 61, 73–77, 90, 113, 183, 190, 198–199, 206
Theatrical metaphor, 196, 205, 213
  actors, 205, 216, 222
  backstage, 196–211, 213–227
  behind-the-scenes, 65, 189, 191–192, 196, 223
  comedy and tragedy, 235
  drama, 158, 213, 233
  dramatic expression, 196, 233
  dramatic performance, 196, 205
  dramatic perspective, 213
  offstage, 214–215
  onstage, 196, 206–207, 214–216, 219, 221, 225
  props, 198, 206, 218
  rehearsals, 202–203, 207, 213, 222
  scripts, 204, 207, 211, 218–219, 225, 234–235
  staging and stage cues, 207, 213

Thompson, J. D., 85, 87
Time, 5, 7, 11, 19, 23–24, 27, 53, 68, 72, 82, 86, 91, 94, 116, 144–145, 149, 152, 169, 172, 182, 199, 203, 225
Trust, 21, 130, 145–146, 159, 164–165, 167, 176, 206–207, 217, 219, 232
Turbulence, 59, 189

Uncertainty, 3, 8, 30, 39–40, 46, 49, 55–56, 70–71, 81, 85, 88, 96–97, 100, 102, 157, 159, 230–231
  introducing, 159
Understanding, 74, 85, 128, 130, 145–146, 152, 159, 164
Unified effort, 46, 68, 72–74, 206
Upgrading materials and techniques, 197–199

Validating worth, 88, 96–97, 99–100
Values, 41–44, 72, 80, 124, 152, 158
Variety, 3, 7, 29, 36, 40, 74–78, 83, 231, 234
Visibility, 33, 127, 162, 176–177, 184–190, 193–194
  controversy, 189
  ego, 187
  enhancing, 191–194
Vision, 163–164, 171, 176, 178
Visiting classrooms and schools, 22, 25, 113, 182, 193
Vulnerability, 4, 176, 181, 223

Weick, K. E., 15, 17
William of Normandy, 233
"Wishful" thinking, 46–47
Wizard of Oz, The, 41
Work schedules, 6–7, 12

Zimmerman, I. K., 196, 212